Transnational Perspectives on Democracy, Citizenship, Human Rights and Peace Education

Also available from Bloomsbury

Critical Human Rights, Citizenship, and Democracy Education,
edited by Michalinos Zembylas and André Keet
Education as a Human Right, Tristan McCowan
Peace Education, edited by Monisha Bajaj and Maria Hantzopoulos

Transnational Perspectives on Democracy, Citizenship, Human Rights and Peace Education

Edited by
Mary Drinkwater, Fazal Rizvi and Karen Edge

BLOOMSBURY ACADEMIC
LONDON • NEW YORK • OXFORD • NEW DELHI • SYDNEY

BLOOMSBURY ACADEMIC
Bloomsbury Publishing Plc
50 Bedford Square, London, WC1B 3DP, UK
1385 Broadway, New York, NY 10018, USA

BLOOMSBURY, BLOOMSBURY ACADEMIC and the Diana
logo are trademarks of Bloomsbury Publishing Plc

First published in Great Britain 2019
Paperback edition published 2020

ISBN: HB: 978-1-3500-5233-8
PB: 978-1-3501-7897-7
ePDF: 978-1-3500-5234-5
eBook: 978-1-3500-5235-2

Typeset by Integra Software Services Pvt. Ltd.

To find out more about our authors and books visit www.bloomsbury.com
and sign up for our newsletters.

Contents

Contributors

Kathy Bickmore is Professor in Curriculum Studies and Comparative International and Development Education programmes at the Ontario Institute for Studies in Education, University of Toronto. Her interests include conflict, peacebuilding and democratic education in K-12 public schools. Current research examines gaps and bridges between young people's lived citizenship experiences in violent neighbourhoods and their school education in Canada, Mexico, Bangladesh and Colombia. She guest-edited *Peace-building (in) Education: Democratic Approaches to Conflict in Schools and Classrooms* (*Curriculum Inquiry* 44: 4 September 2014) and co-edited the book *Comparative and International Education: Issues for Teachers* (expanded 2nd edition 2017, Canadian Scholars Press).

Stephen Chatelier works in China at Utahloy International School, Zengcheng. His PhD, completed at the Melbourne Graduate School of Education, University of Melbourne, focused on postcolonial theory, humanism and education. Stephen's primary research interests relate to ethical and political matters concerning education, as well as the implications of internationalization and globalization for policy, curriculum and pedagogy.

Mary Drinkwater is a lecturer in Curriculum, Teaching and Learning, and in Comparative, International and Development Education at the Ontario Institute for Studies in Education, Toronto, Canada. Her research focuses on issues of arts and cultural practices for democratic and transformative education in Ontario and in Maasailand, southern Kenya. She was the lead editor and has written chapters in *Engaging Children: Creatively and Critically* (Inter-Disciplinary: Oxfordshire, 2013) and *Beyond Textual Literacy: Visual Literacy for Creative and Critical Inquiry* (Inter-Disciplinary: Oxfordshire, 2011). She serves on the executive of the Africa SIG for the Comparative International Education Society.

Karen Edge is Pro Vice Provost (International) at UCL and Reader in Educational Leadership at UCL Institute of Education, London. Karen has conducted research in over thirty countries and recently led a seven-country study of teacher motivation and the influential Global City Leaders Project on Generation X (under forty-year-old) school leaders in London, New York City and Toronto. In 2018, Karen will launch two books on Generation X leaders (Routledge) and city-based education policy contexts and the influence on school leaders (Bloomsbury). She is Past Editor-in-Chief of *Educational Assessment, Evaluation and Accountability* (EAEA) and a current Editorial Board Member for *EAEA, School Leadership and Management* and *Leadership and Policy in Schools*.

Mark Evans is Associate Professor, Teaching Stream in the Department of Curriculum, Teaching and Learning and former Associate Dean, Teacher Education at the Ontario Institute for Studies in Education, University of Toronto. Mark is involved in a variety of education reform initiatives and research studies, locally and internationally. His current teaching and research focuses on global citizenship education, youth engagement and activism, and comparative perspectives and practices in teacher education (mark.evans@ utoronto.ca).

Reva Joshee is Associate Professor in the Department of Leadership, Higher and Adult Education of the Ontario Institute for Studies in Education of the University of Toronto. Her work examines citizenship and diversity policies in Canada, the United States and India. She focuses on linking diversity and citizenship to education for peace. She is also currently Chair of the Advisory Council of the Mahatma Gandhi Canadian Foundation for World Peace and Research Advisor to the International Gandhian Institute for Nonviolence and Peace.

Munir Lalani has recently completed his MPhil (Education) course from the Aga Khan University Institute for Educational Development. Currently, he is working as an academic coordinator at Pathways British School and as a lecturer at Notre Dame Institute of Education. His areas of expertise include curriculum, teaching and learning, and peace education.

Tristan McCowan is Reader in Education and International Development at the Institute of Education, University College London. His work focuses on the areas of access to and quality of higher education, alternative and innovative universities, citizenship education and human rights, and covers a broad range of contexts, particularly in Latin America and Sub-Saharan Africa. He is currently leading multi-country research projects focusing on higher education pedagogy, graduate destinations and the public good in Africa, and is also involved in research on indigenous education in the Brazilian Amazon and Mexico. He is the author of *Rethinking Citizenship Education* (Continuum, 2009) and *Education as a Human Right* (Bloomsbury, 2013), and is editor of *Compare – a Journal of International and Comparative Education*.

Julie McLeod researches in the history and sociology of education, with a focus on youth, citizenship and educational reform. She is Professor of Curriculum, Equity and Social Change in the Melbourne Graduate School of Education and Pro Vice-Chancellor (Research Capability), University of Melbourne. Publications include *Uneven Space-Times of Education: Historical Sociologies of Concepts, Methods and Practices* (2018); *Rethinking Youth Wellbeing: Critical Perspectives* (2015); *The Promise of the New and Genealogies of Educational Reform* (2015); *Researching Social Change: Qualitative Approaches* (2009); *Making Modern Lives: Subjectivity, Schooling and Social Change* (2006).

Sarfaroz Niyozov is Associate Professor and Director of the Institute for Educational Development at the Aga Khan University. He is also a faculty member at the OISE, University of Toronto. His research and teaching interests include comparative, international and development education with particular focus on teacher development, policy borrowing and lending, educational reform, and religious education.

Ann Phoenix is Professor of Psychosocial Studies at UCL Institute of Education, UK and, from 2016 to 2018, the Jane and Aatos Erkko Professor at Helsinki Collegium for Advanced Studies Helsinki University. Her research focuses on narrative analysis, theoretical and empirical aspects of social identities, gender, masculinity, youth, intersectionality, racialization, ethnicization, migration and transnational families. Her most recent book is Phoenix, A., Boddy, J., Walker, C., and Vennam, U. (2017), *Environment in the Lives of Children and Families Perspectives from India and the UK*. Policy Press.

Fazal Rizvi is Professor of Global Studies in Education at the University of Melbourne, as well as an Emeritus Professor at the University of Illinois at Urbana-Champaign. Fazal has written extensively on issues of identity and culture in transnational contexts, globalization and education policy, and Australia–Asia relations. His book, with Bob Lingard, *Globalizing Education Policy* (Routledge, 2010), is used widely in courses around the world. A collection of his essays is published in *Encountering Education in the Global: Selected Writings of Fazal Rizvi* (Routledge, 2014).

Hugh Starkey is Professor of Citizenship and Human Rights Education at UCL Institute of Education, London. He is founding co-director of the International Centre for Education for Democratic Citizenship and editor of the London Review of Education. Since 2016 he has led the Active Citizenship strand of the UCL Global Citizenship Programme. His published books include Osler, A., and Starkey, H. (2010), *Teachers and Human Rights Education*. Stoke-on-Trent: Trentham.

Acknowledgements

This book has a history that spans over a decade. It began with a partnership between the Graduate Schools of Education at University of Wisconsin at Madison, University of Melbourne and the London Institute of Education (now a part of University College London). The origins and purposes of this partnership are described in greater detail in Chapter 1. In the broadest terms, the partnership sought to bring together faculty and students at the three institutions to explore and engage with issues of globalization, and the new possibilities and challenges arising within educational policy and practice in the globalization context. Initially, groups of scholars and students travelled to an assigned university, for an intense Summer course, where they discussed issues of mutual interest. It soon became apparent to these groups that while there were major similarities across the three sites, the differences between them were also significant. The idea of transnationalism emerged as a key concept that revealed that global processes did not make the nation-states obsolete, but created conditions in which forms of connectivity across national borders were intensified.

It was decided that these conditions and their consequences could be usefully explored in an online graduate course that brought students and lecturers from the three universities together to exchange ideas and experiences, and thus develop a deeper understanding of the ways in which global mobilities and transnational connectivities are transforming educational processes, giving rise to new ways of thinking and teaching about democracy, citizenship and human rights in education. Further planning for the possibilities of creating this virtual course brought the Ontario Institute for Studies in Education (OISE) at the University of Toronto into the discussion. The resulting course has been taught over a period of four years and has produced a range of new insights about transnationalism and education, especially as they relate to these thematic areas. The papers included in this volume have emerged from the lectures that have been delivered to the students, using the synchronous teaching platform, Adobe Connect.

We would like to thank each of the lecturers and students who participated in this course, often at times that were not the most convenient. We extend our gratitude to the various educational leaders at the three universities who enabled us to participate in this highly innovative experiment in Comparative and International Education. We would also like to acknowledge the crucial role played by Sarfaroz Niyozov and Mary Drinkwater (OISE) in the initial development of the course, and thank Neil Tinker, Education Commons, at OISE, for his steadfast support in trouble-shooting various technology issues that inevitably arose in working across three continents and time-zones.

And finally, on more personal notes, Mary would like to thank her wife, Eugenia, and her sister, Nancy, for their encouragement and support, throughout the 'virtual teaching', course organization and anxiety over internet connectivity, especially during vacation times in remote locations. Fazal would like to record his appreciation of his wife, Pat Rizvi, who tolerated him teaching a course at 7 am in the morning each week. Karen would like to thank her eight-year-old son, Isaac, who has developed his own international curiosity by popping in to interact with our transnational faculty and students each week instead of going to bed! This book is dedicated to educational activists around the world who have refused to give up on the possibilities of a better future, driven by the principles of democracy, social justice, global peace and human rights.

Part One

Introduction

Transnational Perspectives

Fazal Rizvi, Mary Drinkwater and Karen Edge

Chapter outline

- Introduction
- Transnationalism
- The production of locality
- Transnationalization of student lives
- Rethinking pedagogic challenges
- Evolution of a partnership and pedagogy
- The evolution of the course
- Organization of this book

Introduction

As part of our scholarly work, each of us travels a great deal. Together, we believe there are few parts of the educational world we have not visited over the past decade, in relation to our work as teachers, researchers and university administrators. One of us, Drinkwater, teaches, researches, conducts workshops and presents at conferences, across all levels of education, in North and South America, the UK, Southeast Asia, East Africa and Malta, among other places. Rizvi travels extensively to Asia to carry out his research. He speaks at conferences and advises educational authorities and has maintained his links with American universities where he taught for almost ten years. For Edge, global travel is a core part of her senior administrative role, as vice-provost-International at the University College London, managing its transnational programmes and developing collaborative links with universities around the world, as well as teaching and researching in the fields of Educational Leadership and Comparative and International Education.

One of the major benefits of all this travelling is the opportunity to visit schools around the world and observe the extent to which and how educational systems are changing. On the face of it, however, we find remarkable similarities at the schools we visit. Indeed, many of these schools do not look all that different from the schools we ourselves attended, except, of course, for the evidence of a few more technological gadgets. The content of the textbooks the students use appears remarkably familiar to us, as do the mostly didactic modes of teaching that persist, despite the gadgets. But these appearances can be misleading. To begin with, the schools we visit, especially those in urban areas, are much more culturally diverse than they once were. Teachers tell us moreover that social media is transforming the lives of their students who are now globally connected in ways that are changing their approach to learning. Even the communities that are relatively isolated are not entirely unaffected by the global mobility of ideas and ideologies, cultural tastes and trends and capital and money. This mobility is clearly transforming the schools around the world, though in ways that vary greatly.

To understand how, let us consider a short vignette. Miguel teaches history at a publically funded secondary college in the South Side of Manila, Philippines. The school is located in a desperately poor part of the city. Its students are often forced to leave school early, often in order to supplement family income. The neighbourhood is crime-ridden with heavy presence of police, many of whom are known to be corrupt and violent. The school itself is poorly resourced, with its buildings falling down. It has a library that has few books. Few of its teachers stay on at the school beyond two to three years, becoming disenchanted with the poor conditions they are required to endure.

Miguel is an exception. He has been at the school for nine years and is thought to be one of its longest-serving teachers. He is a deeply committed teacher who enjoys good relationships with his students – but not always with their parents. This is so because most of the mothers of his students are overseas working as maids or cleaners in richer places, such as Hong Kong, Dubai and Singapore, and most of the fathers are drifting through life – alienated, anxious and angry. They are often in trouble with the police for petty crimes and instances of violence, both within and outside their home. The main source of their income is remittance, sent home by the mothers. Miguel is deeply concerned about the dire economic circumstances his students have to endure; yet he is always surprised with the positivity with which they approach life. Most of them have a very buoyant and optimistic 'take' on their future, which, for the girls, lies in following their mothers to go and work abroad. While they know how difficult life is for their mothers, with no security of employment, long hours and exploitative labour conditions, they nevertheless refuse to let this deter them from their plans for this future.

The aspirations the boys have are also linked to a naively romantic view of places like Hong Kong, Dubai and Singapore. If they can't get an opportunity to work abroad themselves, they want to marry a girl who might. For them, Fridays are special because it is on that day the cheques arrive from abroad. There is money to have a party with, and forget their economic and social problems for at least for a day or two, until the routine of desolation and despair sets in again. Miguel knows that only around 10 per cent of his students are likely to get jobs abroad but does not have the heart to puncture their hopes of a brighter future.

What this vignette shows is that the social experiences of students in the school in Manila are deeply shaped by the complex connections they have across national borders through the mobility of money. Their everyday experiences are potentially affected by events taking place in distant localities. In this way, this vignette is illustrative of the ways in which classrooms, schools and communities constitute spaces that are becoming increasingly *transnationalized*, giving rise to a whole range of new pedagogic challenges as well as opportunities. The collection of papers included in this volume addresses some of these challenges and opportunities. Most notably, the papers examine how forces of globalization are transforming the spaces within which education now takes place, and how this demands new ways of thinking about concepts such as human rights, cosmopolitanism, citizenship, social justice and democracy as they relate to issues of educational policy and practice – in ways that are no longer nationally specific but span national and cultural borders. To do this, the papers examine policies and programmes designed to promote education for global citizenship, human rights and democracy in terms of their diverse meanings, contested politics and practical efficacy transformed by transnationalism.

Transnationalism

The idea of transnationalism captures a set of processes relating to social, economic and political connections between people, places and institutions across national borders, potentially spanning the world. These connections have greatly expanded over the past three decades by developments in transport and communication technologies, resulting in unprecedented levels of mobility not only of people but also of money and capital, ideas and ideologies, and media and cultural practices (Urry 2007). This has given rise to systems of ties, interactions and exchange that 'function intensively and in real time while being spread throughout the world' (Vertovec 2009, 3). These systems, however, are not only driven *from above* by governments and corporations, but also *from below* by ordinary people in ways that are often contingent, complex and messy (Smith 2001).

Transnationalism is thus not necessarily an elite phenomenon: it involves ordinary people at all levels of social strata. In her landmark study of transnational villagers, Peggy Levitt (2001) has shown, for example, how it is possible for poor immigrants from the Dominican Republic in Boston in the United States to remain culturally and politically active in the life of the villages from where they have emigrated, through their deliberate and strategic attempts to forge transnational ties and practices. The idea of transnationalism suggests that while a certain level of structural assimilation is always required in the processes of migration, the rejection of cultural and political links is no longer necessary. Indeed, as Levitt (2001) asserts, over the past two decades, transnational activities have been 'reinforced by the growing numbers of global economic and governance structures that make decision-making and problem-solving across border increasingly common' (4). In this sense, transnational cultural and economic links are now increasingly common.

The idea of transnationalism thus describes an emerging social morphology that cuts across national borders through the emergence of a whole range of dynamic networks. According to Faist and his colleagues (2013), transnational space 'consists of combinations of ties and their contents, positions in networks and organizations, and networks of organizations that can be found in at least two nation-states' (13). These spaces involve relatively stable, lasting and dense sets of relationships, formed around kinship groups, circuits of information and services and communities characterized by 'a high degree of intimacy, emotional depth, moral obligation and social cohesion' (Faist et al. 2013, 14). In this way, something like a transnational public sphere has emerged, which appears to have rendered any strictly bounded sense of community or locality obsolete.

That is not to say that the territorially defined local traditions and state regulations and structures are no longer relevant to people's lives. On the contrary, they continue to define the ways in which people make sense of their mobile lives. Indeed, it is invariably from the perspective of a local sensibility that people forge transnational connections. Nation-states clearly continue to perform a major enabling role in transnational mobility and exchange: the importance of national laws, regulations and national narratives cannot therefore be overlooked. National boundaries still demarcate the nationally specific systems of education, health, taxation and border management. The transnational processes have however transformed the nature of the state itself, changing the forms in which its capacity and reach are expressed. Global flows of finance, media images, risks and consumption patterns have destabilized any specific sense of national authority, and have opened up the possibilities of post-national systems of social and economic exchange. What has emerged is a new form of sociality entailing multiple levels of actions across multiple identities and points of reference (Pieterse 2004).

This has also altered the nature of economics and politics. Clearly there have always been important economic dimensions of mobility. Transnationalism has however greatly expanded the amount, scope and forms of economic exchange, producing a range of 'multiplier effects' of cross-border relations (Guarnizo 2003). In monetary terms, global remittances are believed to be approaching $500 billion (Singh 2013), and have become a most visible symbol of the ties that connect globally mobile workers to their countries of origin. However, the raw data on remittances does not fully capture the extent to which transnational mobility of workers entails the development of various spin-off industries and ethnic entrepreneurial activities in areas as diverse as communication, transportation and finance. Indeed, transnationalism has opened up new avenues of capital flows, as well as various new strategies of capital accumulation, demanding national and international policy makers to monitor and control flows of capital in attempts to align these flows to national policy priorities (Castles 2002).

These attempts to align transnational processes to national policy agendas have however proven incredibly complicated. Indeed, transnationalism has created new political spaces in which it has become possible to disseminate and share information, forge new publicity and feedback loops beyond the control of national authorities, mobilize support and enhance public participation and political organization, and lobby government and intergovernmental organizations. The transnational communities are now able to engage in the politics of homeland in a variety of ways. What has long been the case with the Jewish diaspora now also applies to most transnational communities, from Indian and Irish, Jamaican to Japanese. In his book *Fear of Small Numbers*, Appadurai (2006) has shown, however, how this political transnationalism is systematically ambiguous, producing both reactionary and nationalist responses, as well as cosmopolitan and progressive possibilities. The complexity of politics in a more interconnected world demands a fundamental reconfiguration of the conceptual nexus between identity and citizenship, on the one hand, and political order, on the other.

It is no longer possible to assume a linear relationship between nationhood and cultural identity. Transnational consciousness is often marked by dual or multiple identifications, de-stabilizing and de-centring attachments, making it possible to simultaneously be 'at home away from home'. It opens up the possibilities of new subjectivities, linked to what Landold (2001) calls 'circuits of transnational obligations and interests' (217). Transnational social conditions variously reshape people's aspirations and expectations, their sense of moral obligations, their link to institutional structures and their relation to the state. Recent literature on diaspora has highlighted how social norms embedded within the transnational moral economy now have a different form, often disconnected from the requirements of complete social integration. Transnationalism encourages modes of social affiliation and engagement that are selective and strategic, and are not necessarily defined by long-standing cultural obligations. Ray (2007) has argued that while transnational processes are embedded in particular localities, they are no longer *wedded* to them, leading social theorists such as Beck (2001) to conclude that in an era of globalization, individualism has been reinforced, along with 'biographies full of risk and precarious freedom' (23).

The production of locality

What this brief account of transnationalism suggests is that it has changed the nature of people's relationship to space, particularly by creating transnational social fields that connect and position some people in more than one country. As people begin to become more mobile and inhabit multiple places, the potential arises of transforming the very constitution of each of these places. In his work, spanning more than two decades, Appadurai (1996, 2006 and 2013) has investigated the ways in which global cultural flows have destabilized the certainties of nation-states, reconstituting the 'sense of social immediacy, the technologies of interactivity and the relativity of contexts' (Appadurai 1996, 178). This, he argues, has transformed 'the actual existing social forms in which locality, as a dimension or value, is variably realized' (178).

A *locality*, of course, does not exist in any objective sense, as given; rather, it is produced by social subjects who belong to a community of friends and family, and who share various senses of commonality, rites of passage, ceremonies and complex social arrangements. Indeed, Appadurai (1996) posits deliberate practices of performance, representation and action are involved in the production of a locality: 'hard and regular work is done to produce and maintain its materiality' (181). If this is the case, then the relationship between the production of local subjects and the neighbourhoods in which such subjects are produced, named and empowered to act socially is a historically dialectical relationship.

In this sense, Appadurai (1996) views locality as 'a phenomenological property of social life that is produced by particular forms of intentional activity, generating a great variety of material effects' (183). It is always historically grounded and thus contextually specific (Appadurai 2013), inherently involving power relations. A sense of locality is always produced in relation to a broader set of conditions that constitute its wider context. At the same time, local practices and projects generate the shape of the context mediated by a relational consciousness of other localities. The production of localities is, in this way, strategic: it consists in social activities of production, representation and reproduction, defining the material and conceptual boundaries of a neighbourhood. Appadurai (1996) highlights that as local subjects perform the tasks associated with reproducing their neighbourhood in a range of strategic and contingent ways, 'the contingencies of history, environment, and imagination contain the potential for new contexts to be created' (185). If a locality is constituted by a 'structure of feeling, a property of life and an ideology of situated community', then the contextual features of transnationalism must necessarily imply major shifts in the cultural production of localities (Appadurai 1996, 185).

Recent processes of globalization have resulted in a growing disjuncture between territory, subjectivity and collective social movement, reconstituting the conditions in which relations of sociality are performed. These conditions involve high degrees of connectivity and circulation. In his recent writing, Appadurai (2013) argues that 'in our era of globalization, we need to understand more about the ways in which the forms of circulation and the circulation of forms create the conditions for the production of locality' (69). What is distinctive about globalization, Appadurai (2013) insists, is that it involves new transnational forms of circulation that have destabilized the isomorphism of people, territory and legitimate sovereignty that had traditionally defined the moral basis of the modern nation-states. The disciplinary authority of the nation-states has been weakened in an era of relentless human mobility and connectivity across national borders. Transnational mobility has created new opportunities of economic, cultural and political exchange, but has also created inherent instabilities in various social systems. It is now possible for localities to some extent become divorced from regional and national ecologies, developing social ties that are *translocal*, subject to various wider religious, economic and political forces. In this sense, the production of locality is always *emergent* from the changing and strategic practices of local subjects, increasingly influenced by various global forms of circulation. As a 'structure of feeling and property of social life and an ideology of situated community', a locality is performed in a range of shifting cultural, economic and political practices.

Transnationalization of student lives

In the performance of these practices, the role of mobile and globally connected students in schools has grown immeasurably. The students at these schools, and the shifting youth cultures they represent, have arguably become major drivers of change in the reconstitution of localities. This can be readily illustrated through the case of a school in Manila. To begin with, the remittances have been fundamental to the economic development of the locality in which many schools around the globe are now located, rendering their economic and social formation greatly dependent on conditions existing in faraway places. In a sense, the transnational financial flows connect the Southside of Manila to Hong Kong and other places. As a large number of relatives and friends have become reliant upon the generosity of the people who are globally mobile, it substantially alters the balance of power. The processes of decision-making that were once exclusively the province of the elderly men are now shared, with globally mobile and productive women having a substantially say in how the money they have earned is spent.

The remittances economy has also altered relations of power in some additional ways. With the money earned abroad, women from poorer families are now able to buy land which had been held by a very small number of richer families for generations and had been a key source of their power and social status. The remittances economy has greatly destabilized this logic of social stratification. The classed and gendered system that had been incredibly resistant to reform is now changing as a result of transnational economic activity that has the potential to drive social changes towards greater equity that national policy measures have failed to. Remittances have also changed the nature of economic exchange, with new lending and borrowing practices, new entrepreneurial initiatives and new ways of thinking about the value of money. Upon their return to Manila, women are often disinclined to engage in traditional activities, and they consider other ways of investing their money into new careers, mostly in buying and selling consumer goods.

In this way, transnational remittances create pressure towards social change: they have facilitated new social arrangements and emotional ties. Recent migration theorists, such as Faist et al. (2013), have used the term *social remittances* to describe an aspect of remittances that refers to transnational circulation of ideas, norms and behaviours. Migrants, they argue, bring back to their families and communities knowledge and skills that have the potential to contribute to social transformation in such areas as sanitary and health standards and waste management, as well as new ways of thinking about, for example, gender relations and religion. The social effects of remittances can of course be expected to vary across particular individuals and groups. Perhaps, more widely, social remittances create new patterns of consumption. The women bring back with them new media, and new ways of remaining in touch with friends they had made abroad. These new modes of communication link them to a transnational space constituted by people possibly also from around the world. Women return with new consumer tastes in clothes, food, music and other cultural expressions. The nature of their social relationship with families and friends also changes, as they assume a degree of self-importance to which they feel their financial contribution to their locality and their worldly experiences entitles them.

Of course, younger siblings of the returnees keenly observe these rewards of mobility. Inspired by the signs of success, younger people aspire to a similar set of experiences. Their social imagination is fuelled not only by the pretty pictures and videos of tourist sites they consume but also by the highly exaggerated stories of the good life abroad that the returnees feel inclined to narrate. They represent life abroad in a most positive light, in order to socially re-position themselves at home. They tell little of the hardships associated with the exploitive labour conditions, unbearably hot weather, poor living conditions and home sickness. Their interests lie in suppressing those memories, and flaunting instead the wealth and status they bring back. Not surprisingly, therefore, younger students at the school dream only of going abroad enjoying its many attractions, making a lot of money and returning home to enjoy the rest of their lives. The boys however realize that it is not always possible for them to convert fantasies into reality. Given the traditional patterns of gender inequalities in Philippines, this inevitably generates a new politics of resentment.

What this analysis shows is that transnationalism is a *relational* phenomenon around social processes and outcomes that are inherently contradictory. In his widely cited essay *Tourists and Vagabonds*, Bauman (1998) shows how 'the vagabond, the immobile and the badly off, is an *alter ego* of the tourist, the mobile and the well-off' (94). The vagabonds aspire to the lifestyle of the tourist, as they imagine it to be. For vagabonds, there is no other image of the good life, 'no alternative utopia, no political agendas of their own' (94). Increasingly, most young people in Manila, and also in the neighbouring villages, are sucked into the fantasies of global mobility and the good life abroad. Their cultural tastes begin to change and their aspirations become linked to life elsewhere. The mobility of a few, thus, has the potential to transform social relationships across the entirety of Manila, and dictate the contingencies of youth cultures.

Rethinking pedagogic challenges

Of course, such transformations are not limited to students, schools and communities in the Global South. They also affect the communities in the Global North, albeit in ways that are notably different. Let us consider another vignette: relating to Caroline, who teaches English literature in years 11 and 12 at a highly prestigious selective public school for girls in Melbourne, Australia. The school produces outstanding graduates and is consistently ranked among the top. More than two-thirds of the students at the school come from various Asian backgrounds, and Caroline is interested in exploring new pedagogic approaches to the teaching of English in classrooms where most of her students are from non-English backgrounds.

In addition to teaching, Caroline is studying part-time for a postgraduate research degree at a local university, one of the requirements of which is a school-based research project. For this project, Caroline is investigating how her year 11 girls use social media, why they prefer certain websites over others and how social media could be deployed for pedagogic purposes in her Literature class. Even before Caroline commenced her project, she was aware of the fact that the transnational connectivity among her students was extensive, but was nonetheless surprised by some of the results of a survey she conducted as part of her research. She found out that, on average, the girls spend 2.3 hours per day on the web, with only a small proportion of this time linked to their formal studies – mostly when essays or projects are due. Caroline found significant differences in the use of social media between her Anglo-Australian students and those who had either immigrated or were born in Australia of immigrant parents. By and large, the latter group of girls use the social media to remain connected to their friends and relatives around the world, access news and consume popular culture from their countries of origin, such as K-Pop and Bollywood movies. In this way, the cultural products the girls consume are markedly different between the two groups, even if they live in the same physical locality. The friendship groups at the school are thus mostly aligned to their pre-existing social differences, undermining, according to Caroline, the school's attempts to promote intercultural communication and social integration.

For Caroline, her teaching and research have raised some major questions about the ways in which she might approach her teaching. To what extent is the prescribed English curriculum apt for the girls whose cultural experiences are much more globally extended than her own? Which literatures might the students prefer to read, and which issues go under-explored in the formal settings of their classroom? What is the pedagogic potential of their transnational experiences in forging productive cross-cultural dialogues? And how could this dialogue be further promoted? How might their transnational experiences on a daily basis affect their engagement with the issues of cultural difference and social justice, the teaching of which the school is committed?

Caroline's school is proud of its commitment to multiculturalism, and has in recent years embraced the policy rhetoric of global citizenship education. It subscribes to UNESCO's doctrine of global citizenship, which 'aims to empower learners to assume active roles to face and resolve global challenges and to become proactive contributors to a more peaceful, tolerant, inclusive and secure world'. The school regards itself as a democratic school, which encourages its students to participate in various decision-making processes. It has a robust student representative council, supported by the school's principal and council.

The school is also committed to human rights education, helping students to develop a moral sensibility that regards all humanity to be worthy of respect. One of the aims of the school is to provide its students the knowledge and skills they need to understand their rights and to bring about a positive change in their lives and in their communities.

Caroline is among the vanguard of the teachers at the school who is deeply committed to these principles. Yet she is also not convinced that the school has an adequate understanding of these principles, linked to the transnational experiences that her students have on an everyday basis. Her research project has led her to be suspicious of the nation-centric ways in which ideas of democracy, justice and human rights are often interpreted. She is concerned that the pedagogic approach that the school adopts to democracy and global citizenship education, for example, privileges national traditions and interests, regarding those who lie outside the nation-state as worthy of our concerns, but *moral outsiders* nevertheless. She feels that this necessarily introduces the idea of those who are us and those who are not. And crucially she questions the assumption that the world is made up of discrete nation-states, each with its own moral perspective from which to interpret the others. She feels that this positions those whose do not belong to dominant culture as outsiders, worthy of tolerance and respect but they are not unambiguously assured inclusion.

For us, as the editors of this book, the moral, intercultural and pedagogic issues that concern Caroline are of utmost importance in a world in which the social experiences of our students are becoming increasingly transnationalized. The key question that informs the collection of chapters in this book is the extent to which issues of democracy and citizenship education continue to be dominated by national perspective. Is it even possible to transcend this pedagogic tradition and approach them from transnational perspectives, in which global mobility, diversity and connectivity are regarded as normal rather than an exception? If the idea of transnationalism describes a set of processes relating to social, economic and political connections across national borders, resulting from unprecedented levels of mobility of people, money, ideas and cultural practices; and if transnationalism represents new systems of ties, interactions and exchange; and if cross-border mobility has the potential of transforming the social constitution of the entire community, transforming cultural practices, beliefs and aspirations of the young in particular, then how might we think about issues of democracy, human rights and global citizenship education in new ways? This profound challenge forms the basis of this book: to develop an understanding of the ways how we might approach these issues from a transnational perspective.

Evolution of a partnership and pedagogy

This origin of this book lies in a strategic international research partnership (known as the *3 Deans' initiative*) beginning in the early 2000s between the faculties of education at three universities across the United States, Australia and England. One of the outcomes of this research partnership between the Graduate Schools of Education at the University of Wisconsin – Madison, the University of Melbourne and the Institute of Education – IOE (now University

College London – UCL) in London was the development of a course and summer institute with the aim to explore issues of globalization of education policy and practice and possibilities for critical democratic education in transnational settings. Lead programme developers and facilitators for the course included Hugh Starkey (IOE), Diana Hess (UW-Madison) and Julie McLeod (MGSE).

The course brought together internationally reputed education scholars and graduate students from different geographical regions and education systems with a thematic focus on social justice, citizenship and democratic education within a transnational frame. In addition to the face-to-face intensive summer institute, this hybrid course also included some online asynchronous engagement. Policy learning and critiques were plentiful as colleagues engaged in deep and extensive dialogue around cross-cutting globally important issues. Participants deepened their scholarly commitment to transnational issues and nurtured cross-institutional networks. The institutes fostered ongoing collaboration that were consistently rated high by the participants.

While each university was committed to fostering collaboration, shrinking higher education resources necessitated a reduction in travel and hosting costs. Institute participants recommended establishing a joint master's and PhD-level credit-based course focused on globalization and democratic education through virtual classroom technology and pedagogy. At a conference in the summer of 2012, the two deans from Melbourne Graduate School of Education (MGSE) and London Institute of Education (IOE) met with Dean Julia O'Sullivan from Ontario Institute for Studies in Education, University of Toronto (OISE) and presented the idea of this virtual global graduate course. John Portelli, Andy Tolmie and Fazal Rizvi were asked to collaborate to create a draft partnership agreement. This agreement was presented back to the deans for approval and became known as the *Three Deans Partnership*.

Initially, domestic regulatory hurdles created challenges in conceptualizing how a new transnational way of working could be possible. However, there was substantial will from all three universities to catalyse solutions for a jointly curated graduate course. On the OISE side, Associate Dean Jean Watson brought Karen Mundy, Sarfaroz Niyozov and Mary Drinkwater to the design table; on the IOE side, the institutional leads were Andy Tolmie and Karen Edge; and on the MGSE site, the institutional leads were Julie McLeod and Fazal Rizvi.

To test the appetite for a joint course, the international team proposed a session to present the idea for a trial master class at the Comparative International Education Society Conference (CIES) in Toronto in 2014. The master class was intended to be a precursor to a module, open to students at each institution, as a light touch option for exploring the possibility of a live, joint module involving academics from each of the three universities. While the core faculty was to be recruited primarily from these participating universities, the intention was also to invite key comparative international education scholars as guest speakers to deepen the scholarly dialogue.

The initial *Global Masterclass in Democracy, Human Rights and Democratic Education* was launched at the Toronto-based Comparative International Education Society (CIES) conference in 2014. A jointly developed proposal by IOE, OISE and MSGE set out to develop an innovative approach to bring faculty and students across the three universities to explore globalization and social policy issues virtually in real time. The CIES session served as both a test and taster for future iterations of a more robust course. The session involved simultaneous virtual contributions from academics at all three institutions to articulate the historical evolution of the partnership and proposed course and stimulate discussions of current and emerging trends.

The 2014 CIES session provided important contributions to the conference and to the ongoing, iterative design of our nascent transnational innovation. The panel employed live Skype/video conference technology to join scholars from each university in real time. The session was anchored in Toronto by Edge, Niyozov and Drinkwater, with virtual inclusion from Melbourne leads, Rizvi and McLeod. This unique session format launch outlined our intended design for a multi-week innovation and discussed the challenges of live transnational teaching. The panel concluded with the opportunity for participants to ask question, make suggestions and push the idea forward.

The evolution of the course

After CIES, the team set out to create a revolutionary live transnational course for masters and doctoral students across the graduate education units of the three universities. The team recognized current synergies and collaborations and hoped to foster future innovative work. The resulting course aimed to prepare current and future generations of academics and professionals with opportunities and skills to work globally and critically analyse global and national-level education policy. Underpinning the work was our commitment to developing new ways of working in real time across our three times zones. The process was complex and required recognition and careful negotiation of local traditions and regulatory frameworks. Below we highlight some of the key challenges and essential ingredients for cross-institutional, transnational live teaching.

Each institution facilitated its own internal leadership and development of the course. Course leadership was initially provided by Niyozov and Drinkwater (OISE), Rizvi (Melbourne) and Edge (IOE). Senior Teaching Assistants at OISE (Mary Drinkwater) and Melbourne (Mousumi Mukherjee) supported course development and delivery. Drinkwater took the lead in the development of the synchronous and asynchronous pedagogical integration with the technology platform. High-level support from each institutions director/dean was also essential. As with any new endeavour, leadership changes often have deleterious influences on momentum and success. As Niyozov moved to a new overseas position, Drinkwater assumed the lead role at OISE, ensuring continuous leadership in the technology and bringing to the course her own contributions to the themes of democracy.

Creating a course infrastructure that can be translated across three universities, in three different counties, is challenging, given different domestic policies and contexts. The course needed to be validated by each institution's governance structures. After initially exploring validation requirements in Ontario, Canada, and London, UK, the most fruitful strategy identified was for each university to either develop a new shared course or select an existing course within each university that could serve as the shell for our new jointly developed content. By allowing each university to set their own course shell, we avoided transnational validation struggles and perhaps, more importantly, saved time. This pragmatic approach allowed for greater institutional flexibility. For example, IOE adapted the course for its doctoral programme, which would require less validation and time-intensive lobbying internally.

OISE and Melbourne's graduate courses run for twelve weeks, while UCL courses run for ten weeks. We decided to offer a twelve-week course with twelve professors contributing lectures, four per university. We co-created our scholarly wish list and each university lead recruited four colleagues. A session title and readings were shared by each guest and our first course outline was developed. The course emerged as a wide-ranging interdisciplinary audit of related topics focused on globalization, new models of democracy, citizenship and human rights. Drinkwater provided the leadership with respect to the technology infrastructure (Adobe Connect and C2C) along with the combined synchronous/asynchronous pedagogical approach, with input from Rizvi and Edge. The assessment requirements were left to each institution to determine in line with particular university requirements.

Our solutions to contend with delivery across three time zones influenced the allocation of shared responsibility for different course components across partner institutions. The first hurdle was finding a suitable time zone for live teaching between London, Toronto and Melbourne. Our initial course offering occurred at the most suitable time for each location: London (Friday 8–10 pm), Toronto (Friday 3–5 pm) and Melbourne (Saturday 7–9 am). Toronto was the only partner for whom teaching occurred during regular operating hours. As such, Toronto led the technological hosting of the course, as technical support expertise was available without additional overtime costs.

In the end, the course *Democracy, Citizenship and Human Rights Education in an Era of Globalization* was first offered as a credit-based three-institution course from September to December 2014. A second and third offering occurred from January to April 2016, and from January to April 2017. The most recent iteration, offered by OISE and UCL, ran from January to April 2018 with guest lecturers from all three universities. Throughout, the objectives of the module have remained to:

- explore national and transnational perspectives on *Democracy, Citizenship and Human Rights Education in an Era of Globalization*, drawing on experience and scholarship from three continents;
- provide opportunities for in-depth engagement both with leading scholars acting as faculty and with students from other universities;
- build networks of students and faculty to scholarly address the articulation of democratic education not just in the context of the three mentioned countries, but also globally.

Traditionally, course sessions are three hours long. To accommodate time zone differences, we offered two-hour sessions with additional time-flexible wrap-around work. Each session starts with an introduction by a core team member, followed by a forty-five to fifty-minute lecture by one of the twelve guest academics. After the lecture, ten to fifteen minutes are given for *open questions* from any students to the guest lecturers. Each guest concludes their talk with three discussion questions. Participants then work in virtual cross-institutional small groups (*breakout rooms)* on the questions for thirty minutes. A group representative reports back to the large group and poses additional questions for discussion or clarification to the guest lecturer. Prior to and following each of the virtual class sessions, students interact and engage in further dialogue and reflections about the course readings, via our asynchronous platform.

Participants are recruited and registered within their respective universities. All participants are provided with online access codes for the online resource and Adobe Connect systems by the Toronto lead. Each guest receives a written briefing and software test prior to their lecture. The resources and processes refined throughout the lifespan of the course have been used with other OISE modules, developed by Drinkwater. The suite of practices and resources has refined the very complex management of live simultaneous teaching across at least three time zones into a clear, concise and organized operation.

Organization of this book

This book consists of thirteen chapters in the fields of globalization, democratic theory, citizenship, human rights and peace education from the Global North and Global South. With the exception of Munir Lalani and Stephen Chatelier, each of these chapters was originally delivered as a lecture in the course/module. As guest lecturers, most of the authors thus had an opportunity to share their work and engage with the students, and subsequently develop their thinking in the chapters included in this book. The content of these chapters reflects diverse theoretical, methodological and empirical aspects related to democracy, citizenship and human rights education in an era of globalization. They consider, from a transnational perspective, issues of identity, language, conflict and peace-building as they related to demands of cross-sectoral policy and education. There are four major parts to the book: *Introduction, Transnational Perspectives on Democracy and Education, Transnational Perspectives on Citizenship and Education* and *Transnational Perspectives on Peace-building and Human Rights Education.*

Part One introduces the idea of transnationalism using a number of vignettes to show how the space of policy, pedagogy and practice in education has been transformed by transnational and global forces, connectivities and imagination. Furthermore, it highlights the ways in which the global mobility of people, money and ideas has *trans-nationalized* the spaces in which we work, live and learn, creating both challenges of policy and practice, as well as ethical and pedagogic possibilities of transnational dialogues. It describes the development of an innovative virtual pedagogical approach that brought together guest lecturers and graduate students from three universities in Canada, the UK and Australia, and shows how such an approach can contribute greatly to rich and robust dialogue around these issues. It thus encourages similar experiments in pedagogy and politics.

In Chapter 2, Rizvi draws from the work of a range of recent globalization theorists, such as Appadurai, Beck and Faist, to show how notions of mobility, movement, flows and the like are becoming central to our understanding of the global processes that are now re-constituting our communities, social institutions and lives. As we witness ever-increasing levels of mobility, facilitated not only by the revolutionary developments in communication and transport technologies but also by major shifts in the ways in which economic and political relations are now forged, we need to re-think the ways in which contemporary social processes are forged and enacted across transnational spaces. In this chapter, Rizvi argues that these developments have major implications for thinking about the ways in which the political formation of students might be forged and how their normative sensibilities towards citizenship, democracy and human rights might be developed.

In Part Two, authors utilize transnational perspectives to engage with issues of democracy and democratic education in four different contexts. In Chapter 3, Drinkwater offers a new theoretical model for conceptualizing democracy within an era of neoliberal globalization. She begins by discussing the global and Kenyan context which underpin the creation of this new narrative of democracy. Her two-pronged theoretical framework combines traditions of critical theory and decolonial theory. For Drinkwater, critical theory provides tools to identify current inequities in education and to argue for the possibilities for an emancipatory role for education, while decolonial theory illuminates the impacts of the colonial modernity project and acts as a foundation to imagine differently in addressing current injustices in the world. Acknowledging that global neoliberalism is contributing to the thinning of the principles of democracy in society and in schools, Drinkwater suggests a new narrative, or *thicker* conception of democracy, which she calls a *robust global democracy.*

In Chapter 4, McCowan assesses a range of radical alternatives in higher education to neoliberal reforms in Latin America, within the broader context of new social movements, processes of redemocratization following military dictatorships and traditions of popular education. The chapter starts with a discussion of the ideas of Ivan Illich, whose critique of institutionalization in education provides the backdrop for many of these counterhegemonic initiatives. There follows an analysis of a selection of new institutions in Brazil, characterized by distinctive aims or missions, whether relating to a particular ethnic or cultural group, a social or political movement, regional unity and intercultural exchange, or a spiritual calling. The two factors of resources and recognition are found to be critical elements in ensuring their viability and success. Finally, broader implications are drawn out for understandings of educational institutions, in light of Illich's deschooling critique.

In Chapter 5, Joshee takes us into the Canadian context and connects theories of democracy and applying Gandhian principles to democratic policy approaches. The Canadian state has had a long history of engagement with issues of diversity and social justice. The country also has a nominal commitment to peace. This chapter examines the history of policy work in these areas and argues for a new approach to policy that would be peaceful and democratic in its essence.

Building from Gandhian principles and work in democratic and critical approaches to policy, Joshee argues for a policy dialogue approach that would lead to more comprehensive policies for social justice and peace.

The final chapter in this section (Chapter 6) explores the policy implications of the next contexts in which education now takes place for the democratization of education in the UK context. Edge asserts that over the past decade a gradual and accelerating movement to democratize educational knowledge and expertise has paralleled the decentralization of school management in the UK. The weakening of local authorities (LAs) reflects explicit policy ambitions to create even more autonomy for schools from government control – a policy referred to as the *Self-improving School System* (SISS). This chapter highlights policy and practice shifts intended to democratize ownership and expertise within the system by focusing on recent changes in teacher training provision. In parallel, an escalation of social-media-facilitated engagement among educators and the growing weight of these voices will also be highlighted. The potential implications for both trends and their influence on the educational workforce are explored alongside the policy, practice and equity implications.

In Part Three, the focus shifts to the implications of transnationalism and transnational perspectives on citizenship and global citizenship education. In Chapter 7, Evans asserts that various forces of change transcending national boundaries have prompted heightened attention to global dimensions of citizenship. Education for global citizenship has emerged as a prominent line of inquiry as education systems worldwide consider ways forward to deepen global understanding and assist youth to meaningfully engage in, and respond to, questions and issues of civic global interest and importance, in an increasingly globalized world. This chapter focuses primarily on developing understandings of and approaches to educating for global citizenship during formal schooling in Canada. Early engagement with the issues and challenges of complexity, pedagogy and implementation are explored, as academics, policy-makers and educators attempt to better understand its curricular and pedagogical intent and location in formal schooling contexts.

In Chapter 8, McLeod places contemporary educational agendas for global youth citizenship in light of a longer history of curriculum initiatives that have promoted the ideal of internationally minded students in service of cultural and political change. She considers the efforts of international organizations in the interwar years to influence national educational programmes by fostering collaboration through intellectual and cultural exchange. Focusing on the League of Nations and the International Bureau of Education, the chapter examines activities to influence school practices, curriculum and textbooks that aimed to provide greater understanding between nations, support progressive ideas about the purposes of education and lay the ground work to achieve lasting peace through moral disarmament. Developments and discussions in Australia are taken as examples, examined in reference to histories of internationalism in education, questions of race and empire, and theoretical debates regarding the dividing practices of citizenship.

In Chapter 9, Starkey shifts the contextual focus back to the UK, as he unpacks the theme of *Learning to Live Together*, which has been identified by UNESCO as a priority for education in the twenty-first century. This chapter proposes the Universal Declaration of Human Rights and the UN Convention on the Rights of the Child (CRC) as embodying both a utopian vision of freedom, justice and peace in the world and a set of principles that can inform educational decision making. Citizenship education is a site where these principles can be transmitted and implications discussed. Education for cosmopolitan citizenship transcends nationalities and accommodates multiple and flexible identities. It promotes a sense of agency in situations of discrimination and oppression. As a practical example, when schools in England commit to the voluntary Rights Respecting Schools programme they agree to respect, protect and fulfil children's human rights in all activities as the basis for living together. Diversity is recognized and valued as the basis of democracy.

The last chapter in this section, Chapter 10, continues in the UK context, but shifts the connections between global citizenship and transnationalism to what Phoenix calls *language brokering*. Phoenix considers adult retrospective evaluation of childhood experiences and argues that childhood language brokering constitutes acts of citizenship that are of benefit to society and transnational communities. Experiences of language brokering in childhood give adults the impetus to make voluntary contributions to community work in ways that constitute acts of citizenship. Childhood language brokering helps the development of knowledge and skills required to function within and beyond cultural communities and borders, promotes empathy within relationships, connections across lines of difference and commitment to addressing discrimination and inequalities.

In the final section of the book, authors use transnational perspectives to engage on the complexities of peace-building, peace education and human right education in diverse socio-economic and geo-political contexts. In Chapter 11, Chatelier connects again with the UNESCO *Learning to Live Together* theme, but moves the discussion towards the pursuit of a peaceful world. Processes of globalization in recent decades have created particular kinds of challenges to this aim of living together well. The imperative to struggle for global peace and justice remains a priority, as evidenced by contemporary global and geopolitical challenges. While it is not new for humans to encounter differences, the growing interconnectivity and interdependence of humanity across cultures in today's world has intensified the experiences of difference. Can we live together? How important are human rights for this? While European Enlightenment humanism, and the human rights discourse that emerged from it, may have historically been at the heart of UNESCO's mission, the structure of the contemporary world, formed in part through the history of colonialism, demands an alternative. By utilizing aspects of postcolonial theory, this chapter considers the possibilities of, and for a new humanism as a moral resource within an education aimed toward living together well.

In Chapter 12, Niyozov and Lalani draw from a case study in Pakistan to illuminate the complexities of the peace education process within a conflict context. Since its very inception, Pakistan has become victim of conflicts and violence of varying nature. Education has not only failed to address these issues, but in certain cases has promoted biases and prejudice towards minorities. Moreover, in recent times, education has itself become a victim of conflict as educational institutions have also become a target of militants. Government of Pakistan, civil society, private institutions and individuals have taken initiatives for the cause of peace. Niyozov and Lalani describe and discuss issues of funding, contextual sensitivity and innovative pedagogies, including inclusive, non-biased curriculum and critical pedagogical approaches. They argue that the socio-economic restructuring and cultural transformation for a more equitable and inclusive and peaceful Pakistani society will require the participation of all stakeholders, including politicians, clergy and intellectuals.

In the final chapter of this section and book, Bickmore uses a case study situated in three countries to argue that to educate for positive peace is to prepare for and engage in *constructive conflict* communication towards resolution and transformation – to discern and create potential spaces for human action to stop or avoid *violence*. Formal education is shaped by – and can help to re-shape – patterns of social conflict, enmity and social-structural (in)justice in any context. However, it is possible for education to help build young people's *agency* – their repertoire, competence and inclination – for participation in comprehensive democratic peace-building. This chapter draws upon focus group research with youth and teachers in publicly funded Mexican, Bangladeshi and Canadian schools – conflict contexts distinct from the polarized divided societies most often studied. Highlighted here is the problem of gender-based inequity and violence, pervasive in all these contexts. The experienced curriculum described by teachers and students included some lessons on generic interpersonal conflict management skills and values, and fewer opportunities to examine or resist the gender norms and hierarchies at the roots of violent conflict.

References

Appadurai, Arjun. *Modernity at Large: Cultural Dimensions of Globalization.* Minneapolis: Minnesota University Press, 1996.

Appadurai, Arjun. *Fear of Small Numbers: An Essay on the Geography of Anger.* Durham, NC: Duke University Press, 2006.

Appadurai, Arjun. *The Future as Cultural Fact: Essays in the Global Condition.* London and New York: Verso, 2013.

Bauman, Zygmunt. *Globalization: The Human Conditions.* Cambridge: Polity Press, 1998.

Beck, Ulrich. *Globalization.* Cambridge: Polity Press, 2001.

Castles, Stephen. 'Migration and Community Formation under Conditions of Globalization'. *International Migration Review* 36, no. 4 (2002): 1143–1168.

Faist, Thomas, Margit Fauser, and Eveline Reisebauer. *Transnational Migration.* Cambridge: Polity Press, 2013.

Guarnizo, L. E. 'The Economics of Transnational Living'. *International Migration Review* 37, no. 3 (2003): 666–699.

Landold, Patricia. 'Salvadorian Economic Transnationalism: Embedded Strategies for Household Maintenance, Immigration Incorporation and Strategies for Household Maintenance'. *Global Networks* 1, no. 3 (2001): 21–41.

Levitt, Peggy. *The Transnational Villagers.* Berkeley: University of California Press, 2001.

Pieterese, Jan Nederveen. *Globalization and Culture*. New York: Roman & Littlefield, 2004.

Ray, Larry. *Globalization and Everyday Life*. London: Routledge, 2007.

Singh, Supriya. *Globalization and Money: A Global South Perspective*. Lanham, MD: Rowman and Littelfield, 2013.

Smith, Michael P. *Transnational Urbanism: Locating Globalization*. London: Blackwell Press, 2001.

Urry, John. *Mobilities*. Cambridge: Polity Press, 2007.

Vertovec, Steven. *Transnationalism*. London: Routledge, 2009.

2

Global Mobility, Transnationalism and Challenges for Education

Fazal Rizvi

Chapter outline

- Introduction
- Rethinking global mobility
- Transnationalism
- Consequences of transnationalization
- Meeting the new educational challenges
- Cosmopolitan learning
- Conclusion

Keywords: global mobility; transnationalism; transnational space; multiculturalism; cosmopolitanism; cosmopolitan learning

---

Introduction

In his book *The Figure of the Migrant*, the philosopher Thomas Nail (2015) claims that the twenty-first century will be 'the century of the migrant'. He notes that there are more migrants now than ever before in recorded history – around 200 million people, according to the International Organization for Migration (2017). Documented migration is, however, only a small part of the story of the global mobility of people. There is now also an unprecedented number of refugees and undocumented migrants, most of them experiencing uncertain lives in low-income countries rather than in the so-called *developed* world, as is often mistakenly assumed. At the same time, the number of short-term contract workers, both skilled and unskilled, is growing rapidly as the global economy becomes increasingly integrated. People are globally mobile for a wide variety of other reasons as well, including business, education and of course tourism. Indeed, hospitality and tourism has become one of the fastest growing industries in most countries around the world.

The rapid rise in the global mobility of people has consequences that are as far-reaching as they are profound. Mobility has connected people across cultural and national borders in a myriad of ways, especially with the advances in transport and communication technologies. It has reshaped the nature of everyday experiences of not only the globally mobile people, who are now able to remain in touch with friends and families around the world as never before, but also the people who have no desire to move, or who cannot afford to move. It has redefined the ways in which people now think about their localities, consider their sense of belonging, and imagine their futures. It has transformed local and national institutions, including schools, linking them to the dynamic forces of globalization. In short, it has reconfigured the world, economically, politically and culturally, in ways that local and national institutions can no longer ignore.

In recent decades, the idea of transnationalism has been widely deployed to understand these historical shifts. According to Steven Vertovec (2009, 3), transnationalism describes a condition in which, despite great distances and continuing significance of nation-states, certain kinds of relationships across national borders have now become possible, widely enacted and intensified. The idea of transnationalism thus underlines the growing importance of cross-border practices. It suggests that the global mobility not only of people but also of money, ideas and technology has increasingly *trans-nationalized* the spaces in which most of us now live and work. The trans-nationalization of identities, social practices and institutions has opened up new possibilities but has also created new challenges. It has resulted in outcomes that are both positive and negative.

In this chapter, I want to discuss some of the educational challenges to which transnationalism has given rise, especially with respect to the ways in which moral and political pedagogies might now be envisaged, relating not only to local and national imperatives but also to global social imaginaries. My key argument is that, in the contemporary pedagogic settings, issues of democracy, citizenship and human rights can no longer be addressed in terms that are based either on a set of universal principles or are relative to particular localities, but demand relational cosmopolitan learning both within and across national borders and cultural traditions.

Rethinking global mobility

In recent decades, governments around the world have become increasingly anxious about growing level of migration into their countries. Yet even as migration has become a volatile political issue, they have found it difficult to curtail migrant numbers. At the same time, they have begun to recognize that the nature of migration is no longer the same as it once was. International migration has now become part of a broader range of practices and institutions surrounding the global mobility of people, linked to the processes of globalization. Moreover, migration represents only a small proportion of the people who are now globally mobile. People move for a wide variety of additional reasons, including business, education, work and tourism. Indeed, in this broader sense, mobility has now become a major driver of economic growth and prosperity of nations. This is so because the various contemporary forms of mobility are now interrelated and are linked in a variety of complicated ways to the dynamic processes of globalization (Appadurai 1996). Mobility affects communities in both economically well-off countries and those that are not, though in ways that are radically different. In this way, it is multi-directional, multi-dimensional and multi-causal.

The complex reasons that encourage people to move are linked to the understanding they have of their circumstances and opportunities, but also to their aspirations that are at least partly influenced by that understanding. For many refugees in search of security, for example, a neighbouring developing country is often the first port of call, even as many aspire to go eventually to a more economically advanced country. Almost 60 million people are now registered with the United Nations Commissioner for Refugees (2018), with fewer than 3 million allowed to find refuge in a developed country. Beyond the registered refugees, there is of course an indeterminate number of the so-called 'undocumented' people living and working in a country where they were not born, often in search of economic opportunities and better life for their children. The number of short-term visitors and sojourns has also exploded in recent decades.

Even a cursory visit to a large airport indicates how business executives are now constantly on the move, as indeed are the workers recruited and employed by transnational corporations. Many people, professionally educated as well as those who are not, no longer hesitate, as they once did, to take employment opportunities abroad. According to the World Tourism Organization (2018), international tourists, measured in terms of arrivals from another country, expanded twenty-fold between mid-1950s and mid-2010s. International conferences and conventions have become commonplace despite the enhanced possibilities of online communication. And the number of international students is now more than 3 million, up from just 300,000 in 1970 and is expected to more than double by the mid-2020s (Shields 2013).

There is of course nothing new about the movement of people, both within and across nations. Historically, people have always moved, in search of security, jobs, business and other opportunities; interested in experiencing exotic locations and the cultural *others*; acquiring new knowledge and cultural tastes. Equally, people have been forced to move as part of colonial conquests and indentured labour. The contemporary dynamics of mobility is continuous with some of these processes but is now much more intricate and complicated. Not only has the numbers of mobile people increased significantly, but so has the ways people think about and approach mobility. In the past, cross-border movement was relatively permanent. It is now more contingent and flexible, with new information and communication technologies enabling people to keep their options open and retain links with their countries of origin. Almost twenty years ago, Aihwa Ong (1999) argued that, in the era of globalization, mobile individuals develop a flexible notion of citizenship often designed to accumulate capital and power. As Ong (1999) argues, the logic of capital accumulation is to 'induce subjects to respond fluidly and opportunistically to changing political-economic conditions' (33). Powerful incentives now exist for individuals to emphasize practices that favour 'flexibility, mobility and repositioning in relation to markets, governments and cultural regimes'. This has transformed the nature of migration, complicating the traditional pull–push explanations.

What is thus now clear is that the intricacies of global mobility can no longer be understood in terms of the dynamics of the mobility of the people only. Needed also is an account of how the mobility of people is necessarily linked to the global circulation of money and capital, media and technology, ideas and ideologies, and so on, in ways that are often disjunctural (Appadurai 1996). Also important to understand are the ways in which global mobility is both driven by and has the potential to transform the desires, hopes and aspirations of people, along with their cultural tastes and traditions. National and cultural borders invariably do not have the same degree of significance for those who are constantly on the move. Their sense of opportunities often lies in their understanding of the shifting nature of the global economic and political systems. The global capital flows have resulted in changes in the modes of production and consumption, affecting the structures of opportunity, and the life chances of both the people who are mobile and those who are not (Dicken 2015). This is so because in a period of rapid economic globalization, technological shifts, post-Fordism and the hegemonic dominance of neo-liberal policies, not only has the nature of work and work conditions been transformed, but so have people's aspirations and desires and the strategic calculations they now make about how best to relate to the globalizing conditions.

The revolutionary developments in information technology and the new social media have also had a major impact in the construction of desires, wants and aspirations, as people are now able to access information and develop new perspectives on career and even citizenship possibilities. In this way, the cross-border movement of people is at least partly driven by consumerist desires and subjective awareness of global opportunities. The globalization of media has altered the ways in which people are now able to imagine their futures, just as corporations are able to take advantage of the possibilities of cross-border investment and trade. They are able to move sites of production and value the mobile people who are able to work in teams that are often globally assembled. Furthermore, the global mobility of people has become a core driver of the services-based knowledge economy, in which the modes of production and consumption are now globally determined. The diaspora communities that are globally 'dispersed but connected' (Rizvi, Kam and Evans 2016) are now viewed as a major asset that many governments and various development agencies have begun to exploit (Wilson 2012).

This explains the difficult political position in which governments often find themselves with respect to the global mobility of people. While they are aware of the populist xenophobic sentiments within their communities, they also realize that, in an increasingly globalized economy, cross-border mobility is important for national economic development and prosperity, since people who are mobile are not only able to provide a range of much-needed skills and labour but also the knowledge of global markets, intercultural understanding and commercial networks. Communication technologies have enabled people to remain in touch with their families and friends around the world, and they do not feel any compulsion to abandon their sense of belonging and even citizenship, as the policies of assimilation once required them to. Through social media, they are now able to keep in touch with the shifting cultural trends at 'home', remain up to date with cultural, social and political events, often participating in political activity there even more confidently than from abroad. They thus relate to the idea of 'home' in deeply complicated ways. As Ostergaard-Nielson (2003) points out, the politics of homeland takes a variety of forms, including campaigns to effect social and political change.

Transnationalism

What this account suggests is the experiences of migration are not what they used to be. The ideas of moving from one place to another on a permanent basis, leaving the home community and assimilating into the host community on a permanent basis, is no longer necessary. It is now possible to remain connected to both communities (Nagel and Mavroudi 2016). Furthermore, even as governments try to control migration number, they find it difficult to restrict the number of people who are globally mobile. This is so because the global economy is now fundamentally shaped around various forms of mobility, of people as well as money, things and ideas, often in ways that have contradictory forms. So, on the one hand, cross-border mobility has now become a part of a global culture of rampant consumerism, and, on the other, it is the only option people have when they experience major environmental, economic and political turmoil. One of the most serious effects of climate change, for example, is likely to be the global flows of people in numbers that are unimaginable.

These realizations have led a number of recent social theorists to re-think not only the idea of migration but also the nature of sociality itself. Nicholas Papastergiadis (2000), for example, suggests that recent global transformations require new ways of thinking about movement and new ways of accounting for migration, since the traditional push–pull and structural theories, the distinctions between economic and forced migration, and the representations based on classic South–North flows, are no longer adequate. More radically, the late John Urry (2007) called for a new 'mobilities paradigm' in the social sciences, beyond the 'methodological nationalism' that has traditionally characterized them (1). Consistent with Urry's critique of methodological nationalism, Steven Vertovec (2009) has argued that the increasing level of people mobility has 'transnationalized' space, both the places to which people move and the places they leave, connecting them inextricably – culturally, politically and economically.

In recent years, the idea of transnationalism has thus emerged as a powerful concept with which to understand how the world is now constituted by cross-border relationships, patterns of economic, political and cultural relations and complex affiliations and social formations that potentially span the globe. It names the multiple and messy proximities through which human societies have now become globally interconnected and interdependent. In contrast with some of the more enthusiastic rendering of globalization that asserted the demise of nation-states (Ohmae 1996), the idea of transnationalism suggests that nationally specific laws, regulations and narratives retain their salience, but now need to be conceptualized differently, as essentially linked and responding to the seemingly ubiquitous forces of globalization. It points to a condition in which certain kinds of relationship have been globally intensified and now take place in a space that is spatially stretched. In this sense, the idea of transnationalism implies systems of ties, interactions, exchange and mobility that spread across national borders and potentially span the world.

Vertovec (2009) discusses what he calls a number of different *takes* on transnationalism. First, he suggests, transnationalism may be viewed as a kind of social formation spanning borders. He asserts that 'dense and highly complex networks spanning vast spaces are transforming', giving rise to 'many kinds of social, cultural, economic and political relationships' (5), producing in a transnational public sphere that has rendered a strictly bounded sense of community obsolete. Second, transnational networks have produced a type of consciousness, marked by multiple senses of identification, comprising of ever-changing representations. Third, Vertovec (2009) adds that transnationalism involves a mode of cultural reproduction, associated with 'a fluidity of constructed styles, social institutions and everyday practices' (7). Fourth, transnationalism is linked to new practices of capital formations that arguably involve globe-spanning structures or networks that have largely become disconnected from their national origins. Thus, new global systems of supply, production, marketing, investment and information management have become major drivers for much of the world's transnational mobility and practices. Fifth, transnationalism may be viewed as a site for political engagement where cosmopolitan anti-nationalists often exist alongside reactionary ethno-nationalists within various diasporas, representing the dynamism of the relationships between different sites of political activity. And finally, and perhaps most importantly for my argument, transnationalism has reconstructed localities, spaces of living, working and learning, as a result of the mobility of both people and ideas, as well as the practices and meanings derived from multiple geographical and historical points of origin. Vertovec (2009) thus maintains that transnationalism has changed 'people's relations to space particularly by creating transnational "social fields" or "social spaces" that connect and position some actors in more than one country' (12).

Vertovec insists, correctly in my view, that the idea of transnationalism does not imply a coherent theory as such but names a *theoretical lens*. It directs our attention to a range of cross-border transactions as a process. Faist, Fauser and Reisnauer (2013) use the verb *trans-nationalization* to refer to a set of processes through which 'sustained ties, events and activities across the borders of several nation-states' are forged and maintained (10). The processes of transnationalization involve nation-states but are not always controlled by them. Nation-states seek to 'regulate borders, places of residence, economic activities, and access to rights' (11), but cannot always dictate the activities of non-state agents. In this way, trans-nationalization is different from inter-nationalization which names ties, events and processes that are managed exclusively by nation-states and their agents. The nation-states are of course always nervous about losing control over non-state activities since they are often unable to regulate the emerging transnational spaces in which people are able to develop new and multiple forms of sociality across borders. Indeed, as Ray (2007) points out, these spaces represent 'accomplishment of everyday life involving human agents engaged in the active construction of global forms of sociality' (71).

The idea of transnationalism thus implies the importance of a spatial analysis of contemporary social processes. It suggests that sociality now takes place in spaces where the contingencies of everyday life are lived, felt and experienced through transnational relations and networks. The role that these relations and networks now play is important in making sense of our histories, social relations and aspirations. This relational view of space thus represents a useful theoretical lens with which to understand the contemporary drivers, forms and consequences of global mobility, and the challenges they pose for institutions such as education. Such a spatial analysis underscores the importance of human agency, and points to the connections between macro-economic and geopolitical transformations, on the one hand, and the patterns of social action, on the other. It suggests a need to account for the ways in which human agents and groups of people interpret, engage with and negotiate various forces of globalization, at the level of everyday practices, social relationships and collective action. It highlights the ways in which patterns of social interaction are changing, and now occur in spaces that can no longer be understood exclusively in national terms. It thus suggests the need to describe the messiness of living and acting in a world mediated by transnational ties and activities.

Consequences of transnationalization

Such a transnational perspective helps in an understanding of the processes that are now reconstituting localities, resulting in a re-alignment of political, ethnic and personal identities more conducive to navigating the shifting landscapes of our experiences, practices and opportunities. These transformations are however not arbitrary but involve creative articulations between subjects and the shifting regimes of trans-nationalizing practices and institutions such as the family, the nation-state and at the broadest level global capitalism. In this way, transnational practices lie at the heart of contemporary global processes in the production and negotiation of cultural meaning within the hegemonic framework of late capitalism. The processes of trans-nationalization are complicated and messy because they are accompanied by various dilemmas for people who are pulled in the direction of cultural flexibility, on the one hand, and uncertainty and confusion, on the other, producing a wide variety of complex and dynamic social configurations, the consequences of which are both positive and negative.

Aihwa Ong (1999) illustrates the uncertain consequences of trans-nationalization by referring to Hong Kong Chinese immigrants to the United States, who 'seem to display an élan for thriving in conditions of political insecurity, as well as in the turbulence of global trade', but also recognize how their mobility is always unsafe, full of risks (37). Similarly, Beck (2000) has used the phrase 'place polygamy' to underscore the ways in which, under the conditions of global capitalism, people may be able to live in more than one place at once, but live at the edges of risk, subject to the arbitrary exercise of state power. When citizenship, a notion that has traditionally linked each citizen to a singular national origin, becomes *flexible* and involves multiple senses of belonging, it should be noted that a feeling of security is also lost. We should therefore be cautious about valorizing the experiences of mobility and of trans-national dwelling.

Also important is to note that global mobility is not available equally to everyone, and is inflected by gender, class and race considerations. Transnational spaces can, for example, often be unsafe and insecure for women, as has been pointed out by Massey (2007). Various racial and ethnic groups and social classes also experience mobility differently, with its social consequences unevenly distributed. Under the conditions of globalization, according to Bauman (2000), voluntary mobility is available largely to elites, a new global cosmopolitan class of people. He euphemistically calls them *tourists*, the mobile people who contribute in one way or another to the development of a consumer economy. In a globalized era, for the mobile tourists—the trans-national businessmen, culture managers and knowledge workers—Bauman (2000) asserts that the 'state borders are levelled down, as they are dismantled for the world's commodities, capital and finances' (89). But for subaltern groups, the *vagabonds*, mobility may be desired but remains unattainable, or is forced under the most dangerous of conditions.

The processes of trans-nationalization of course do not only affect those who are physically mobile across national boundaries but also those who are not. To begin with, the people who do not travel are equally implicated in the relations of global capitalism. Not only do the flows of capital across borders, but also the globally reconstituted labour processes, have the potential to reshape entire communities, even in the poorest parts of the world. Communities in Africa, for example, live under the shadows of global capitalism, as Ferguson (2006) points out. Global capital flows have resulted in changes in the mode of production and consumption, affecting the structures of opportunity, and the life chances of people throughout Africa and elsewhere. A large number of villages and poorer urban communities have become dependent on financial remittances from relatives who have moved to richer countries in search of work and financial security. These relatives have also been a source of social remittances, foreign ideas, images and cultural practices. The social media plays a major role in transforming cultural tastes and aspirations of young people in the remotest villages.

In this way, the processes of trans-nationalization have the potential to transform most, if not all, localities, affecting all aspects of our lives, including our identities, social relations and institutions such as schools. They have certainly transformed cities, creating urban conglomerates at the intersection of global flows of finance and capital (Sassen 1991). It is in these *global* cities where most international immigrants and refugees settle, and where people from diverse backgrounds live across multiple time horizons, creating conditions not only of opportunities but also of risk and vulnerability. Vertovec (2006) argues that, as a result of global mobility of people, major cities around the world, such as London, have become 'super-diverse', consisting immigrants not only from poorer backgrounds but also extremely rich people with larger disposable incomes. They contribute a great deal to making cities richer, converting them into creative and dynamic places where new cultural practices and tastes emerge, as a result of hybridity of traditions (Pieterese 2005). In these cities, the rich immigrants often exist alongside refugees, international students and tourists, putting pressure on local governments to provide services adapted to a super-diverse and shifting situation with extremely heterogeneous neighbourhoods and hugely varied needs.

With the global mobility of people and the trans-nationalization of communities around the world, cultural diversity is becoming *the new normal*, with cultural heterogeneity best regarded as an exception. Yet trans-nationalization also has the potential to unsettle the long-established communities, raising anxieties about migration, both documented and undocumented, as has become increasingly evident over the past decade. Governments have therefore sought to 'control their borders', often with extremely authoritarian measures, in an attempt to reduce the percentage of migrants as a share of the total population in their communities. The current rise of populist political movements, such as those exemplified by Brexit in the UK, the rise of Trump to the presidency of the United States and other ethno-nationalist movements in places as diverse as South Africa and India, is arguably driven by what Appadurai (2006) calls the 'fear of small numbers'.

Transnationalism has thus given rise to a new contradictory politics that involves, on the one hand, a growing recognition that the global economy depends heavily on the mobility of people, along with the unhindered flows of capital and ideas. It is widely acknowledged that mobility is a source of cultural exchange and creativity, of economic dynamism: that cultural diversity is a major driver of social and economic productivity and prosperity (Cope and Kalantzis 2000). Mobile people, such as denizens, global business people and international students and migrants, are major carriers of information and ideas, money and capital, and are able to connect economic, political and cultural practices across vast distances. At the same time, transnationalism has resulted in major concerns of security, sustainability and adaptation, and also the emergence of a reactionary anti-globalization politics (Shipman 2017).

This politics has highlighted new concerns about the nature and scope of citizenship, as well as about governance and political representation. Because places are no longer internally homogeneous and bounded identities, they are now constructed out of material and symbolic resources that reach beyond local boundaries, and are forged in transnational spaces, which are mediated and mitigated by the cultural turbulence of globalizing forces, connections and desires, as well as an inward-looking xenophobic creation to them. In this context, transnationalism has not only created a climate of fear of the *other*, but has also unsettled the international moral norms of democracy, social justice and citizenship that had been developed following the turmoil of the Second World War.

Meeting the new educational challenges

These contradictory consequences of transnationalism have serious implications for educational policy and practice. How do we prepare students to live and thrive in such a contradictory world? In his highly influential book, published in 2000, the French sociologist, Alain Touraine (2000), asked perhaps the most pressing and profound question facing human societies today: can we live together? Touraine's question was located within a dilemma, of how we might live together in a globalizing society in which we are increasingly aware of our interconnectivity and interdependence, and yet confront conditions in which our differences are being heightened, as communities increasingly define their identities against the encroaching forces of globalization, and against each other. Touraine argued that, in transnational spaces, our cultural distinctiveness is increasingly under attack by the homogenized mass culture, making us increasingly introverted as we fight to defend ourselves against outside forces. In political terms, the basic issue we confront is how we should develop policies that acknowledge that in a globalizing world our problems and their solutions transcend national boundaries, but which nonetheless recognize that we will inevitably interpret the world from a particular position, and that most of us wish to remain attached to cultural and national particularities, to the social and cultural norms with which we are comfortable.

In the 1990s, Francis Fukuyama (1992) and Samuel Huntington (1996) provided contrasting responses to these challenges. Following the fall of the Berlin Wall, Fukuyama (1992) spoke optimistically about the 'end of history', of the deep ideological conflicts between capitalism and communism and a global convergence towards market rationality and liberal democracy. He thus assumed that world culture was increasingly moving towards a shared set of moral and political values. In contrast, Huntington (1996) insisted on the opposite. The world was now witnessing a major 'clash of civilizations', he argued, which is likely to shape all aspects of our lives. Huntington predicted that in the future the world would experience more rather than less conflict, and that the fundamental source of this conflict would no longer be ideological, or even economic, but rather cultural. He insisted that the differences between civilizations were not only real but also basic. They revolved around issues of history, culture, tradition and most notably religion. Huntington (1996) asserted that people of different civilizations had 'different views on the relations between God and man, the individual and the group, the citizens and the state', as well as 'different views on the relative importance of rights and responsibilities, liberty, authority, equality and hierarchy' (6). So far from being on the verge of a global convergence, we were now witnessing a clash between contrasting perspectives on identity and civilization heritage. The political analyses of both Fukuyama and Huntington cast a very depressing shadow on education since neither global homogeneity nor permanent conflict appear to be apt solutions to the educational challenges of transnationalism. In many systems of education, multicultural education has been proposed as the solution to the challenge put forward by Touraine. From the perspective of transnationalism, the main problem with multiculturalism however is that it takes the nation-state to be its entire moral universe. In this way, it often appears divorced from the processes of transnationalization that are increasingly affecting the ways in which many people think about their identity, their sense of belonging and the cultural spaces they inhabit. So if multiculturalism is to survive as a useful policy concept then it cannot remain tied simply to the agenda for managing inter-ethnic relations *within the nation-state*. For it to be useful in dealing with the transnational exchange, it needs to interpret the local and the national within the wider global context. It has to deal, for example, with the transnational spaces that enable many people to now belong simultaneously to more than one country and interpret their sense of belonging with respect to economic, social and political relations in ways that span across national boundaries.

In the past, multiculturalism was seen as a way of reconfiguring the relationship between the dominant culture and minority communities within the nation-state (Rizvi 1985). It was concerned with the issues of cultural maintenance and equality of access and opportunity of minority groups. The question we now need to ask is whether it is possible for multiculturalism to enlarge its political agenda, to reflect the realities of the transnationalization. Can multiculturalism respond effectively to those new patterns of cultural interaction and communication that are facilitated not only by the flows of people across the globe but also by the flows of finance, technologies and media images? In my view, it cannot to do this unless it embraces a more dynamic view of cultural identity that is located within the conditions of transnationalism. This demands critical engaging with ideas and images that circulate around the world and paying attention to the problems of inclusion and exclusion in the emerging transnational spaces. It necessitates rejecting a view of intercultural relations that is inherently naturalistic and anthropological, conceptualized as a *way of life*. By ignoring and obscuring the historical and political construction of cultural identities, multiculturalism had always reified culture (Hall 1996). Its essentialism implied that society was fundamentally constituted by an uninterrupted accord between diverse cultural traditions and that, as a consensual social site that could accommodate differences in an impartial manner. However, as a number of critics (e.g. Papastergiadis 2000) have pointed out, this pluralism ignores the workings of power and privilege. It presupposes harmony and agreement as natural states within which differences can co-exist without disturbing the prevailing structural norms.

If multiculturalism cannot adequately meet the challenges of transnational spaces then we need alternatives that preserve some of its pluralist sensibilities, but view culture as a dynamic relational concept – forged, maintained and developed in response to changing social and material conditions, often in relation to other cultural traditions with whom it interacts in transnational spaces. For the philosopher Martha Nussbaum (1996) the idea of cosmopolitanism is not wedded to a national framing in the ways multiculturalism is. She stresses the importance of an education that takes seriously the notion of a globally inter-related moral order, in which the entire humankind is treated with moral concern. She thus rejects the assumption that citizens have a duty to identify themselves first and foremost as citizens of a particular nation. Indeed, Nussbaum (1996) regards any attempt to accord one's own traditions 'special salience in moral and political deliberations' as 'both morally dangerous and, ultimately subversive of some of the worthy goals patriotism sets out to serve' (11): morally dangerous because it reinforces the unexamined assumption that one's own preferences and ways of acting are somehow natural and perfectly rational and subversive because it overlooks the fact that, in the longer term, even our most local of interests are tied to the broader concerns of others.

Nussbaum insists however that this does not mean giving up local affiliations in order to be a citizen of the world. She recognizes that local traditions could be a source of great richness in the world. However, she insists that they can also produce much conflict, especially if they were celebrated in an uncritically partisan fashion. For Nussbaum, cosmopolitanism represents a set of universal moral principles that apply to all societies, even if their concrete expressions vary. She links the idea of cosmopolitanism to notions of social solidarity, cohesion and a global sense of belonging. In this way, she challenges the spatially specific reference to define social solidarity. If communitarism is based on the idea of solidarity across a given community (Etzioni 2004), and nationalism implies developing a sense of belonging to a nation (Smith 2010), Nussbaum believes that cosmopolitanism appeals to solidarity and belongs to the whole cosmos or the universe. As appealing as Nussbaum's notion might appear, a number of scholars (e.g. Fine 2007) have pointed out that this association between cosmopolitanism and the universal has contributed to the development of a highly abstract understanding of cosmopolitanism that overlooks issues of historical difference and political contestation. Furthermore, the notion of cosmos is difficult to grasp in practical and experiential terms. It is consequently difficult to utilize it in educational settings (Rizvi 2009), especially with respect to the development of a sense of belonging.

Cosmopolitan learning

Nussbaum believes that education has an important role to play in disseminating an understanding of the universal principles associated with cosmopolitanism. Her conviction is based on a genuine belief in a common humanity that transcends differences in cultural traditions and political configurations. However, lacking such universal principles, is it possible to craft a narrative of cosmopolitanism that promotes an understanding and appreciation of our connectedness at the global level but does not assume abstractionism, together with a perspective that insists on a universal moral order? We need to recognize the enormous diversity that exists in the world in the ways in which moral and political regimes are forged, and that these regimes are increasingly coming in contact with each other. Perspectives towards the notions of citizenship, democracy and human rights vary greatly across communities and nations, even as, in transnationalizing spaces, their economic and political interests might at times converge. So if our principles cannot be assumed to exist in a transcendental space then an alternative is clearly needed.

To articulate such an alternative, a number of scholars have in recent years sought to develop a concept of 'everyday cosmopolitanism' (e.g. Skrbis and Woodward 2013). Such a concept suggests that our moral principles are always tentative and subject to revisions and that they can only emerge out of an empirical understanding of the nature and causes of political disputes and cultural conflicts, along with conversations within and across cultures about how disputes can be managed and conflicts overcome. It points to the realization that most people are already engaged in cosmopolitan encounters in their everyday life and are already developing an incipient organic sense of cosmopolitanism with which to engage the world of cultural difference. The idea of 'everyday cosmopolitanism' thus refers to those practices of cosmopolitanism that are now routine and are part of an emerging 'global consciousness' (Robertson 1991). Normatively, this consciousness has the potential to promote the importance of a broad sense of openness towards other people, cultures and ways of life. But such an openness demands an empirical understanding of the ways in which everyday cosmopolitan encounters produce social meaning and increasingly affect many of our dispositions, experiences and aspirations.

Such a grounded approach to cosmopolitanism appears more plausible, readily accessible to students than the moral universalism proposed by Nussbaum. It also rejects a relativism that might recognize the existence of cultural diversity but refuse to engage with it in any seriously critical way. Instead, it suggests that the educational challenges of transnationalism can only be met through attempts to develop in students the capacities to interpret and negotiate intercultural encounters. As I have already noted, in the current condition of ubiquitous global mobility, there is nothing unusual about such encounters, nothing extraordinary. Rather they are often routine ways of engaging with the contemporary realities of everyday life. If this is so then cosmopolitan learning should be situated within the actual lives of young people, highlighting how their lives are part of wider social, political and economic relations, in increasingly transnational spaces. It should accept the fact that everyday experiences can open up the possibility for multiple engagements with cosmopolitanism, and to approaches to cosmopolitan learning that are always situated and context-specific. It is through this interaction with specific experiences, desires and expectations that normative principles can be contextualized and become meaningful and relevant to the lives of students.

This view of cosmopolitanism is in line with what the moral philosopher Kwame Appiah (2006) calls 'rooted cosmopolitanism'. From Appiah's perspective, cosmopolitanism does not contradict patriotism or other allegiances. Rather it embraces the notion of multiple and overlapping belongings. This involves a significant shift from the either/or logic, in which the demarcation of symbolic borders is often assumed to be a precondition for identity formation, to the both/ and logic of 'inclusive differentiation' (Beck 2006). It suggests that the strong opposition between cosmopolitanism (as detachment) and national identities (as attachment) is mistaken and misleading. Cosmopolitanism is instead seen as performative. It is messy, complex and put into play in everyday decisions. It is not an outcome; it is not an individual attribute, but rather a practice, a disposition that is always in process of changing as people interact across different contexts. So, a cosmopolitan does not describe people, but suggests a way of engaging with others. As Skrbis and Woodward (2013) put it, there is no such thing as an *end point* in cosmopolitanism. It is an ongoing project, both at the social and the individual level. In this way, the cosmopolitan project in education involves developing the capacity of students to participate in open-ended conversations with others without necessarily reaching an agreement or defining universal maxims. Appiah (2006) uses the notion of conversation, both in its habitual meaning, and also 'as a metaphor for engagement with the experience and the ideas of others' (85), to show how intercultural dialogue is essential for developing cosmopolitan sensibilities. In this way, cosmopolitanism is about developing awareness of the complexity of life decisions, the value of considering other points of view, and the consequences of our everyday decisions and actions for those that are close, but also for those that are far away in space and time.

Cosmopolitan learning thus does not involve the acquisition of a fixed set of values and dispositions, but an attempt to help student to develop a sense of how they are located in a world of transnational exchanges. It demands making everyday cosmopolitan experiences – including its banal, consumerist and elitist forms – visible, open to scrutiny and competing interpretations. Once cosmopolitan experiences are made visible, the next step is to promote a critical and reflexive practice, avoiding binary thinking associated with an ethical good/bad approach, and getting deep into the messiness and complexities of moral everyday decisions in which different values and the rights of different groups may be in conflict but also overlap, both within and across national borders. This exchange should take the form of open-ended collective conversations that provide students an opportunity to discuss cosmopolitanism in relation to real lived experiences of the participants, reflecting about the complexities that are inherent to every decision, no matter how trivial or profound. These types of conversation should be aimed at overcoming purely individualistic notions of global responsibility, in which global problems are couched in individualistic, psychological and moralistic terms but should instead help students to realize that the global problems, inequalities, risks and challenges can only be understood in ways that are historicized and politicized.

To do this, a critical contextually specific understanding of transnational interconnectivity and interdependence is necessary, helping students to come to terms with their *situatedness* in the world – of their knowledge and their cultural practices as well as the unique positions they occupy in relation to social networks, political institutions and social relations that are no longer confined to particular communities, but span the globe. It should be possible to do this pedagogic work through networked learning, both formal and informal, bringing together people from different cultural backgrounds. Such learning must necessarily encourage students to think outside their own parochial boundaries and cultural assumptions, to consider how the processes of transnationalization affect communities differently, and to examine what the sources of these differentiations and inequalities might be. Instead of learning about cultures in an abstract manner, cosmopolitan learning implies the need to create opportunities for students to explore the criss-crossing of transnational circuits of communication, the flows of global capital and the cross-cutting of local and transnational social practices, and their differential consequences for different people and communities.

Such learning must involve students considering the contested politics of place making, the social constructions of power differentials and the dynamic processes relating to the formation of individual, group, national and transnational identities, and their corresponding fields of difference. In this sense, cosmopolitan learning should be concerned with the development of attitudes and skills for understanding, not other cultural traditions per se, but the ways by which global processes are creating conditions of economic and cultural exchange that are transforming our identities and communities; and that, reflexively, we are contributing to the production and reproduction of those conditions.

Conclusion

The spaces in which we live, work and learn are becoming transnationalized. The processes of transnationalization, however, have both positive outcomes, but also negative consequences. They have given rise to new opportunities and expressions of creativity, but they have also raised the spectre of an ugly reactionary politics, with the revival of ethno-nationalist and xenophobic traditions among people who are fearful of cultural diversity and exchange. These contradictory aspects of transnationalism have deep implications for thinking about educational policy and practice, especially as they relate to issues of democracy, citizenship and human rights education. In spaces that are increasingly characterized by ubiquitous mobility, diversity and connectivity, the issues of moral and political pedagogy take on centre stage. The urgent questions educators around the world now face is how they might help their students to think seriously and critically about processes of transnationality, in pedagogic spaces that are themselves transnational.

I have examined a number of approaches to the ways in which the political formation of students might be forged, and how their normative sensibilities towards citizenship, democracy and human rights might be developed. In particular, I have considered the idea of cosmopolitanism, which has a long history but a highly contested meaning. It has variously been promoted as a political philosophy, a moral theory, a cultural disposition and an educational orientation. As a moral doctrine, cosmopolitanism suggests a duty of all human beings to help each other, or at least, be respectful of each other's values and ways of life regardless of political borders and cultural differences. In recent years, renewed interest in cosmopolitanism has been based upon the realization that the world is becoming increasingly interconnected and interdependent, and that most of its problems are global in nature, requiring global solutions.

I have argued that a normative agenda for cosmopolitanism needs to acknowledge that the processes of transnationalization are already giving many young people in particular an incipient organic sense of cosmopolitanism with which to engage with the world of cultural difference. Following a number of recent scholars, such as Skrbis and Woodward (2013), who have used the term 'everyday cosmopolitanism' to refer to those discourses and practices of cosmopolitanism that have become routine and are taken for granted in many parts of the world, I have argued the need to take this insight seriously, not least because it has profound consequences for the social constitution of our identities and institutions. I have argued that cosmopolitanism can be viewed as a form of learning through which students are encouraged to understand their *situated-ness* in a world in which cultural diversity has become normal, but cultural exchanges are shaped through power relations that are diffuse, transnationally stretched and increasingly unequal. I have suggested that cosmopolitan learning should therefore involve teaching students how to engage *empirically* with the ways in which ordinary cosmopolitan encounters produce meaning and have impact on human practices, dispositions and experiences in historically and politically specific ways; and that it is only through open-ended but critical conversations that a shared understanding of our global problems and their solutions are possible.

References

Appadurai, Arjun. *Modernity at Large: Cultural Dynamics of Globalization.* Minneapolis: University of Minnesota Press, 1996.

Appadurai, Arjun. *Fear of Small Numbers.* Durham, NC: Duke University Press, 2006.

Appiah, Kwame. *Cosmopolitanism: Ethics in a World of Strangers.* New York: W.W. Norton, 2006.

Bauman, Zygmunt. *Globalization: The Human Consequences.* Cambridge: Polity Press, 1998.

Bauman, Zygmunt. *Globalization: The Human Consequences.* Cambridge: Polity Press, 2000.

Beck, Ulrich. *What Is Globalization?* Cambridge: Polity Press, 2000.

Beck, Ulrich. *Cosmopolitan Vision.* Cambridge: Polity Press, 2006.

Cope, Bill and Mary Kalantzis. *Productive Diversity.* Sydney: Pluto Press, 2000.

Dicken, Peter. *Global Shift: Mapping the Mapping the Changing Contours of the World Economy* (7th edition). London: Guildford Press, 2015.

Etzioni, Amitai. *The Common Good*. Cambridge: Polity Press, 2004.

Faist, Thomas, Margit Fauser, and Eveline Reisenauer. *Transnational Migration*. Cambridge: Polity Press, 2013.

Ferguson, James. *Global Shadows: Africa in the Neo-Liberal World Order*. Durham, NC: Duke University Press, 2006.

Fine, Robert. *Cosmopolitanism*. London: Taylor and Francis, 2007.

Fukuyama, Francis. *The End of History and the Last Man*. New York: Free Books, 1992.

Hall, Stuart. 'New Ethnicities'. In *Stuart Hall: Critical Dialogues in Cultural Studies*, edited by David Morley and K.-C. Chen, 441–449. London: Routledge, 1996.

Huntington, Samuel. *Clash of Civilizations and the Remaking of the World Order*. London: Simon and Schuster, 1996.

International Organization for Migration. Data. https://migrationdataportal.org/data?i=stock_abs_&t=2017, 2017.

Massey, Doreen. *World City*. Cambridge: Polity Press, 2007.

Nagel, Caroline and E. Mavaroudi, *Global Migration: Patterns, Processes and Politics*. London: Routledge, 2016.

Nail, Thomas. (2015) *The Figure of the Migrant*. Stanford: Stanford University Press.

Nussbaum, Martha. 'Patriotism and Cosmopolitanism'. In *For Love of Country?* edited by Joel Cohen, 3–17. Boston, MA: Beacon Press, 2002.

Nussbaum, Martha. 'Patriotism and Cosmopolitanism'. In *For the Love of Country: Debating the Limits of Patriotism*, edited by M. Nussbaum and J. Cohen, 1–14. Cambridge MA: Beacon Press, 1996.

Ohmae, Kenichi. *The End of the Nation-state: The Rise of Regional Economy*. New York: HarperCollins, 1996.

Ong, Aihwa. *Flexible Citizenships: The Cultural Logics of Transnationality*. Durham, NC: Duke University Press, 1999.

Ostergaard-Nielsen, Eva. 'The Politics of Migrants' Political Practices'. *International Migration Review* 37, no. 3 (2003): 760–786.

Papastergiadis, Nicholas. *The Turbulence of Migration: Globalization, Deterritorialization and Hybridity*. Cambridge: Polity Press, 2000.

Pieterese, Jan Nederveen. *Globalization and Culture*. London: Routledge, 2005.

Ray, Leslie. *Globalization and Everyday Life*. London: Routledge, 2007.

Rizvi, Fazal. *Multiculturalism as an Educational Policy*. Geelong: Deakin University Press, 1985.

Rizvi, Fazal. 'Towards Cosmopolitan Learning'. *Discourse: Studies in the Cultural Politics of Education* 30, no. 3 (2009): 253–268.

Rizvi, Fazal, Kam Louie, and Julia Evans. *Australia's Asian Diaspora Advantage*. Melbourne: Australian Federation of Learned Academies, 2016.

Robertson, Roland. *Globalization: Social Theory and Global Culture*. London: Sage, 1991.

Sassen, Saskia. *The Global City: New York, London and Tokyo*. Princeton: Princeton University Press, 1991.

Shields, Robin. *Globalization and International Education*. London: Bloomsbury, 2013.

Shipson, Tim. *Fall Out: A Year of Political Turmoil*. London: William Collins, 2017.

Skrbis, Zlato and Ian Woodward. *Cosmopolitanism: Uses of the Idea*. London: Sage, 2013.

Smith, Anthony. *Nationalism: Theory, Ideology, History*. Cambridge: Polity Press, 2010.

Tomlinson, John. *Globalization and Culture*. Chicago: Chicago University Press, 2000.

Touraine, Alaine. *Can We Live Together? Equality and Difference*. Stanford: Stanford University Press, 2000.

United Nations Commissioner for Refugees. Figures at a Glance. http://www.unhcr.org/figures-at-a-glance.html, 2018.

Urry, John. *Mobilities*. Cambridge UK: Cambridge University Press, 2007.

Vertovec, Steven. *The Emergence of Super-diversity in Britain*. Oxford: COMPAS, Working Paper WP-06-25, 2006.

Vertovec, Steven. *Transnationalism*. London: Routledge, 2009.

Wilson, Kalpana. *Race, Racism and Development: Interrogating History, Discourse and Practice*. London: Zed Books, 2012.

World Tourism Organization. Data. http://www2.unwto.org/content/data, 2018.

Part Two

Transnational Perspectives on Democracy and Education

3

Towards a Narrative of a Robust Global Democracy: Critical Democratic and Decolonial Perspectives

Mary Drinkwater

Chapter outline

- Acknowledgements and introduction
  - Political shifting in the purposes of education: Colonial modernity, classical liberalism, neoliberalism
  - Emergence and spread of the many faces of globalization
- Kenyan context and the impetus for a new narrative of democracy for education
- Theoretical framework (critical, decolonial)
- Erosion of thick democracy in schools: Impact of colonial modernity and neoliberalism
- Moving towards a new narrative of a robust global democracy
  - Deweyan contributions
  - Ancient Greek (paideia) contributions
  - African and indigenous contributions
  - Arendtian contributions
  - Plurality, politics and criticality in democracy
- Summary

Keywords: robust global democracy; critical democratic theory; decolonial theory; neoliberal globalization; social transformation; Kenya

Acknowledgements and introduction

In keeping with decolonial practices, I begin by acknowledging the *indigenous peoples* of *Turtle Island* (now known as the geo-political regions of Canada and the United States) from which I am writing. I also acknowledge the Maasai peoples from southern Kenya, who have *named me* as a member of their community and who have contributed significantly to my learnings over the past nine years. My own transnational mobilities and the invitation to become a member of another cultural community, quite different in many ways from the community and culture in which I was born and raised, brings about some of the *complexities* in *identity* that Rizvi speaks about in the opening chapter of this book. It also brings about tremendous opportunities for reflection on differences, particularly in ways of *knowing* and *being*. Based on these reflections, I develop and share with you, for your own reflections, a different narrative of democracy.

The impetus for the creation of this new narrative of democracy arose during my doctoral thesis research work (Drinkwater 2014) in two Maasai communities in southern Kenya between 2009 and 2012. At the time, I was searching for a conception of democracy that opened possibilities for the use of the arts and cultural praxis in formal and non-formal educational programmes around the world, as a way to *give voice, touch 'the intimate senses', connect the head, heart & hand, critically engage,* and *act* for the purpose of informing and contributing to social change. Under the multidimensional impacts of the processes of *globalization* and *global mobilities* (Rizvi 2018), current dominant conceptions of democracy, such as liberal democracy, representative democracy and even critical democracy, are narrowly focused on the *nation-state* and limit opportunities to consider our roles as *global citizens* in what Kymlicka (2001) calls the *global commons*. Under the impacts of both industrialization and neoliberal globalization, Amutabi (2017), Brown (2006), Mignolo (2011) and Niyozov and Dastambuev (2012) raise concerns in the global commons related to issues such as environmental sustainability, cultural diversity, human rights violations, regional and global conflict and peace-building processes. I introduce this new narrative of democracy to challenge and possibly disrupt dominant conceptions of democracy and inform curricular and pedagogical approaches for more *democratic and transformative* purposes of education in the transnational contexts in which we are living.

This chapter includes five major sections. The first section provides an historical overview of some of the significant global political/ideological shifts which have influenced the purpose of education, particularly with respect to notions of *democracy* and *democratic education*. The second section outlines the context underpinning the creation of this new narrative of democracy. The third section introduces a two-pronged theoretical framework, combining critical theory and decolonial theory on which the narrative of a robust global democracy is constructed. The framework draws on *critical theory* as a theoretical approach to identify current inequities in education and to offer a *discourse of possibility* for an emancipatory role for education. *Decolonial theory* illuminates the impacts of the *colonial modernity project* and acts as a foundation to *imagine differently* to begin to address current inequities and injustices in the world. The fourth section reviews literature to support the argument that neoliberal globalization contributes to an erosion or *thinning* of the concept and principles of democracy in society and schools. In the final section, drawing on the work of critical and decolonial scholarship from the global north and global south, I begin to create a new narrative, or *thicker* conception of democracy, which I call a *robust global democracy.*

Political shifting in the purposes of education: Colonial modernity, classical liberalism, neoliberalism

To understand the context of democratic education within the current global educational context, I present a brief history of the development of *modern* educational systems using Wallerstein's (1974) world systems theory. As Wallerstein (1974) argues, each major political and ideological shift catalysed the establishment of a new World Order. The ontological and epistemological underpinnings of modern educational systems have been impacted and influenced by these political and ideological shifts.

During the mid-eighteenth century, the move from feudalism to Enlightenment was viewed by many critical and decolonial theorists as a move towards what Mignolo (2011) calls *colonial modernity*. Within this colonial modernity World Order, the governance structure was informed by classical liberalism theorists (Brown 2003). The liberal ideology advocated for universal rights including freedom and equality. A set of principles governing the limitations of state power was enshrined within the 'Rule of Law' of the nation-state (Brown 2003). The features of a truly liberal democracy included:

> Civil liberties equally distributed and protected; a press and other journalistic media minimally free from corporate ownership on one side and state control on the other; uncorrupted and unbought elections; quality public education oriented, inter alia, to producing the literacies relevant to informed and active citizenship; government openness, honesty and accountability; a judiciary modestly insulated from political and commercial influence; separation of

church and state; and a foreign policy guided at least in part by the rationale of protecting these domestic values. (Brown 2003, para. 30)

The legitimation of any government purporting to follow the principles of a liberal democracy requires the consent of those it governs. As a means of increasing the efficiency of gathering the input of large numbers of citizens, many liberal democratic states adopt a system of *representative democracy*. As Brown (2006) argues, over the years, nation-states around the world explicitly espousing a liberal democratic model have faced challenges related to majority rule, while respecting minority rights; strengthening communities, while liberating individuals; and empowering government, while at the same time limiting the power of the state.

Another major shift in the World Order followed the end of the Second World War, as governments began to search for ways to rebuild their economies. As Klees (2008) asserts, fierce debates arose between liberal and conservative neoclassical economists, largely situated in the United States, around the role of government in the development of efficient and equitable economic systems. As the humanistic, social justice and human rights focus of the welfare state began to erode, the competitive, market-based technology-driven paradigms of the International Monetary Fund (IMF), the World Bank and the Organization of Economic Cooperation and Development (OECD) signalled the emergence of the hegemony of Western capitalism (Zajda 2009). In the 1970s, a conservative economic view became strengthened through the development of 'public choice theory' (Klees 2008). Public choice theory was based on a belief that even though the free market might fail to operate efficiently and equitably in the absence of government intervention, 'government was so incapable of making successful interventions that it was better not to have it intervene in the first place' (Klees 2008, 311). A significant shift in global public policy began in 1980. The neoliberal approach to economic policy emerged with the elections of Ronald Reagan (USA) and Margaret Thatcher (UK) and the predominance of conservative and public choice economists in positions of political and economic power. Market-based principles of efficiency, standardization, accountability, user fees and privatization began to increasingly inform public policy analysis and development. As Klees (2008) argues, over the past quarter-century, neoliberal ideology and economic principles have increasingly been influencing educational policy reform around the world.

Emergence and spread of the many faces of globalization

The forces of globalization have indeed influenced the spread of educational policies. However, it is important not to essentialize globalization but to observe and critique the various processes of globalization and how they are managed: who and what benefits, and who and what is marginalized, eroded or destroyed. Niyozov and Dastambuev (2012) assert that many of the issues and concerns within the highly interwoven processes of globalization arise from the 'unprecedented intensification and extensification of cross-border interactions and flows between humans (individuals, communities, nations, interest groups, transnational agencies) and human products (goods, ideas, technologies and cultures)' (Introduction and method, para. 2).

Niyozov and Dastambuev (2012) discuss the face of globalization. Indeed, this metaphor of the human face contributes to the complexity of the analysis of the processes of globalization on the human condition. Rizvi (2018) highlights the diverse impacts of *global migration and mobilities*. In recognizing the importance of counter-narratives to neoliberal globalization processes, Niyozov and Dastambuev (2012) argue that 'while globalization may be inevitable and even desirable, neoliberalism is not and should not be its only face and outcome' (Introduction and method, para. 2).

Kenyan context and the impetus for a new narrative of democracy for education

The impetus for the need to create a new narrative of democracy arose during my doctoral research work in Kenya between 2009 and 2012. This important historical period for Kenya reflects what Nasong'o and Murunga (2007) call its 'struggle toward democracy'. Although Kenya gained independence in 1963 and espouses democratic nation-state status, Kenya has been challenged by critical educators and civil society organizations for its true commitment to the ideals, principles and practices of truly robust democracies (Amutabi 2017; Murunga and Nasong'o 2007). The 2013 report of the Truth, Justice and Reconciliation Commission (2013) identified four decades of significant issues with corrupt leadership, ethnic conflict, human rights atrocities and the brutal post-election violence in 2007–2008.

Many of the major structural and pedagogical elements within Kenyan education systems remained largely unchanged since independence (Nasong'o and Murunga 2007). Kenya released its new *Basic Education Curriculum Framework* (2017), with only four references to *democracy* within the middle years integrated social studies curriculum. Although a significant step was taken along the road towards democracy in Kenya with the adoption of the new constitution in 2010, Drinkwater (2014) found that the policy discourse within the constitution and the 2013 Kenyan Education Bill reflects a thin notion democracy and democratic education. This erosion of democracy in education is not isolated to Kenya.

Theoretical framework (critical, decolonial)

To open possibilities for exploring democratic and transformative education within a transnational context, I developed a two-pronged theoretical framework to construct a new narrative of robust global democracy. The rise of critical theory grew from aspects of the social theory work of Marx and Freud. Foundational intellectuals of the Frankfurt School in the 1920s, including Horkheimer, Adorno and Marcuse, began to challenge the impacts of the hegemony of the ideology of capitalism. Horkheimer (1982) described a theory as critical in so far as it seeks 'to liberate human beings from the circumstances that enslave them' (244). Gramsci (1971) argued for the need to develop what he termed *organic individuals* who possessed the tools necessary to engage in educational, social and cultural action, which included the exercise of critical (dialectical) consciousness aimed at social transformation.

Critical theorists of the 1980s and 1990s, such as Freire (1998, 2000), Giroux (1989, 1991), Greene (1988) and Kincheloe (1999), assert that critical scholars have a role in continuing to explore and illuminate issues of power, oppression and marginalization in education. Using a *discourse of possibility*, they argue instead that teachers and education should play a liberatory role in confronting and challenging the hegemony of colonial Eurocentrism and neoliberalism to enable schools to become venues for hope, resistance and democratic possibility. Critical theorists argue that this shift towards a more emancipatory role for education would require a new conception of human agency which places increased responsibility on students, teachers, educational leaders and communities to become critically engaged in the social transformation process (Darder, Baltodano and Torres 2009). These theorists advocate for the importance of linking individual lived experience to critical analysis, reflection and growth. Their work reinforces the need to de-link and reopen ways of thinking that challenge and disrupt the status quo in areas of equity and social justice, in ways that illuminate power imbalances, within more democratic and socially transformative purposes of education.

Decolonial theory, like critical theory, recognizes that education is not politically neutral and also aims to disrupt hegemony for social transformation towards a more just and inclusive society. However, decolonial scholars narrow their focus specifically towards colonialism/imperialism as the root cause of current global inequities and injustices. This theoretical sense requires imagining what De Lissovoy (2010) calls an 'ethic of the global' contextually set to recognize the 'relations of power that have shaped history, and in particular the political, cultural, economic, and epistemological processes of domination that have characterized colonialism and Eurocentrism' (279). Although the dismantling of colonial structures began during the eighteenth and nineteenth centuries, as many colonized countries gained independence, new forms of colonialism or imperialism continue to create power imbalances and inequities for people and nations. A deeper critique of these arising global social inequities has led scholars from multidisciplinary fields of feminist theory, critical theory and critical race theory to push more strongly for changes in policy and pedagogy towards decolonialism (Abdi 2012; Moya 2011; wa Thiong'o 1986).

Decolonial theory necessitates a thinking which de-links and opens the doors to other truths which challenge the colonial or imperial truth. Maldonado-Torres (2011) states that while this theoretical and philosophical decolonial turn has distinct features it had existed through various forms of expression of opposition to 'the colonizing turn in Western thought' (1). The links between critical theory and decolonial theory become clear in Mignolo's (2009) paper 'Epistemic Disobedience, Independent Thought and Decolonial Freedom', which posits the need for political and epistemic de-linking, as well as decolonializing and decolonial knowledges as 'necessary steps for imagining and building democratic, just, and non-imperial/colonial societies' (159).

Erosion of thick democracy in schools: Impact of colonial modernity and neoliberalism

Many nation-states continue to call themselves democratic. However, Brown (2006) suggests that the increasing ideological shift towards neoliberalism continues to erode liberal democratic principles and practices. Critical and decolonial scholars believe that the conception of a liberal democracy may not be *thick* or *robust* enough to be able to re-engage the public to challenge hegemonic ideologies (Thayer-Bacon 2008). Public education systems need to develop the skills, knowledge, attitudes and values to confront the current World Order dominated by global neoliberalism and begin the social transformation to create a more socially just and inclusive global community and sustainable environment.

The current conception of democracy expressed in many schools and nation-states, which purport to be democratic, often conflates citizenship with democracy (Westheimer 2008). Although the rhetoric of democratic citizenship is used, Lawy and Biesta (2006) argue that 'current educational policies and approaches to citizenship education are commonly founded on the assumptions of *citizenship-as-achievement,* a conceptualization with the emphasis on social engineering, upon the "manufacture" of compliant yet "active" citizens' (42). Lawy and Biesta (2006) also suggest that to view young people as moving into citizenship status represents an impoverished view of what it means to be a citizen that necessarily marginalizes and excludes them from mainstream life.

In drawing from personal experience with educational methods of other cultures, Thayer-Bacon (2008) highlights that many of the educational policies and pedagogical approaches adopted in schools in democratic nation-states are informed by liberal democratic ideology privileging 'rationalist and individualist understanding of democracy' (ix). Further, she asserts that the 'individualist legacy of liberal democracy, as conceived by Locke and Rousseau, ignores and excludes the needs of American students raised in cultures with strong communal traditions' (Thayer-Bacon 2008, back cover).

One of the most marginalizing approaches under colonial systems of educational reform was the promotion of teaching and learning approaches based on *deficit mentality* (Paris 2012). Deficit approaches view languages, literacies and cultural ways of being of students not belonging to dominant, hegemonic (White, Eurocentric) culture as deficiencies to be overcome by learning the legitimized, dominant, standardized, core curriculum on which they would be assessed. The ultimate goal of deficit approaches was the eradication of linguistic and cultural practices from students' homes and communities for replacement with those viewed as 'superior practices' (Paris 2012).

Critical scholars posit that the *thin* conception of democracy currently informing educational policy and pedagogy is insufficient. Even in educational systems in nations self-identifying as democratic, school-based spaces and opportunities for students to critically question and engage in robust dialogue related to larger historical, political and social forces contributing to marginalization and increasing inequities is becoming increasingly constricted (Thayer-Bacon 2008). Analysing data from Canadian schools, Westheimer (2008) found that the 'very foundations of democratic engagement, such as opportunities

for independent thinking and critical analysis have become less and less common'
(6). These findings indicate that the 'goals of K-12 education have been shifting
steadily away from preparing active and engaged public citizens and towards
more narrow goals of career preparation and individual economic gain' (6–7).

Moving towards a new narrative of a robust global democracy

Preparing youth to participate as active and engaged global citizens for social
transformation requires educational systems to be informed by a more robust
and global conception of democracy. As Anyon (2005) argues, many successful
socio-historical transformations have resulted from the democratic actions of
social movements. Our schools and communities do not sit in isolation from
these social movements. On the contrary, the combined effects of the globalization
and the evolution of global information technology increasingly enable schools,
communities and interest groups to engage, mobilize and take action around social
and political issues, in what Kymlicka (2001) calls *the global commons* at the local,
national and global scale. The challenge exists to revisit, reflect and re-conceptualize
the notion of democracy which is informing our educational systems in order to
thicken, deepen and globalize the purpose of education for social transformation.
I take my inspiration from these social movements. I draw from the concepts and
writing of theorists and scholars from the global north, global south and indigenous
communities to build this new narrative of democracy.

My notion of a *robust global democracy* emerges from various scholars
including Dewey (1916/2005), Mignolo (2009), Louw (1999, 2006), Mucina
(2011), Price (2007), Grande (2004), Arendt (1958), Mouffe (2002) and Portelli
and Solomon (2001). The multicultural and multidisciplinary aspects of these
authors' works contribute to a broader understanding of what it means to be a
democratic person and have implications on how democratic learning and the
goals of education within a democratic society are understood. The conception
of democracy put forward by Dewey (1916/2005) illuminates a *social* aspect;
notions of democracy and *paideia*, from the fifth century and fourth century
BC in Greece, add what may be termed a *reciprocal* aspect; notions arising from
within the African ethic of *ubuntu* (Louw 1999, 2006; Mucina 2011), combined
with the work of indigenous scholars, Price (2007) and Grande (2004) illuminate
a *collective* aspect; conceptions espoused by Arendt (1958) can be described as
adding *human-* and *action-oriented* aspects; and, those of Mouffe (2002) and
Portelli and Solomon (2001) add *plural, critical* and *political* aspects.

Deweyan contributions

Dewey (1916/2005) speaks to the importance of education in societies espousing democratic principles and renouncing external authority. Dewey (1900/1971) argues that the goal of education in democratic societies must be to develop individuals who have the knowledge, skills, interests and dispositions to take up this way of living. In this form of understanding democracy, education becomes a question of thought as much as governance. It is tied to ethical responsibility as much as to questions of society and socialization. Dewey (1916/2005) believed that 'a democracy is more than a form of government; it is primarily a *mode of associated living*, of conjoint communicated experience' (53).

For Dewey (1916/2005), the democratic subjectivity of an individual must include *social intelligence*. Through the interactions with others, individuals have the opportunity to think, reflect and make meaning of their environment. Biesta (2007) extends Dewey's work to suggest that during the process of *communication* through discussion, dialogue and interaction, that patterns of thought and action can be either formed or transformed. Democratic education for the development of *intelligence* must include opportunities for students to experience a multiplicity of social interactions and perspectives in order to develop both critical and creative thinking skills (Dewey, 1916/2005). Therefore, education within a democratic society, with many shared interests and a primary interest in the common good, must promote the *free and full interplay of associations* in order to secure a *liberation of powers* (Dewey 1916/2005). For Dewey (1916/2005), the transformative purpose of education rests on the social awareness of individuals so that each individual 'has to refer his own action to that of others and to consider the action of others to give point and direction to his own' (53).

Dewey (1938) stressed the importance of *experience* within the schooling environment, particularly that which linked to the lived experiences of students. Dewey also introduces the notion of *plasticity* to the idea of education as growth. Plasticity refers to the ability to retain lessons from one experience that could help when facing future difficulties. It is not simply in the learning from one experience, but as Dewey (1916/2005) suggests, it is through the process of open-ended reflective thinking through multiple experiences, particularly *social experiences*, that enables an individual to 'modify actions' and 'develop dispositions' (29). For Dewey, genuine education could not come from what Freire (1970/2000) referred to as a *banking education* in which formal education is separated from experience. Dewey conceptualizes education as being a lifelong pursuit in which the development of these democratic dispositions illuminated what Baldacchino (2008) describes as a view of society which has a 'ground of continuous possibilities' (151).

In order to open up the possibilities for students to use and grow from their own local experiences, educational systems must recognize and value the pluriversality of local languages and cultures. Dewey noted that when vital interests and experiences were disconnected from the classroom, students lost interest in being engaged in their learning. Dewey (1917/1980) references the disengagement students experience when classroom-based language of instruction is different from their *mother tongue*, stating: 'Since the language taught is unnatural, not growing out of the real desire to communicate vital impressions and convictions, the freedom of children in its use gradually disappears' (55–56).

In addition to opening itself up to pluriverse ways of knowing and being, Baldacchino (2008) identifies in Dewey's writings a key element which connects to what I refer to as an ethic of a *globality of humanity* (Drinkwater 2014). Baldacchino (2008) views Dewey's idea of communication and communicated experiences being built around a 'consensus for difference', which should inform our thinking 'as a way of acting and defining our case as human beings, as the rational co-inhabitants of one world' (153). Within this narrative of a robust global democracy, this consensus of difference requires an understanding and acceptance of the need for pluriverse voices and perspectives, while acknowledging that the tensions created while experiencing and engaging with difference are necessary in order for individuals to learn and grow. In creating this new narrative of democracy, acknowledging and respecting the plurality of the members of the global polis and the commonality of our humanity, Dewey's belief in a *consensus for difference* remains an important principle as a *social* aspect.

Ancient Greek (paideia) contributions

Centuries ago, in ancient Greece, Plato began to build the model for a utopian society identifying an important role for education in a democratic state to extend beyond formal settings. In *The Republic*, Plato describes a system of education built on *paideia*. As Hancock (1987) notes, the concept of *paideia* saw 'the city-state and the citizen existing in an educational relationship in which both the society and the individual had reciprocal obligations to improve one another' (para. 2). Fotopoulos (2012) describes *paideia* as an 'all-round civic education that involves a life-long process of character development, absorption of knowledge and skills and – more significant – practicing a "participatory" kind of active citizenship, that is citizenship in which political activity is not seen as a means to an end but an end in itself' (83). This participatory element pushes the narrative of democracy beyond narrow notions of *representative democracy* towards more *participatory democracy*. However, Fotopoulos (2012) stresses that *paideia* pushes even further to promote the development of strong moral values, including those of cooperation, mutual aid and solidarity, which are consistent with individual and collective autonomy in a *demos*-based society.

In both nation-states and globally, under the influence of global neoliberalism, Fotopoulos (2012) argues the need to revisit the role that *paideia* can play in addressing inequalities arising from economic democracy. If political democracy is defined as the authority of *demos* (citizens) in the political realm, Fotopoulos (2012) posits

> economic democracy can be defined as the authority of the *demos* in the economic realm – which implies the existence of economic equality in the sense of equal distribution of economic power. Economic democracy can be described as an economic *structure* and a *process* which, through direct citizen participation in the economic decision-taking and decision-implementing process, secures an equal distribution of economic power among citizens. (97)

Under increasing globalization of the market economy, resulting inequalities are influencing the demos at the local, national and global levels with rising levels of inequity. The development of a global *demos* with moral values promoted by paideia, and a high level of robust democratic engagement is ever more vital. In constructing a new narrative of a robust global democracy, the lessons arising from *paideia* speak to the importance of *equality, equity* and the notion of a *reciprocal* relationship between the society and the individual.

African and indigenous contributions

In expanding the narrative of a robust global democracy, bringing in the voices and theories of decolonial scholars reinforces the knowledge and voices of those marginalized under colonialism/Eurocentrism/imperialism which must be reignited, promoted and valued (Abdi 2012; Battiste 2010; Dei and Simmons 2011; Maldonado-Torres 2011; Mignolo 2011; wa Thiong'o 1986; Wane 2009). As Mignolo (2009) argues, 'the need for political and epistemic de-linking ...

as well as decolonizing and decolonial knowledges, [are] necessary steps for imagining and building democratic, just, and nonimperial/colonial societies' (7).

Centuries prior to Dewey, and prior to the colonial encounter, many indigenous societies established their own forms of governance based on their philosophical, ontological and cosmological understanding of the relationship between individuals, their society and their environment. Many traditional African societies espouse the importance of a *collective* responsibility or social ethic for individuals as members of a society. In Zulu, the phrase *Umuntu ngumuntu ngabantu* means 'a person is a person through other persons' (Louw 2006, 161). The central concept of *ubuntu* means *humanity, humanness* or even *humaneness*, and articulates a basic respect and compassion for others. Ubuntu reflects a social ethic which not only describes human being as *being-with-others*, but also prescribes how individuals should relate to others. The ethic of *ubuntu*, officially recognized in the 1997 South African Governmental White Paper for Social Welfare, bears many similarities to the concept which I am putting forward in this chapter of a robust global democracy grounded in a globality of humanity:

> The principle of caring for each other's well-being ... and a spirit of mutual support ... Each individual's humanity is ideally expressed through his or her relationship with others and theirs in turn through a recognition of the individual's humanity. *Ubuntu* means that people are people through other people. It also acknowledges both the rights and the responsibilities of every citizen in promoting individual and societal well-being. (Republic of South Africa 1997, Article 24)

Recognizing the forces of globalization and decolonizing the post-industrial notion of democracy, which has dominated Northern and Western nation-states for over a century, requires the creation of an alternative radical narrative of democracy.

Within this more inclusive and global conception, Price (2007) draws on Mignolo asserting the need for 'stories from below [that are] an empowered counter narrative to globalisation from above' (10). For centuries prior to the post-industrial Western model of democracy, many Fourth World or indigenous cultures had their own models of governance and decision-making. Beliefs drawn from indigenous ontology and cosmology could contribute further to the conception of a global democracy by placing the responsibility for decision-making for the sustainability of the earth and the peaceful co-existence of humans and their environment in the hands of humans (De Lissovoy 2010).

Many indigenous scholars have written about the continuing and historic contributions of Fourth World or indigenous peoples to the conceptualization, approach, principles and content of a range of democratic ideals (Battiste 2008; Grande 2004; Louw 2006; Price 2007). Dewey's description of democracy as being more of a *way of life* than a form of governmentality blends well with the conception of an indigenous Confederacy or *way of being and governing* (Price 2007). Price (2007) describes the democratic ideal of the Haudenosaunee (Iroquoian) peoples as the equitable distribution of power and 'an inclusive social, economic, political, and environmental democracy, with an ideal trinity of protection, provision, and participation for its entire people' (17). Further, it models what Arendt (1958) stressed as critical to the development of democratic subjectivities, the freedom to speak, think and act. Price (2007) identifies a number of core distinguishing content qualities of these democratic communities including: generalized and empowered dialogue, respect for diversity, equity, ecological justice and peace.

Price (2007) builds a notion of a critical red democracy from the work of Grande (2004), who linked the Haudenosaunee democratic tradition, critical pedagogy and transformative praxis. For the Haudenosaunee peoples, the guiding values and principles included participation by all members, collective thinking and decision-making by consensus. The spiritual beliefs of the Haudenosaunee people include the need to recognize and seek the wisdom of all members of society, those living, those whose spirits have passed on and those still to come. As Price (2007) recounts 'all people and points of view must be heard and respected including the interests of the coming seven generations and maintaining the respect for the past seven generations' (17). The deep spiritual respect for and connection with the land and its natural elements guided decision-making in this conception of democracy. In this new narrative of democracy, the principles inherent in a robust global democracy must be extended to all global peoples in order to open a much broader, deeper, critical, decolonial dialogue and participation to re-create and sustain a global consciousness in our *shared environment* for social and ecological justice.

Arendtian contributions

Arendt (1958) pushes Dewey's *social* conception of democracy further by arguing that for an individual to develop a democratic subjectivity he or she must be able to *act*. In this historical-philosophical analysis of the link between politics and the human condition, Arendt posits that the Western philosophical and political traditions have devalued the role of human action, the *vita activa*. In *The Human Condition*, Arendt (1958) classifies human activities into the three categories of labour, work and action. According to Arendt (1958), under the current conditions of modernity, the primary purposes of labour and work have been to both *produce* and *consume* driven by the forces of industrialization and capitalism. Arendt (1958) asserts that the fruits of many of these efforts of labour and work are 'impermanent, perishable and sometimes exhausted as they are consumed or destroyed' (ii. Work, para 2). Increasingly, these aspects of labour and consumption of the human condition do not possess the qualities necessary for a sustained existence in a shared global environment.

Arendt continually attempts to reinstate the important role of public and political action for the purpose of the common or public good. In writing about the *vita activa,* Arendt (1958) describes *action* as being one in which 'an individual takes initiative, begins something new or brings something new into the world' (15). As human beings, we each have the ability to create something uniquely different. Both Arendt (1958) and Dewey (1916/2005) believe that in order to develop an individual's democratic subjectivity, this creative action must be taken in a situation in which others can be subjects as well. Hence, individuals must be able to *take action* in a social situation where others present are able to respond to or take up this action further without being controlled or restricted. Biesta (2007) explains Arendt's notion of *democratic subjectivity* and contends that the actions of the individual must be related 'to the life of the polis, the public sphere in which we live – and have to live – with others who are not like us' (14). It is in this sense of social interaction that Arendt's work begins to coalesce with many of the critical theorists who see democratic education existing for the purpose of transforming society and for continually creating new possibilities based on interactions between others *in the polis*. Arendt's contribution to the conception of a *robust global democracy* rests in the argument for the need to overturn the current hierarchy of human activity to put *action* at the top of the pyramid (above labour and work) to regain the public and political *freedom* and *creative agency* necessary to assume the responsibilities inherent in a democratic subjectivity. For Arendt, this freedom does not rest simply at the level of the *individual,* as an inner, private or contemplative phenomenon, but entails a much more active, worldly and public freedom.

Arendt's (1958) understanding of action excludes acting in isolation. As Biesta (2007) writes, 'in order to act, in order, therefore, to be someone, to be a subject, we need others who respond to our beginnings' (13). As this understanding of social action becomes integrated into the work of Freire (1970/2000) and other critical pedagogues, the rich dialogue, debate and discussions arising from the multiple perspectives they bring to the table deepens the understanding and informs a plan of action for social transformation. Arendt (1958) argues further that it is the *otherness* in others that informs their response to our actions and if we deny or limit the action of others then we deprive ourselves of the possibility to develop our subjectivity. She concludes that 'plurality is the condition of human action' (p. 188).

Plurality, politics and criticality in democracy

Mouffe (2002) takes Arendt's (1958) notion of plurality and offers a model of *agonistic pluralism*, which provides the ideal to strive for in any discussion, dialogue or debate which purports to be democratic. This notion of agonistic pluralism reflects Dewey's (1916/2005) democratic principle of a *consensus for difference.* Mouffe (2002) asserts all political identities entail the creation of an *Us* that can only exist by distinguishing itself from a *Them*. This relationship has the potential to become *antagonistic* anytime that the *Other* begins to be perceived as questioning our identity and threatening our existence. Mouffe (2002) argues that once the dimension of *the political* is acknowledged, the main challenge facing democratic politics becomes how to 'domesticate hostility and to defuse the potential antagonism in human relations' (8). The goal is to not allow conflict to 'take the form of *antagonism* (struggle between enemies) but of *agonism* (struggle between adversaries)' (Mouffe 2002, 9). As part of the *agonistic struggle,* Mouffe (2002) argues that conflict cannot and should not be eradicated as it is the very condition of a vibrant democracy.

In their notion of what they call *participatory democracy,* Portelli and Solomon (2001) build on the importance of plurality as they link the individual, school and community as part of an ongoing reconstructive process 'associated with equity, community, creativity, and taking difference seriously' (17). A significant component of this conception of participatory democracy is that of *critical inquiry* in which students and teachers develop knowledge, skills, values, dispositions and actions that are called for by a reconstructive conception of democracy. In the current transnational and global context, Rizvi (2009) believes it is even more pressing for democratic practices to consider alternatives that are informed by how people come to know, understand and experience themselves both as members of a community and citizens of one or more nation-states.

Summary

In summarizing this new narrative for a *thicker* and more *global* narrative of democracy, the key elements would include *experience and social interaction; action for freedom and social transformation*; an *acceptance of the non-neutrality of the political* and an understanding of the need for *agonistic struggle;* an ethic of the *globality of humanity*; a collective focus on the *global common good*; and an acceptance of the value of *pluriversality* and *coexistence.*

Recognizing the forces of neoliberal globalization and decolonizing the post-industrial notion of democracy will require the creation of an alternative radical narrative of democracy. Drawing from the wisdom of our indigenous brothers and sisters, and academic scholars and theorists from the global north and south, the principles inherent in a robust global democracy must be extended to all global peoples in order to open a much broader, deeper, critical, decolonial dialogue and participation to re-create and sustain a global consciousness in our *global commons* for social and ecological justice. Preparing youth to participate as active and engaged global citizens for social transformation requires educational systems to be informed by a more robust and global conception of democracy. However, for this to happen, as critical and decolonial theorists have argued, a paradigmatic shift will be needed in educational systems around the world towards an ethic which accepts, respects and embraces difference; believes in the globality of humanity; works in the context of a recognition of the relations of power that currently exist and those that have shaped history; and aims to de-link from the colonization of knowledge.

References

Abdi, Ali A. 'Clash of Dominant Discourses and African Philosophies and Epistemologies of Education: Anti-colonial Analyses'. In *Decolonizing Philosophies of Education*, edited by Ali A. Abdi, 131–146. Rotterdam, NLD: Sense, 2012.

Amutabi, Maurice N. *Africa in Global Development Discourses*. Nairobi, Kenya: Centre for Democracy, Research and Development (CEDRED), 2017.

Anyon, Jean. *Radical Possibilities: Public Policy, Urban Education, and a New Social Movement*. New York, NY: Routledge, 2005.

Arendt, Hannah. *The Human Condition*. Chicago, IL: University of Chicago Press, 1958.

Baldacchino, John. "'The Power to Develop Dispositions": Revisiting John Dewey's Democratic Claims for Education'. *Journal of Philosophy of Education* 42, no. 1 (2008): 149–163.

Battiste, Marie. 'The Struggle and Renaissance of Indigenous Knowledge in Eurocentric Education'. In *Indigenous Knowledge and Education: Sites of Struggle, Strength, and Survivance*, edited by Malia Villegas, Sabina R. Neugebauer, and Kerry R. Venegas, 85–91. Cambridge, MA: Harvard Educational Review, 2008.

Battiste, Marie. 'Nourishing the Learning Spirit: Living Our Way to New Thinking'. *Education Canada* 50, no. 1 (2010): 14–18.

Biesta, Gert. 'Foundations of Democratic Education: Kant, Dewey, and Arendt'. In *Democratic Practices as Learning Opportunities*, edited by Ruud Van Der Veen, Danny Wildemeersch, Janet Youngblood, and Victoria Marsick, 7–17. Rotterdam, NLD: Sense, 2007.

Brown, Wendy. 'Neo-liberalism and the End of Liberal Democracy'. *Theory & Event* 7, no. 1 (2003). Doi: 10.1353/tae.2003.0020.

Brown, Wendy. 'American Nightmare: Neoliberalism, Neoconservatism, and De-democratization'. *Political Theory* 34, no. 6 (2006): 690–714.

Darder, Antonia., Baltodano, Marta., Torres, Rodolfo. 'Critical Pedagogy: An Introduction'. In *The Critical Pedagogy Reader*, 2nd edition, edited by Antonia Darder, Marta Baltodano, and Rodolfo Torres, 1–26. New York, NY: Routledge, 2009.

De Lissovoy, Noah. 'Decolonial Pedagogy and the Ethics of the Global'. *Discourse: Studies in the Cultural Politics of Education* 31, no. 3 (2010): 279–293.

Dei, George J. S. and Simmons, Marlon. 'Indigenous Knowledge and the Challenge of Rethinking Conventional Educational Philosophy: A Ghanaian Case Study'. In *Regenerating the Philosophy of Education: What Happened to Soul?* edited by Joe L. Kincheloe and Randall Hewitt, 97–111. New York, NY: Peter Lang, 2011.

Dewey, John. *Experience & Education*. New York: Macmillan, 1938.

Dewey, John. *The School and Society*. Chicago, IL: University of Chicago, 1971. Original work published in 1900.

Dewey, John. 'The Need for Social Psychology'. In *John Dewey. The Middle Works, 1899–1924*, Vol. 10, edited by Jo Ann Boydston, 53–63. Carbondale and Edwardsville: Southern Illinois University Press, 1980. Original work published 1917.

Dewey, John. *Democracy and Education*. Stillwell, KS: Digireads.com Publishing, 2005. Original work published in 1916.

Drinkwater, Mary A. 'Democratizing and Decolonizing Education: A Role for the Arts and Cultural Praxis: Lessons from Primary Schools in Maasailand, Southern Kenya'. PhD diss., Ontario Institute for Studies in Education, University of Toronto, 2014.

Fotopoulos, Takis. 'From (Mis)Education to "Paideia"'. *Counterpoints* 422 (2012): 81–119.

Freire, Paulo. *Pedagogy of Freedom: Ethics, Democracy and Civic Courage*. Lanham, MD: Rowman & Littlefield, 1998.

Freire, Paulo. *Pedagogy of the Oppressed* (30th anniversary edition). New York, NY: Continuum, 2000. Original work published 1970.

Giroux, Henry A. *Schooling for Democracy: Critical Pedagogy in the Modern Age*. London: Routledge, 1989.

Giroux, Henry A. 'Democracy and the Discourse of Cultural Difference: Towards a Politics of Border Pedagogy'. *British Journal of Sociology of Education* 12, no. 4 (1991): 501–519.

Gramsci, Antonio. *Selections from the Prison Notebooks*. London: Lawrence & Wishart, 1971.

Grande, Sandy. *Red Pedagogy: Native American Social and Political Thought*. Lanham, MD: Rowman & Littlefield, 2004.

Greene, Maxine. *The Dialectic of Freedom*. New York, NY: Teachers College Press, 1988.

Hancock, Don. 'The Greek Concept of *Paideia* and Modern Continuing Education'. *Research Annual, Texas Association for Community Service and Continuing Education* 3, no. 1 (1987). Retrieved from http://boomerfrigate.tripod.com/paideia.htm.

Horkheimer, Max. *Critical Theory*. London, UK: Continuum, 1982.

Kenya. Ministry of Education. *Basic Education Curriculum Framework*. Nairobi: Ministry of Education, 2017. http://www.education.go.ke/index.php/downloads/file/315-basic-education-curriculum-framework.

Kincheloe, Joe L. 'Critical Democracy for Education'. In *Understanding Democratic Curriculum Leadership*, edited by James. G. Henderson and Kathleen R. Kesson, 70–84. New York: Teachers College Press, 1999.

Klees, Steven J. 'A Quarter Century Neoliberal Thinking in Education: Misleading Analyses and Failed Policies'. *Globalization, Societies, and Education* 6, no. 4 (2008): 311–348.

Kymlicka, Will. *Politics in the Vernacular: Nationalism, Multiculturalism, and Citizenship*. Oxford: Oxford University Press, 2001.

Lawy, Robert and Gert Biesta. 'Citizenship-as-practice: The Educational Implications of an Inclusive and Relational Understanding of Citizenship'. *British Journal of Educational Studies* 54, no. 1 (2006): 34–50.

Louw, Dirk J. 'Ubuntu: An African Assessment of the Religious Other'. Paper presented at the *Paideia Project-World Congress of Philosophy, Boston University, 1999*. Retrieved from https://www.bu.edu/wcp/Papers/Afri/AfriLouw.htm

Louw, Dirk. J. 'The African Concept of *Ubuntu* and Restorative Justice'. In *Handbook of Restorative Justice: A Global Perspective*, edited by Dennis Sullivan and Larry Tifft, 161–173. New York: Routledge, 2006.

Maldonado-Torres, Nelson. 'Thinking through the Decolonial Turn: Post-continental Interventions in Theory, Philosophy, and Critique – An Introduction'. *Transmodernity: Journal of Peripheral Cultural Production of the Luso-Hispanic World* 1, no. 2 (2011): 1–15.

Mignolo, Walter D. 'Epistemic Disobedience, Independent Thought and Decolonial Freedom'. *Theory, Culture & Society* 26 (2009): 159–181. Doi: 10.1177/0263276409349275

Mignolo, Walter D. 'Border Thinking, Decolonial Cosmopolitanism and Dialogues among Civilizations'. In *The Ashgate Research Companion to Cosmopolitanism*, edited by Maria Rovisco and Magdalena Nowicka, 329–348. Farnham, UK: Ashgate, 2011.

Mouffe, Chantal. *Politics and Passions: The Stakes of Democracy*. London: Centre for the Study of Democracy, University of Westminster, 2002.

Moya, Paula M. L. (2011). 'Who Are We and from Where We Speak'. *Transmodernity: Journal of Peripheral Cultural Production of the Luso-Hispanic World* 1, no. 2, (2011): 79–94.

Mucina, Devi D. 'Ubuntu: A Regenerative Philosophy for Rupturing Racist Colonial Stories of Dispossession'. PhD diss., Ontario Institute for Studies in Education, University of Toronto, 2011.

Nasong'o, Shadrack W. and Godwin, R. Murunga. 'Prospects of Democracy in Kenya'. In *Kenya: The Struggle for Democracy*, edited by Godwin R. Murunga and Shadrack W. Nasong'o, 3–16. London, UK: Zed, 2007.

Niyozov, Sarfaroz and Nazarkhudo Dastambuev. 'Exploiting Globalization While Being Exploited by It: Insights from Post-Soviet Education Reforms in Central Asia'. *Canadian and International Education* 41, no. 3 (2012): 1–22.

Paris, Django. 'Culturally Sustaining Pedagogy: A Needed Change Instance, Terminology, and Practice'. *Educational Researcher* 41, no. 3 (2012): 93–97. Doi: 10.3102/0013189X12441244

Portelli, John P. and Solomon, R. Patrick. 'Introduction'. In *The Erosion of Democracy in Education: From Critique to Possibilities*, edited by John P. Portelli and R. Patrick Solomon, 15–27. Calgary, AB: Detselig, 2001.

Price, Jason M. 'Democracy: A Critical Red Ideal'. *Journal of Thought* Spring-Summer, (2007): 9–25.

Rizvi, Fazal. 'Global Mobility'. In *Globalization and the Study of Education*, edited by Tom Popkewitz and Fazal Rizvi, 268–289. New York: Wiley Blackwell, 2009.

Rizvi, Fazal. 'Global Mobility and Its Educational Challenges'. In *Transnational Perspectives on Democracy, Citizenship, Human Rights and Peace Education*, edited by Mary Drinkwater, Fazal Rizvi and Karen Edge, 27–47. London: Bloomsbury, 2018.

Thayer-Bacon, Barbara J. *Beyond Liberal Democracy in Schools: The Power of Pluralism*. New York, NY: Teachers College Press, 2008.

Truth, Justice and Reconciliation Commission (TJRC). *Report of the Truth, Justice and Reconciliation Commission*, Vol. 1, Nairobi: TJRC, 2013. http://www.tjrckenya.org/images/documents/TJRC_report_Volume_1.pdf

Wa Thiong'o, Ngugi. *Decolonizing the Mind: The Politics of Language in African Literature*. Portsmouth, NH: Heinemann, 1986.

Wallerstein, Immanuel. *The Modern World System: Capitalist Agriculture and the Origins of the European World Economy in the Sixteenth Century*. New York: Academic Press, 1974.

Wane, Njoki N. 'Indigenous Education and Cultural Resistance: A Decolonizing Project'. *Curriculum Inquiry* 39, no. 1 (2009): 159–178. Doi: 10.1111/j.1467873X.2008.01443.X

Westheimer, Joel. 'What Kind of Citizen? Democratic Dialogues in Education'. *Education Canada* 48, no. 3 (2008): 6–10.

Zajda, Joseph. 'Globalisation, and Comparative Research: Implications for Education'. In *Globalisation, Policy and Comparative Research: Discourses of Globalization*, edited by Joseph Zajda and Val Rust, 1–12. Dordrecht, NLD: Springer, 2009.

4

Countering the Mainstream in Higher Education: Experiences in Brazil

Tristan McCowan

Chapter outline

- Introduction
- Higher education in Brazil
- Initiatives within the mainstream system
  - The thematic federal universities
  - Alternatives within the private sector
  - Challenges faced
- Exodus from the mainstream
- Liminal experiences
  - *The Landless Movement*
- Resources, recognition and embodiment
- Acknowledgement

Keywords: alternative higher education; deschooling; indigenous education; Ivan Illich; Latin American education; radical universities

---

Introduction

Education for social transformation has often operated around the fringes of the mainstream system. Non-formal adult education has been particularly prominent in this regard, influenced by Paulo Freire's (1972) notion of conscientization, and ideas that political change starts with the collective transformation of consciousness of the oppressed, and a dialectic of reflection and action. Social movements, women's groups and trades unions have been other important sites of these forms of radical education work over the past century. While these ideas have been incorporated into the practice of some educators in formal institutions – for example, 'critical pedagogy' in higher education – they have been peripheral in relation to human capital-based skills development and traditionalist conservative conceptions. But is this an expression of the ongoing struggle for the centre ground, or is there something in formal education that acts against this transformatory role?

One theorist who argued strongly for the latter position was Ivan Illich. He went beyond the – now commonplace – unveiling of the hidden curriculum of schools and its role in the reproduction of socio-economic inequalities, to point to an even deeper and more pernicious problem: the very existence of an 'institution' of learning. For Illich (1971), the issue was not just that schools were failing on the meritocratic dream of enabling social mobility for all, but that they were squeezing out meaningful learning – for everybody, and not just those at the bottom of the pile. Institutionalization of education was seen to lead to reliance on expert teachers and the consequent undermining of people's faith in their ability to learn for themselves and from each other. Most dangerously, the process perpetuated its survival into the future in an inexorable cycle, with each generation having to send its children through the same soulless procession of grades so as to ensure that they obtain the qualifications needed to earn a livelihood.

While some may consider these questions now buried along with the neo-Marxist critiques of the same period, there is an enduring relevance to Illich's account of institutionalization. Despite the continuing expansion of formal education systems, concerns over obsession with qualifications and testing – raised in Ronald Dore's *Diploma Disease* (1976) – continue unabated, while attention has now been drawn to the cultural imperialism of the Western-style schooling being spread globally through the Education for All initiative. Even in high-income countries there are worries about the limitations of formal education in fostering creativity. What's more, the possibilities of responding to these concerns and fulfilling Illich's ideals of peer learning and conviviality have been vastly increased with developments in information and communications technologies, particularly the internet.

In higher education, these new modes of learning have been particularly prominent. With the phenomenal expansion of enrolments in tertiary education in recent decades – now reaching 35.69 per cent gross enrolment ratio globally (UIS 2017) – it would at first sight appear that the 'university'[1] as institution has definitively won the day. Nevertheless, there are signs of a lingering, or perhaps a new, scepticism about the institution, motored by the ideal of the Silicon Valley innovator, untroubled by formal qualifications, and seeing higher education as much as an impediment as a facilitator of developing a successful start-up business. The emergence of online courses, in particular MOOCs – and the challenges they pose to the university as a physical space, as a validator of knowledge and a community of scholars – along with the entry of new for-profit providers offering pared-down value-for-money tuition, have led to a process some have termed the 'unbundling' of the traditional university (Barber et al. 2013; MacFarlane 2011; McCowan 2017). Furthermore, there are those who argue that young people are better off not going to university at all, and organizations such as *Uncollege* in the United States support young people to pursue other avenues.

These developments undoubtedly present a challenge to the conventional institution of university. However, there is an important distinction between these changes and the original ideas of Illich – along with those of others who developed the deschooling thesis in association with him (e.g. Prakash and Esteva 2008; Reimer 1971) – namely, the value attached to equality. The original critique of schooling was one rooted in the institution's regressive effects on equality in society, and the potential of a deschooled society for upholding social justice; the new deschoolers, on the other hand, have as their arch-virtue 'innovation', understood to a large extent as the creation of new products that will be successful in the market, and will bring success to their creators within a capitalist economy.

This chapter focuses on forms of alternatives to conventional higher education that adhere to Illich's egalitarian principle. Often associated with indigenous groups, political and social movements, NGOs and radical educators, these institutions represent fundamentally different ways of viewing the aims of higher education, the basis of valid knowledge, the role of the lecturer, forms of governance and indeed the nature the institution itself. They are 'radical' in the sense that they aim to get to the root of the educational and social problems of the contemporary world, and challenge and transform core aspects of these spheres, rather than 'tinker' around the edges, bringing mild and incremental reform (Teamey and Mandel 2014). For example, UNITIERRA (the University of the Land) in southern Mexico is an institution with no entry requirements and no formal qualifications on exit, which functions through a combination of seminars and workshops, and pairing of 'students' with professional mentors in the workplace (Esteva 2007). Other examples of alternative universities around the world are Swaraj University (India), Gaia University (international),

Schumacher College (UK) and the University of the Third Age (international). Importantly, these initiatives involve not only the development of alternative *means* for achieving the aims of higher education (e.g. new modes of delivery), but question and reframe the very *ends* of the endeavour.

For the most part these initiatives are responding to broadly recognized concerns about inequitable access, irrelevant curricula, restricted epistemological perspectives, poor graduate outcomes and ineffective governance that have accompanied the recent rapid expansion of higher education systems, particularly in low- and middle-income countries. However, instead of proposing reform efforts at the national and institutional levels within the mainstream system, they have involved the creation of entirely new forms of institution. These institutions are significant not only in providing solutions to the problems outlined above, but also in challenging our very conception of university and opening new possibilities of development for the future. However, as will be explored further below, they also encounter a range of significant problems in achieving their aims and ensuring their very survival.

In providing an analysis of some examples of these alternative universities, this chapter focuses specifically on the case of Brazil, a country in which the political conditions are conducive to this form of experimentation: combining a decentralized education system with opportunity for innovation at the local level, some financial support from the state (at least until the recent economic downturn) and strong civil society organizations and social movements campaigning for educational alternatives. These conditions have led to the emergence of a number of innovations at all levels of the education system, ones which have intrinsic interest and value for educational practitioners and researchers worldwide, but which also provide a useful context in which to analyse the dynamics of educational alternatives. The chapter does not attempt to provide an exhaustive list of alternative higher education institutions in the country, or to provide a comprehensive analysis of the dynamics of the higher education system, but to explore the theoretical questions of institutionalization through the selected cases.

The aims of this study are threefold. First, it documents a range of examples of alternative institutions so as to provide an account of their characteristics and contribute to the mapping of these institutions worldwide, in the context of a significant lack of research in the area. Second, the chapter analyses their potential and their prospects for survival and success, focusing on the fundamental preconditions of *resources* and *recognition*, and the dangers that compromises made to ensure their practical viability may pose to the embodiment of their mission. Last, implications are drawn out for theoretical debates around institutionalization of education, and for Illich's proposal for deschooling. This is an exploratory qualitative study, investigating theoretical concerns from the literature within an empirical context, as well as generating new theoretical ideas from the themes emerging from the data collected. The study draws on documentary and web sources, as well as institutional visits and interviews with academic staff, senior leadership, creators and activists of the institutions, carried out between 2011 and 2015. Interviews were transcribed and analysed in Portuguese, and the quotations appearing in this chapter are the author's translation; while the real names of the initiatives have been used so as to enable contextual understanding, all respondents remain anonymous.

The specific question addressed in relation to the third of the aims outlined above is that of how institutionalization affects the process of radical reform. Is radical education with the power to transform societies possible within the mainstream? Does the existence of an institution of higher education ultimately militate against the creation of real alternatives for meaningful learning? And if so, can initiatives survive and prosper outside of this institutional framework? What is to be gained and lost by operating inside or outside of the mainstream? In order to answer these questions, cases have been selected to represent three types of institution: those within the mainstream, those outside of it and those with a liminal existence between the two. As explored in Huisman et al. (2002), existing theories of institutional change predict different possible trajectories of alternative universities. On the one hand, neo-institutional approaches predict a gradual merging back to the norm, whether through coercive, mimetic or normative isomorphism. On the other hand, critics of these approaches present different scenarios, asserting that there are 'ways for universities to be and stay different from the idea of the traditional university' (318). These dynamics of movement towards and away from the norm will be explored in the cases that follow. However, there will not be extensive engagement with the analytical frameworks of institutional theory; instead, the focus will be on the more normative ideas of Illich and others who assert the desirability, and even the necessity, of the construction of learning opportunities outside mainstream institutions. Not all of the cases covered in this chapter exemplify attempts to *deschool*, but they nevertheless represent sites for exploring the implications of institutionalization and deinstitutionalization for radical reform.

Illich's critique, in fact, goes beyond education to encompass the entirety of modern industrial societies and their conceptions of 'development'. For Illich, the problem with institutions is that they undermine people's confidence in themselves and destroy *conviviality*. This latter concept is central to Illich's (1973) work, signifying the

> autonomous and creative intercourse among persons, and the intercourse of persons with their environment; and this in contrast with the conditioned response of persons to the demands made upon them by others, and by a man-made environment. I consider conviviality to be individual freedom realized in personal interdependence. (18)

In the sphere of education, conviviality can be achieved not by institutional forms, but only through webs of interaction that will lead to unfettered access to learning. Institutions undermine these elements in the first place through the creation of experts, who define what is legitimate to learn, then deliver and certify it, and safeguard their own position by delegitimizing the claims of others. Commodification is another aspect of institutionalization, in this case in packaging knowledge for the purpose of sale and thereby cutting off its lifeblood in the organic relationships of learning between human beings. As Finger and Asún (2001) state: '[I]nstitutions create the needs and control their satisfaction, and, by so doing, turn the human being and her or his creativity into objects' (10).

The ultimate consequence of institutionalization for Illich (1973) is counterproductivity, through which instead of promoting the good it is intended to support an institution ends up working against it: 'When an enterprise grows beyond a certain point on this scale, it first frustrates the end for which it was originally designed, and then rapidly becomes a threat to society itself' (4–5). The analysis presented in this chapter focuses on the ways in which initiatives challenge (or accommodate themselves to) the seductive but constraining process of institutionalization, and seek to provide a space for the flourishing of conviviality and meaningful learning.

An initial task is to define what is meant by 'alternative' in this context. Clearly, 'alternative' is a relational concept, in this case relative to what might be considered the standard or mainstream form of higher education institution (HEI). While of course there is significant diversity of HEIs even within specific countries, we can identify some salient common characteristics in, for example, admissions requirements based on academic merit, courses leading to a nationally recognized diploma at undergraduate or postgraduate level, the division of courses into recognized academic fields or professional areas and the existence of academic staff specializing in research and teaching in their academic field. An alternative institution, therefore, would be one in which either one or more of these common features is significantly departed from, providing a challenge to conventional conceptions of access, curriculum and governance.[2] Of course, in this sense it is wrong to think about a dichotomy of 'alternative' and 'traditional' universities, with institutions locating themselves along a continuum and sometimes with a complex interplay of different elements.

Readers may justifiably question whether these institutions are really 'universities' at all, and there may be other labels such as 'adult education' that some may prefer to assign. In fact, in some cases this is exactly the effect intended by the proponents, to apply the term 'university' in an unusual context, so as to challenge, subvert and in some cases satirize the concept. This was the case of Tent City University, for example, established during the Occupy Movement in London in 2011, which was a large open-fronted tent with a mini-library, providing a space for talks from invited speakers, workshops and discussion groups open to those involved in the occupation and the general public.

Before addressing the characteristics of these alternative institutions, there will first be a brief background discussion of higher education in Brazil.

Higher education in Brazil

Brazil is unusual in the contemporary period for having a stark division between public and private sectors in higher education. Public universities – whether federal- or state-run institutions – are entirely free of charge for students, but have highly restrictive admissions policies based on competitive public examinations. Private universities, on the other hand, have ample spaces but charge fees on a broad scale from low-prestige economical institutions to high-ranking expensive ones. The private sector has, since the 1990s, absorbed the considerable demand for higher education from growing numbers of secondary school leavers, and now accounts for 74 per cent of undergraduate enrolments (Carvalho 2006; INEP 2014; McCowan 2004; Sampaio 2014). Approximately half of the private sector is for-profit, being an extremely lucrative sector for investors, with the largest higher education companies having significant holdings on the Brazilian stock exchange. There are also a number of religious universities in Brazil – most important of which the Catholic universities (*Pontifícia Universidade Católica*, PUC) – which are distinct from the for-profit sector in their ethos and range of activities, and have a greater resemblance to the public universities in terms of their research and community engagement.

Despite the rapid expansion of access in Brazil – with undergraduate enrolment increasing from 3 million in 2001 to over 7 million in 2013 – the net enrolment rate is still only 18 per cent (IBGE 2016), with lower-income students excluded for the most part from both public and private institutions. Brazil is one of the most unequal countries in the world in terms of income distribution, and these inequalities are reflected in the higher education system. Racial/ethnic background is also a significant factor in higher education access, with African Brazilians and indigenous peoples having disproportionately low rates of enrolment. These questions have been addressed through a range of policies – most dramatically, the 2011 law obliging federal universities to have a 50 per cent quota for students from public schools and from disadvantaged racial groups[3]– yet inequalities remain acute.

In terms of the curriculum, the country is characterized by a high degree of 'classification' in Bernstein's (1971) conception, with few cross-disciplinary courses, and with the exception of the recent initiatives outlined below, little in the way of a liberal arts model. In spite of theoretical influence of thinkers such as Paulo Freire, pedagogy in universities also remains predominantly traditional, with emphasis on knowledge transmission through lecturing. The new private universities offer mainly evening courses for working students, operating on what could be described as a 'high school' model, with little in the way of independent study and broader campus experience. In terms of management, while private institutions follow a corporate model, public institutions are highly democratic as regards selection of office-holders – with rectors elected by staff and students – although their operations and funding are regimented by the national legal framework. Public institutions also have a strong commitment to community engagement and public benefit more broadly, a legacy of the reforms at the University of Córdoba in 1918 that influenced universities across the region (Bernasconi 2007; Figueiredo-Cowen 2002).

More broadly, Brazil has been the site for a range of radical experiments, socially and educationally, since the ending in 1985 of two decades of military dictatorship. This period has seen the emergence of strong mobilizations of trade unions, indigenous peoples, African descendants and many other social movements, in addition to the founding of the Workers' Party (PT[4]), which came to power at the national level with the election of Lula da Silva in 2002 (Gandin 2006; Ghanem 2013; King-Calnek 2006; McCowan 2009; Singer 2016). These movements have interacted strongly with the field of education, calling for expanded access for disadvantaged groups as well as transformation of curriculum and governance in schools and universities. A number of the initiatives below have emerged directly or indirectly from these broader social movements.

Initiatives within the mainstream system

This first section addresses experimentation within the mainstream, focusing on a small number of institutions in Brazil, within both public and private sectors, that retain most of the features of conventional institutions – and so are far from Illich's ideal of deschooling – but nevertheless innovate in particular ways. These operate within the legal framework of higher education institutions and accreditation, using the conventional sources of funding, but present innovations in relation to curriculum, access and governance.

The thematic federal universities

In response to the stagnation of the public sector in higher education since the 1990s, the Lula government instigated a programme known as *Reuni*,[5] which implemented a range of measures to increase the number of places available in public institutions. Alongside this programme, a number of new federal institutions were created, among which a small number of *thematic* universities, focusing on a distinctive remit or mission. The creation of these institutions was spurred on by social movements campaigning for the rights of specific groups, as well as by broader movements within the government and ruling Workers' Party to transform federal universities. The latter movements targeted the highly restricted access in these institutions – introducing more equitable forms of entrance requirements in the form of the national secondary leaving examination *Enem* in place of the institution-specific *vestibular* examinations, which favoured those students who could afford preparatory courses; and changes to the narrow disciplinary nature of the curriculum by introducing a liberal arts conception through ideas of the *Universidade Nova* (New University), as seen in the Federal University of Southern Bahia (Santos and Almeida Filho 2008; Tavares and Romão 2015).

The most prominent of these new institutions is the University of Latin American Integration[6] (UNILA). Founded in 2010 in the symbolic location of the triple border of Brazil with Paraguay and Argentina near the Iguaçu Falls, the institution aims to provide a space for teaching, research and community service linked not to the national context but to pan-Latin American concerns (Comissão de Implantação da UNILA 2009a, 2009b; Trindade 2009). While funded entirely by the Brazilian government, it is a bilingual institution (Portuguese and Spanish, with some limited engagement with indigenous languages too) aiming to have half of the student and staff body from other countries in Latin America.

The curriculum offered is distinct from conventional universities, through the emphasis on interdisciplinarity, the 'common cycle' of Latin American studies that all students undergo in their first year, and the pan-Latin American focus of the specific degree courses, including Latin American Cultural Diversity, Rural Development and Food Security, and Engineering for Sustainable Energy. In line with its interdisciplinary focus, the university has moved away from the traditional faculties and departments towards centres of interdisciplinary studies.

The university also has a social justice agenda, aiming to serve the local population which would not normally have access to a federal institution (many of the inhabitants of Foz de Iguaçu are descendants of the migrant workers who built the Itaipú dam), as well as maintaining a range of community engagement activities. Motter and Gandin (2016) highlight the distinctiveness of the institution in reverting the dominant forms of internationalization in higher education globally, promoting South–South cooperation and engaging with neighbouring and more distant countries in a spirit of solidarity rather than income generation or competition. While certainly not rejecting all aspects of institutional education, UNILA does resist and provide an alternative to the commodification that was a source of concern for Illich (1971).

UNILA has nevertheless encountered a range of challenges. In spite of constitutional guarantees of autonomy to the sector, as a federal university it exists within a set of strongly defined legal and academic boundaries. Senior managers and lecturers interviewed all pointed to tensions between the political forces that had given rise to the university and the needs of the institution in terms of achieving its mission. The job security, prestige and relatively generous remuneration make working in a federal university highly attractive to early career academics, but there is no guarantee that those applying for the posts will genuinely buy into the vision of pan-Latin American solidarity, or have the appropriate knowledge and experience. As one lecturer stated:

> I don't have a very refined political sense, maybe because my discipline is biology. So I still have a bit of difficulty in understanding this sphere of Latin America. One of the problems here at UNILA is exactly this: not even the lecturers really know what Latin America is.

Conversely, the relatively remote location of the university in relation to the population centres of Brazil has in some cases made it hard to attract the experienced staff required. Other challenges include the fact that the university does not have control over selection of students from the other countries so cannot ensure the same principles of equity are applied. Bureaucratic barriers include difficulties of contracting visiting professors from other countries in Latin America, and recognition of diplomas across the region, as well as accreditation of new and experimental areas of study. An example of these constraints was given by a member of the senior leadership team:

> In Brazil, to buy a product we have to get three quotes. Take a book about 'Political crisis in the new regional parties in Peru', which for some reason we want to get. It doesn't exist in Brazil. How are you going to get three quotes for this from northern Peru?

Empirical research with students shows that there are also challenges in relation to the integration of the multi-national student body, the balanced use of different languages and unevenness of academic preparation between the different countries (Vianna and McCowan 2012). Respondents also pointed to anxiety in the students at undertaking only generic courses in the first year and not being able to focus on their chosen discipline until the second year. Finally, there are significant cost implications in funding the non-Brazilian students, particularly in terms of maintaining the generous support package of accommodation and other services.

Created at a similar time to UNILA was another thematic university, this time with a focus on Africa. The University of Lusophone Afro-Brazilian International Integration (UNILAB[7]) is aimed at articulation with the Portuguese-speaking countries of Africa, primarily Angola, Mozambique, São Tomé and Príncipe, Guinea-Bissau and Cape Verde, but with links to other Portuguese-speaking countries, such as East Timor. The location[8] of the university is again symbolic, in this case in Redenção, Ceará, in the impoverished northeast of Brazil, the first city in the country to abolish slavery in 1883. Like UNILA, it aims to have half of its students from Brazil and half from overseas, funded by the Brazilian government. Aware of the dangers of brain drain, provisions are in place to ensure the relocation of the overseas students back to their countries of origin, and their insertion in areas of work beneficial to local development. Not only does the university aim to strengthen links between Brazil and Africa, but also to provide a focal point for engagement with African cultures and history within Brazil. Courses and research again are focused on themes of relevance to inclusive development in all of the countries: research groups include Agro-Ecology and Organic Produce; Popular Education, Micro-Finance and Solidary Economy, and African Thought and Philosophy. Unusually for Brazil, students undertake a third term each year engaging in interdisciplinary academic, cultural and community development activities.

There are currently a little over 4,000 students, with nearly half of these studying at a distance. UNILAB has been highly successful in relation to widening participation. The proportion of students from disadvantaged backgrounds is extremely high, with 90 per cent of the initial cohorts from lower-income families,[9] a very unusual figure for a federal university, especially before the compulsory introduction of quotas. Nevertheless, it faces some similar challenges to those of UNILA, in terms of developing a high-quality university in a remote area away from metropolitan centres, preventing the shift back towards conventional curricula and maintaining state support for this radical vision in the face of a changing political landscape.

Other examples of thematic federal universities include the Federal University of the Southern Frontier (UFFS[10]), a multi-campus institution focusing on the agricultural worker population of southern Brazil, and the Federal University of Western Pará (UFOPA,[11] originally intended as the University of Amazonian Integration) aiming for transnational cooperation between the countries of the Amazon rainforest.

Alternatives within the private sector

These alternative universities within the mainstream do not only appear within the public sector. There are also private institutions with distinct characters – as might be expected given the greater autonomy of the sector.[12] Founded in 2003, the Zumbi dos Palmares University in São Paulo, for example, is an institution focusing on the African Brazilian community. In the context of disproportionately low rates of access to higher education for the black population, this institution allows an opportunity for accessing higher study, in the model of the historically black colleges and universities in the United States, with 90 per cent of students being of African descent. Yet it has a further function acting as a focal point for the valuing and development of African Brazilian history, thought and culture.

Other alternative institutions within the mainstream include the 'community universities' in the south of the country, private institutions set up by local communities to provide access to university for young people in the absence of state provision, and provide a boost for local industry, with a high degree of community involvement in governance. These institutions are by now well established and have their own national association,[13] with twenty-five institutions across the country, including for example the University of Caxias do Sul, founded in 1967 with as many as 37,000 students (Schmidt 2009).

Challenges faced

These institutions in the mainstream have a number of substantial benefits, including a steady funding stream (from state funds in the case of the federal institutions, or from student fees in the case of the private ones) and the convenience of using existing structures and procedures of curriculum and management. However, they face a constant struggle against the *centripetal forces* of the system, in order to maintain the distinctiveness of their vision and uphold their principles in all areas of their work. First, there is the question of the bureaucratic frameworks and pedagogical cultures pulling practice back towards the 'norm'. The framework of recognition of degrees, for example, and assumptions about modes of study and assessment present clear limitations on the ability of the taught courses to take on new formats that may be appropriate for their aims. One lecturer at UNILA, for example, expressed his frustration at the fact that their attempt to develop an alternative assessment scheme was ultimately thwarted by the constraints of the national framework. Selection of students is also determined to a large extent by federal policy. The challenges of the bureaucratic framework within which the federal universities operate can also be seen in the innovative Federal University of Southern Bahia, created in 2013, as emphasized by the first Rector of the institution, Naomar de Almeida Filho (Tavares and Romão 2015).

Second, while funding provides security, it also creates forms of allegiance, accountability or dependence on the funder. In the case of the federal government, the existence of these institutions has been enabled by the propitious political climate during the administration of the Workers' Party – which has had close articulation with progressive academics – as well as availability of government funds. That scenario is precarious to say the least, and since the impeachment of President Dilma Rousseff in 2016 there have been threats from the government of closure or reverting to conventional universities. In the private institutions there is greater autonomy, but nevertheless the customer power associated with full-fee paying students presents a different form of constraint.

Exodus from the mainstream

However, there are alternative institutions that have been developed entirely outside of the mainstream education system. These are less prominent, less well documented, and as discussed above, might in some people's view have a dubious claim to being universities at all. Nevertheless, in using the label 'university', they make an important statement about the nature of their institution, and the challenges being made to our conventional conceptualizations. In both of the cases outlined below, the aim is to provide a space for 'convivial' learning (Illich 1973), in which human beings share and develop unmediated by rigid institutional forms.

The Intercultural Indigenous University of Maracanã Village (UIIAM[14]) was established in a spirit of defiance of the political and educational establishment. As stated by one of the organizers: 'We don't want to do it within the state, ours is direct action. We don't want to compete for that power, because, besides not believing in it, we want to create alternatives for the people in the struggle.' It grew out of the occupation in 2006 by various indigenous groups[15] of the former Museum of the Indian near the Maracanã football stadium in Rio de Janeiro. Some of the occupiers rejected the government's offer to create an indigenous cultural centre in exchange for vacating the building so it could be turned over to private developers. The building has become the focal point of a movement for political resistance, but also an educational centre, where people can come to do courses on indigenous culture. The initiative for the university grew organically out of these ad hoc educational activities. The aims of the initiative are:

> 'Indianization' ... which is 'Humanization', that is, recognition, affirmation, identity, reinvention of reality through the perspective and principles of living of indigenous culture, which by its very nature is the negation of capitalist society, and the valuing of life and well-being. (Interview with activist of Maracanã Village)

This initiative responds not only to the lack of mainstream opportunities for indigenous people, but also to the absence of indigenous knowledge and culture within the curriculum. Students come from the local area, but also from various other parts of the country, and even internationally.

The reference to 'humanization' above invokes the influence of Paulo Freire (1972, 1994), whose ideas on dialogue, conscientization and praxis in the context of adult education underpin the pedagogy of many of these initiatives.

A second example of this form of institution is the Pampédia Free[16] University in São Paulo. Like Maracanã Village, it started by offering regular workshops for the general public – although with a distinct underpinning political and epistemological view. It draws on the ideas of seventeenth-century Czech educator Jan Comenius and his concept of universal education (*Pampaedia*). It also has influences from Allan Kardec and Spiritism, a religious tradition that is highly popular in Brazil – based on the notion that humans are engaged in a process of constant improvement through incarnation through history in different bodies – although the university adheres strongly to principles of interreligious dialogue and is not restricted to spiritists. The principles of Pampédia University revolve around democratization of knowledge, interdisciplinarity, pluralism, spirituality, ethics and dialogue. Run by university lecturers, teachers, designers, artists, therapists and journalists, who coordinate the initiative in their spare time, it has a permanent building in the city of São Paulo in which seminars, discussions and workshops are held, as well as a range of online learning opportunities.

> Our idea ... is to have knowledge organised in an interdisciplinary, organic way in the form of interdisciplinary groups and thematic axes that interlink. And the student on entering the Free University can make his or her own pathway through this content, and choose between face-to-face workshops, distance courses, tutoring .... (Interview with founder of university)

Emerging from an alternative publishing house and an earlier educational initiative, the 'Pampédia Free Space', it now has a more formalized offering, with fee payments for courses, although with no formal accreditation. In fact, freedom from the constraints of conventional assessment and Ministry of Education recognition is one of the key principles of the university: in the words of the founder of university, 'what we are emphasising here is what the student produces, not the diploma'. Consequently, the university works in accordance with the idea that people can become professionals through portfolios of work and not only through certificates. Current courses include 'Spiritist Pedagogy', 'Deconstructing Nietzsche', 'Peace Education and Conflict Mediation' and 'Education and Spirituality'. There is even a proposal to set up a 'free PhD' in the near future, involving the writing of a thesis (or some other form of intellectual, artistic or social product) but without formal accreditation.

These initiatives have either not been able to join the mainstream, have not attempted or in some cases have been offered but have deliberately rejected the chance. The latter is the case of Maracanã Village, who see a splinter group's acceptance of the government's proposal for a cultural centre as a 'sell-out' and an unacceptable compromise of the political and cultural principles of the movement. The advantage of not being part of the mainstream is that the initiatives are relatively free of constraints to embody the vision that they hold to: they retain their authenticity and are not compromised or pulled in contrary directions.

Nevertheless, there are some obvious challenges, first of which is resources. These initiatives function on a shoestring budget, and therefore rely on donated or occupied buildings, volunteered staff time of lecturers from other universities or of activists, and minimal teaching resources and equipment. This lack of physical and human resources imposes limits on the nature and range of courses taught, and consequently (or for reasons of the interests of the creators) they largely focus on humanities and social science related areas.

The second major challenge is the lack of a recognized diploma. As these institutions do not have legal recognition, there are restrictions on its ability to certify the learning that has taken place – beyond the value perceived by learners and teachers. The disadvantage for students is that – unless the ideas of portfolio work proposed by Pampédia take root – they cannot then convert that learning into other forms of opportunity in the mainstream society, such as employment and further study. This constraint has an obvious impact on demand for the courses, and explains the low uptake, particularly among school leavers.

The perspective of these radical initiatives would be that seeking mainstream assessment and certification is not necessary and would signify undermining their mission: they do not need endorsement from the state and, indeed, such an endorsement would undermine their authenticity and autonomy. In order to challenge the deeply unjust foundations of modern society – even while standing within – it is seen to be necessary to create alternative forms of conducting and evaluating learning and human development, ones that do not rely on instrumental rewards within the competitive, capitalist system.

Liminal experiences

Finally, there are some initiatives that aim to respond to the dangers and limitations of standing either within or outside the mainstream by having one foot in each. They aim to obtain some of the benefits of mainstream support, while maintaining a significant degree of autonomy.

The landless movement

The Movement of Landless Rural Workers[17] (MST or Landless Movement) emerged in the early 1980s so as to challenge the inequitable distribution of land in the country and the predicament of millions of peasants who had been pushed off the land into day labouring or into the urban shantytowns. In addition to an intense programme of land occupation and resettlement, the movement places a strong emphasis on education. It has extensive experience of running educational initiatives for adults, including basic literacy, but also has a large network of its own state-funded schools (McCowan 2009). Its educational ideas are strongly influenced by Freire and aim to promote conscientization of students, as well as a valuing of the rural context and strengthening of the identity of the social movement.

In more recent years it has also moved into the sphere of providing higher education. The model it uses is to provide its own courses, but in partnership with recognized public institutions – including prestigious state and federal universities such as the State University of São Paulo and the University of Brasília. Most commonly, it runs teacher education courses, according to its distinctive philosophy of 'Pedagogy of the Land', but it also has a range of other degrees, including social work and law, in addition to non-accredited courses. The principal site for the delivery of these courses is the Florestan Fernandes National School, which was constructed in the state of São Paulo by volunteer workers from the movement, and opened in 2005. Over 24,000 people have studied at the institution. However, even within this autonomous institution, the validation for the degree courses is provided by recognized universities. This accreditation allows the landless people to gain public recognition, move on to further study, and even (though not encouraged by the movement) to forms of urban employment outside of agriculture and activism for the movement.

Resources, recognition and embodiment

All of the initiatives outlined above aim to challenge the contemporary direction of travel of education systems: the unfair distribution of the fruits of education, the marginalization of alternative forms of knowledge and meaningful learning, and the reduction of space for conviviality (Illich 1973). Yet they do so in very different ways. One way we could classify the institutions analysed above is by their aims, mission or values – whether to preserve and develop a culturally specific form of knowledge, to foster social transformation or to provide spiritually liberating learning.

However, as seen above, they also differ in terms of the institutional forms their innovations have taken, and their approximation towards or distancing from the mainstream, and it is this that has been the primary focus of analysis in this chapter. The initiatives that reject mainstream forms to a large extent adhere to the ideas expressed by Illich (1971) that:

> School prepares for the alienating institutionalization of life by teaching the
> need to be taught. Once this lesson is learned, people lose their incentive to grow

in independence; they no longer find relatedness attractive, and close themselves off to the surprises which life offers when it is not predetermined by institutional definition. (67)

The ultimate aim of these initiatives is to embody their fundamental purpose: for example, in the case of the Maracanã Village, to represent the space of respectful, non-authoritarian relations, inclusive and valuing of diverse cultures and enabling emancipatory learning; in the case of the community universities, to provide an institution attentive to and governed by the local community, enabling access for young people and boosting employment and local economic growth; and in the case of UNILA, to foster cultural and political integration across Latin America.

In order to achieve these aims, two principal elements need to be present: *resources* and *recognition* – relating respectively to what might be described as 'input' and 'output' factors. The primary resource is the teacher, in whatever form that figure may appear: if full-time staff are needed then there are significant costs in providing for their upkeep. Those institutions that rely on voluntary work of staff whose primary source of income is derived elsewhere suffer from the competing demands for their time. In addition, there are physical resources, including buildings, equipment and teaching materials. Depending on the model of higher education, these can be minimal, and those institutions relying primarily on oral interaction of small groups can survive with simple multipurpose accommodation. However, there are obvious limitations of the forms of study possible in this kind of environment.

Having said this, in some cases these radical initiatives outside the mainstream challenge the very idea that physical infrastructure and full-time paid staff are actually necessary for a university. The notion of university that they hold to is something altogether more fluid, it is a movement, a relationship between people, a spirit of learning, rather than a campus, a building and a degree. Nevertheless, even in this more fluid conception, some human and physical resources – not least of which people's *time* – are still required for them to function.

In addition to resources, these initiatives also need recognition, in the sense of public acknowledgement of the value of the learning taking place. In the first place, this is to ensure demand from prospective students and the motivation to commit to the studies seriously on the part of the learners. Demand, however, is also largely dependent on another form of recognition: the formal approval of the course of study in the external society, primarily in the labour market. This form of recognition expresses itself most obviously in the form of the degree diploma, along with – in many cases – the approval of a relevant professional body. Given the centrality of formal qualifications to most opportunities relating to formal employment and further study, the absence of this kind of recognition of learning can place 'graduates' at a significant disadvantage in their subsequent lives. This level of risk would make this form of higher learning most readily available to the most privileged (who can afford to let go of the security of a salaried job) or to the most desperate (who would have had no other chance of higher education in any event). Many of these initiatives rightly focus on the intrinsic value of higher learning: yet if they do not attend additionally to the instrumental needs of their students (and sadly, perhaps even desires for positional advantage), then it is rare that they can attract much interest from their target population.

The counterargument is that if an institution always compromises its beliefs in order to 'fit in' with the rest of society, then no real change will ever take place. Initiatives such as Maracanã Village forcefully critique other indigenous groups who have accepted government funding and in the process compromised their political and cultural vision. In this way, 'institutionalization' poses a constant threat to these radical initiatives, while at the same time, avoiding institutionalization can leave them isolated and impotent.

'Embodiment' – the actual manifestation of the goals and principles the initiative is promoting, whether dialogue, co-operativism, enquiry or equality – is subject then to the threat of progressive encroachment of resources and recognition. Resources are of course essential, and in most cases, acquiring more resources will enable an initiative to either enhance the quality of its work or expand availability and accessibility. However, over-attention to the question of resources can lead to dangers: it is rare for investment to be made without conditions, and initiatives will end up adapting the vision of their work, along the line of the saying 'he who pays the piper calls the tune'. Alternatively, if resources are gathered through charging fees to students there are obvious implications for equity.

Recognition also poses risks. As with resources, desire to obtain recognition of learning from national higher education boards or professional associations can lead to an undesirable adaptation of values or course content. The existence of the instrumental product of the course the diploma – can also serve to undermine the intrinsic value of the venture for students and lecturers. Furthermore, as with all educational undertakings, the existence of a final summative assessment – particularly if it is a badly designed one – can have a negative impact on learning, with unintended backwash effects. The Landless Movement has appeared to have resolved this tension by partnering with established universities to provide formal accreditation, although not all are in agreement with this kind of solution: the organizers of Pampédia Free University originally had such a partnership, but extricated themselves from it on account of the financial cost and constraints on their pedagogical practice.

The threats posed by emphasis on capturing resources and ensuring recognition are not confined to alternative institutions by any means. While not perhaps providing a compelling argument for abandoning institutions altogether, these considerations do vindicate Illich's concerns about the encroaching dangers of the process of institutionalization, and the need to be constantly vigilant that the aim of meaningful learning for all is not being undermined by the structures created to promote it.

What we are faced with, therefore, is the image of a grape held in a large hand: the hand can support and protect the grape, but if the fingers squeeze too hard, the grape will be crushed.

The features of mainstream higher education institutions – their bureaucratic structures, channels of financial, physical and human resources, accreditation and prestige – can act to ensure the viability and sustainability of higher learning; yet if care is not taken, these very same features can undermine or even destroy the learning they are supposed to promote. Alternative higher education seeks to recuperate what is perceived to be the forgotten essence of higher learning, or to provide a space for new or previously marginalized epistemological perspectives. It remains to be seen whether these courageous visions can survive outside the protective cover of the mainstream, or alternatively retain their authenticity within it.

Acknowledgement

An extended version of this chapter was published in 2016 in the journal *Other Education*, 5 (2), 196–220.

Notes

1   Tertiary education customarily includes a range of non-university institutions, including polytechnics, single discipline faculties and teacher education colleges. This chapter will not focus on the specific differences between these types.
2   This chapter will not follow the distinctive usage of the term 'alternative provider' in the UK, referring to the new private entrants into the higher education system

(many of which are for-profit), that have joined the established universities and further education colleges in offering degree courses.

3 Within the 50 per cent quota, the proportions of students entering must be in line with the racial/ethnic composition of the state in question.

4 Partido dos Trabalhadores.

5 Programa de Apoio a Planos de Reestruturação e Expansão das Universidades Federais.

6 Universidade Federal da Integração Latino-Americana.

7 Universidade da Integração Internacional da Lusofonia Afro-Brasileira.

8 An additional campus has been established in São Francisco do Conde, Bahia.

9 Family income of up to three minimum salaries.

10 Universidade Federal da Fronteira Sul. UFFS has a total of over 8,000 students. It goes beyond the legal requirement (of 50 per cent) and reserves 90 per cent of its places for students from public schools.

11 Universidade Federal do Oeste do Pará.

12 Religious higher education institutions, particularly Catholic ones, are common in Brazil. This study will not consider them as 'alternative', however, due to their formative role in creating the 'mainstream' institution and because in practice they customarily have only a few distinctive features in terms of curriculum and governance.

13 ABRUC (Associação Brasileira de Universidades Comunitárias)

14 Universidade Intercultural Indígena Aldeia Maracanã.

15 In addition to the Amazon rainforest and other rural areas, there are a large number of indigenous people now located in the shantytowns or periphery areas of large cities: the last census showed 15,000 indigenous people of the city of Rio de Janeiro (Interview with activist of Maracanã Village).

16 The term 'free' is used here in the sense of liberty, rather than in the sense of being without cost.

17 Movimento dos Trabalhadores Rurais Sem Terra.

References

Barber, Michael, Katelyn Donnelly, and Saad Rizvi. *An Avalanche is Coming: Higher Education and the Revolution Ahead*. London: Institute for Public Policy Research, 2013. https://www.ippr.org/files/images/media/files/publication/2013/04/avalanche-is-coming_Mar2013_10432.pdf.

Bernasconi, Andres. 'Is There a Latin American Model of the University?' *Comparative Education Review* 52, no. 1 (2007): 27–52.

Bernstein, Basil. 'On the Classification and Framing of Educational Knowledge'. In *Knowledge and Control*, edited by Michael F. D. Young. London: Collier-Macmillan, 1971.

Carvalho, Cristina A. 'O PROUNI no Governo Lula e o Jogo Político em torno do Acesso ao Ensino Superior'. *Educação & Sociedade* 27, no. 96 (2006): 979–1000.

Comissão de Implantação da UNILA. *A UNILA em Construção: um Projeto Universitário Para a América Latina*. Foz do Iguaçu: IMEA, 2009a.

Comissão de Implantação da UNILA. UNILA: Consulta Internacional. Contribuições à concepção, organização e proposta político-pedagógica da Unila. Foz do Iguaçu: IMEA, 2009b.

Dore, Ronald. *The Diploma Disease: Education, Qualification and Development*. London: George Allen and Unwin, 1976.

Esteva, Gustavo. 'Reclaiming our Freedom to Learn'. *Yes Magazine*. 7 November 2007.

Figueiredo-Cowen, Maria de. 'Latin American Universities, Academic Freedom and Autonomy: A long-term myth?'. *Comparative Education* 38, no. 4 (2002): 471–484.

Finger, Matthias and José M. Asún. *Adult Education at the Crossroads: Learning Our Way Out*. London: Zed Books, 2001.

Freire, Paulo. *Pedagogy of the Oppressed*. London: Sheed and Ward, 1972.

Freire, Paulo. *Pedagogy of Hope: Reliving Pedagogy of the Oppressed*. New York: Continuum, 1994.

Gandin, Luis A. 'Creating Real Alternatives to Neo-liberal Policies in Education: The Citizen School Project'. In *The Subaltern Speak: Curriculum, Power, and Educational Struggles*, edited by Michael W. Apple and Kristen Buras, 217–242. New York: Routledge, 2006.

Ghanem, Elie. 'Inovação em escolas públicas de nível básico: o caso Redes da Maré (Rio de Janeiro, RJ)'. *Educação e Sociedade* 34, no. 123 (2013): 425–440.

Huisman, Jeroen, Jorunn D. Norgård, Jogen Rasmussen, and Bjorn Stensaker. 'Alternative' Universities Revisited: a Study of the Distinctiveness of Universities Established in the Spirit of 1968'. *Tertiary Education and Management* 8, no. 4 (2002): 315–332.

IBGE. Pesquisa Nacional por Amostra de Domicílios 2015. Rio de Janeiro: IBGE, 2016.

Illich, Ivan. *Deschooling Society*. New York: Harper & Row, 1971.

Illich, Ivan. *Tools for Conviviality*. New York: Harper & Row, 1973.

INEP. *Censo do Ensino Superior. 2013*. 2014. Accessed 23 October 2015. http://download.inep.gov.br/educacao_superior/censo_superior/apresentacao/2014/coletiva_censo_superior_2013.pdf.

King-Calnek, Judith. 'Education for Citizenship: Interethnic Pedagogy and Formal Education at Escola Criativa Olodum'. *Urban Review* 38, no. 2 (2006): 145–164.

Macfarlane, Bruce. 'The Morphing of Academic Practice: Unbundling and the Rise of the Para-academic'. *Higher Education Quarterly* 65, no. 1 (2011): 59–73.

McCowan, Tristan. 'The Growth of Private Higher Education in Brazil: Implications for Equity and Quality'. *Journal of Education Policy* 19, no. 4 (2004): 453–472.

McCowan, Tristan. *Rethinking Citizenship Education: A Curriculum for Participatory Democracy*. London: Continuum, 2009.

McCowan, Tristan. 'Higher Education, Unbundling and the End of the University as We Know It'. *Oxford Review of Education* 43, no. 6 (2017): 733–748.

Motter, Paulino and Luis A. Gandin. 'Higher Education and New Regionalism in Latin America: The UNILA project'. In *Global Regionalisms and Higher Education: Projects, Processes, Politics*, edited by Susan Robertson, Kris Olds, Roger Dale and Que A. Dang. Cheltenham: Edward Elgar, 2016.

Prakash, Madhu S. and Gustavo Esteva. *Escaping Education: Living as Learning in Grassroots Cultures* (2nd edition). New York: Peter Lang Publishing, 2008.

Reimer, Everett. *School is Dead*. Penguin: Harmondsworth, 1971.

Sampaio, Helena. 'O global e o Local No Ensino Superior no Brasil: Apontamentos Preliminares'. Paper presented at the 38th ANPOCS conference, 27–31 October 2014. Caxambu, Brazil. https://www.anpocs.com%2Findex.php%2Fpapers-38-encontro%2Fgt-1%2Fgt25-1%2F9065-o-global-e-o-local-no-ensino-superior-no-brasil-apontamentos-preliminares%2Ffile&usg=AOvVaw3ixa EkeNaGk6qS4YM5CeWD.

Santos, B. S. and Almeida, Filho N. *A Universidade no século XXI: para uma Universidade nova*. Coimbra: Almedina-CES, 2008.

Schmidt, João P., ed. *Instituições Comunitárias: instituições públicas não-estatais*. Santa Cruz do Sul: EDUNISC, 2009.

Singer, Helena. 'Innovative Experiences in Holistic Education Inspiring a New Movement in Brazil'. In *The Palgrave International Handbook of Alternative Education*, edited by Helen Lees and Nel Noddings. London: Palgrave Macmillan, 2016.

Tavares, Manuel and Tatiana Romão. 'Emerging Counterhegemonic Models in Higher Education: The Federal University of Southern Bahia (UFSB) and Its Contribution to a Renewed Geopolitics of Knowledge (interview with Naomar de Almeida Filho)'. *Encounters in Theory and History of Education* 16 (2015): 101–110.

Teamey, K. and U. Mandel. 'Challenging the Modern University, Perspectives and Practices from Indigenous Communities, Social and Ecological Movements'. Paper presented at the Forum on Higher Education and International Development, London, 24 October 2014.

Trindade, Helgio H. C. 'UNILA: Universidade para a Integração Latino-Americana'. *Educación Superior y Sociedad* 14, no. 1 (2009): 147–153.

UNESCO Institute for Statistics. Statistical tables. Gross enrolment ratio by level of education, 2017. http://data.uis.unesco.org/index.aspx?queryid=142.

Vianna, Juliana and Tristan McCowan. 'The University of Latin American Integration: A New Model of Higher Education against the Odds'. Paper presented at the European Conference on Educational Research, Cádiz, 19 September, 2012.

5

Democratic Approaches to Policy and Education: Diversity, Social Justice and Peace

Reva Joshee

Chapter outline

- Introduction
- What is peace?
- A brief overview of Canadian policies on diversity and social justice
- From social justice to social cohesion
- Policy process for peace
- Moving forward to Canadian peace policy
- Notes

Keywords: policy; peace; social justice; Gandhian approaches; democratic policy process; participatory policy analysis

Introduction

The Canadian state has had a long history of engagement with issues of diversity and social justice. At the same time, as the informal national motto ('Peace, order and good government')[1] indicates, peace is a valued ideal. While diversity and social justice have found their way into policies broadly defined as citizenship, peace has not had a policy presence except where direct violence is being addressed, most often in a case of war or international conflict. Moreover, policies addressing diversity and social justice have had a problematic history. For years I have contended that teaching and thinking about diversity through the lens of a

Gandhian-inspired understanding of peace would create a more robust approach to social justice (Joshee 2004, 2006, 2012; Joshee and Thomas 2017). Here I will extend my argument to policy. In particular, I am advocating the adoption of new policy processes that would help to create the kind of peace and social justice policy I envisage and would be peaceful in their nature. In this chapter I will begin with a brief discussion of what I mean by peace, provide a short overview of the history and contemporary situation with regard to cultural diversity and social justice policies,[2] and conclude by discussing an approach to policy that is consistent with peace.

What is peace?

In Canada, as in most nation-states, we tend to understand peace policy as part of foreign policy that responds to current or potential armed conflict (Bjorkdahl 2013; Zimelis 2012). In the case of regions with protracted internal conflict, such as Northern Ireland, Cyprus and Israel, peace policy may be framed in terms of addressing that conflict (Byrne and Irvin 2001; Levin 2005; Zembylas et al. 2011). In addition, current discourses frame peace as part of a security agenda (Badescu 2010; Imboden 2012; Regehr 2004) where security is seen largely as a response to actual or perceived threats of terrorism. While there have been some attempts in Canada to create a broader and more comprehensive peace policy, most notably the proposal supported by the Canadian Peace Initiative to create a Department of Peace (Arbess and Hoffman 2017), the focus of this work has continued to be framed by responses to international conflict, with some acknowledgement of indigenous issues in Canada. In other words, peace is largely constructed as the absence of war; this is what is called 'negative peace' (see Diehl 2016).

Since the early 1990s, peace educators and researchers in Canada and elsewhere (e.g. Bickmore 2006; Diehl 2016; Galtung and Ikeda 1995; Paulson and Bellino 2017; Smith and Carson 1998; Toh and Floresca-Cawagas 2000) have advanced a broader and more proactive view. Following from the work of Galtung (1969), educators are called upon to understand and address the underlying causes of direct violence, namely, cultural and structural violence. Social injustice of any kind is understood as a form of structural violence. Smith and Carson (1998) have argued that cultural violence includes the denial of the traditions and culture of a people. In other words, racism, sexism, homophobia, transphobia, ableism and state-sponsored assimilation are all forms of structural and cultural violence. Paying attention to structural and cultural violence also causes us to think more deeply about notions of agency as they pertain to violence. For example, if a young person grows up as a member of a marginalized community and is consequently denied opportunities because of her social location, and if that same young person is then set up to fail in school, who is to blame for her failure? Is this young person a dropout, or is she a pushout? In Galtung's (1969) view, structural and cultural violence are silent and unchanging.

More recently, Nixon has advanced a notion he calls 'slow violence' (Nixon 2011). Nixon's slow violence differs from Galtung's structural violence in two important ways: first, it is more concerned with time than agency, and second, it is not viewed as indirect violence. Nixon (2011) explains slow violence as 'a violence that grows gradually and out of sight, a violence of delayed destruction that is dispersed across time and space, an attritional violence that is typically not viewed as violence at all' (2). In other words, slow violence takes place at a rate that is typically outside our attention span. He argues that we generally only understand violence in terms of the spectacular – bombs being dropped, mass shootings and explosions. Slow violence, on the other hand, happens over the course of years or even decades. Nixon is particularly concerned with environmental degradation. He notes that slow violence generally happens to people and places that most of the world (read: the elites) see as unimportant or expendable. The violence also goes unnoticed because those to whom it happens are not seen as credible witnesses; their stories are not listened to or heard.

In recent work with colleagues (Joshee and Thomas 2017; Joshee, Shane, Shirvell and Thomas 2016), I have coined the term 'slow peace' to talk about an approach to peace that engages with key Gandhian principles and with Nixon's (2011) notion of slow violence. While there are several Gandhian principles that inform slow peace, the most central for this discussion is the notion of *ahimsa*. Gandhiji[3] did not invent the idea of ahimsa. It has existed since at least the sixth century BCE as part of Hindu, Jain and Buddhist philosophical traditions. While Gandhiji and others have translated it into English as *nonviolence*, I find this translation inadequate because, as Chapple (1993) has noted:

> In western cultures, nonviolence usually denotes passive, non-resistant civil disobedience, pacifism, and conscientious objection to war. It is particularly associated with the Christian teachings of the Religious Society of Friends (Quakers) and other radical reform movements that rely on Biblical injunctions to 'love your neighbour as yourself' and to 'turn the other cheek'. In India, nonviolence … is a personal commitment to respect life in its myriad forms. (xiii)

A commitment to ahimsa, from this perspective, is built on a belief in the unity of life, nonviolence in thought, word and deed, sacrifice of self in the service of others, equity, love of one's opponents, compassion and forgiveness, respect for the just laws of the State, and openness and communication. It concurrently requires a recognition that the common life force is expressed in the world in myriad ways and that our task as educators and policy actors is to understand, accept and support the diversity around us. This simultaneous insistence on one and many requires the rejection of the either/or way in which we usually frame the world in favour of an approach that considers each and.

A commitment to ahimsa has to be at once personal and political. It requires attention to one's own development and everyday actions while striving to address issues at a larger level. The precepts of slow peace encourage stepping back to understand the taken-for-granted practices that contribute to various forms of slow violence, with particular attention to the ways in which those practices are embodied in the work we do as educators, researchers and policy actors. In particular, I have advocated that it is important to focus on specific forms of violence writ large and to proceed by thinking about day-to-day practices that sustain these types of violence. For example, I have focused on neoliberalism in education as a form of slow violence. One of the ways I try to interrupt this form of violence is by pushing back against the calls for speed and efficiency in our work. Increasingly I build in time in all my classes for slowing down and reflecting on what we are learning and how it relates to our own practices. Finally, to be effective as a framework for approaching policy, slow peace requires all policy actors, not just those who are state-based, to commit to sustained action through a variety of forms and methods (Joshee and Thomas 2017). I will return to slow peace in the discussion of policy process later in the chapter.

A brief overview of Canadian policies on diversity and social justice

In 1867 the British North America Act (now known as the Constitution Act) was passed by the British Parliament; it created the Dominion of Canada as a federal state with a parliamentary system of government. At the outset, Canada was part of the British Empire; policy development was the purview of men, generally of British origin, who were loyal to the crown and empire and who were guided in part by a commitment to creating a 'white' Canada (Price 2013). Not surprisingly, a key policy focus in relation to people who were not of British origin was that of Anglo-conformity, and assimilability was a key criterion in deciding who would be allowed to settle in Canada. This had several implications with regard to citizenship policy. For Francophones, it was a recanting of the original pact between British and French Canadians, whereby Canada was meant to be a nation based on cultural and linguistic duality. It led French Canadians across the country to develop an attitude of protectionism towards their identity (McLean 2007). For First Nations, Inuit and Metis peoples, it meant a continuation of policies and programmes meant to *civilize* all aboriginal peoples. There is a growing recognition in Canada that this approach led to cultural genocide (Truth and Reconciliation Commission of Canada 2015). For immigrants, the policy focus was assimilation (Joshee 2004).

In the late 1930s, with the threat of war looming, some Canadian government officials determined it would be important to find ways to work with people who were of neither British nor French origin. This led to engagement with a small group of men who were more or less sympathetic to the *foreign-born* population and the development of policies that began to shape the Canadian version of integration, the idea that immigrants did not have to give up their ancestral culture or language in order to be Canadian (Joshee 1995). This work was extended following the adoption of the Canadian Citizenship Act (1947) and through an incremental process of policy development involving a few key community-based agencies (namely the Canadian Citizenship Council and the Canadian Association for Adult Education); citizenship education policy for adults became largely associated with what would now be called equity-focused work in immigrant integration and intergroup relations (Joshee 1995; Schugurensky 2006). Notably, the one group whose education fell outside of this general trend was adults of First Nations, Inuit and Metis origin. As Bohaker and Iacovetta (2009) have noted, 'there were also critical differences between the immigrant and Aboriginal [citizenship] campaigns, including the virtual absence of any explicit discourse of cultural pluralism or unity-in-diversity in the Aboriginal programs for the period under review. Instead, these programs were characterized by a more marked policy of racial assimilation into white society' (443).

With the work of the Royal Commission on Bilingualism and Biculturalism (1963) – known as the B&B Commission – from the mid-1960s to the early 1970s, there was a new focus on policies related to identity and diversity in relation to ethnic groups of immigrant origin. There were also formal opportunities for ethnocultural groups from across the country to influence policy development through participation in Commission hearings and written submissions. The B&B Commission, which was established partly in response to unrest among Francophones in Quebec, made recommendations that created more cultural and linguistic security for Francophone communities outside of Quebec, especially because of the provisions that pledged to support increased efforts in bilingual education (in French and English) (Cardinal 2013; Hayday 2013). But the fact that the mandate of the B&B Commission (1963) had been expanded to include 'the contribution of other ethnic groups' (the title of book four of the B&B Commission Report) was seen by many Francophones, particularly in Quebec, as a direct threat to the status of their culture. Notably, this Royal Commission, which was meant to address the contributions of all groups to the building of Canada and Canadian culture, made no mention of indigenous people.

The introduction of the federal multiculturalism policy in 1971 focused attention on two areas: nonofficial (or heritage) languages and the sharing of culture. The first resulted in programmes both within and outside of formal schooling. The second created renewed interest in multicultural concerts and food fairs, events that had first been promoted across the country by the railway companies in the 1930s (Burnaby 2008; Joshee 2004). Additionally, the creation of the multiculturalism programme and work by officials in that programme created links between numerous ethnocultural groups and the government of the day. Through conferences, advisory councils and formal consultations, people from minority ethnocultural groups were being given even more opportunities to engage in policy conversations.

Meanwhile, Druick (2007) asserts that the same government that was promoting diversity among the settler population had in 1969 introduced a White Paper to dismantle the Indian Act and 'afford First Nations people complete citizenship through total assimilation' (151). The White Paper was an attempt to dismantle all previous legislation regarding the Indigenous populations of Canada and would have resulted in negating the status of Indigenous peoples as the First Peoples of Canada. In particular, it was seen as an attempt to remove the possibility that First Nations might pursue land claims. Indigenous groups across the country wrote responses to the 1969 White Paper and a key national body at the time, the National Indian Brotherhood (later renamed the Assembly of First Nations), organized a campaign against the federal proposals and developed its own agenda for change. This led to the development of a joint committee of the National Indian Brotherhood and the federal cabinet. This committee was touted as being a unique opportunity for joint policy development, but it was disbanded in 1978 without having made any significant policy agreements (Weaver 1982)

Following the adoption of the Canadian Charter of Rights and Freedoms in 1982, educators began to use this document as the basis for discussions of human rights and multiculturalism within citizenship education (Bromley 2011). Hughes and his colleagues (1998) have noted that, through the 1990s, curriculum documents across the country defined citizenship in terms of 'freedoms, justice, due process, dissent, the rule of law, equality, diversity, and loyalty' (4). Lévesque (2003) has noted that there is some evidence that this emphasis helped to create a 'rights-based consciousness' among Canadian students (110). Despite the broader lens of diversity, however, there is evidence to suggest it did little to enhance understanding of Francophone or First Nations claims (Lévesque 2003).

Briefly then, from the late nineteenth century through most of the twentieth century the Canadian state used a variety of approaches from cultural genocide to human rights in its attempts to address social injustice. For the most part, policy development was directed by state actors with limited input from community-based actors. In practice, all of these approaches divided society into two groups, variously labelled, 'Canadian and foreigner', 'dominant and minority', 'privileged and marginalized' or 'oppressors and oppressed' and generally constructed the quest for social justice as a battle between 'us' and 'them' (Kunz and Sykes 2007).

From social justice to social cohesion

Since the 1990s, discussions of social justice have largely been supplanted by discussions of social cohesion (Joshee and Sinfield 2010). As Shuayb (2012) has noted, 'the theory underpinning the social cohesion agenda in neoliberal states is market and economic driven. Its main objective is economic prosperity and the maintenance of the status quo through increased distribution of social goods, which should help address the inequalities' (13). Shuayb (2012) argues that social justice is absent from the conversations on social cohesion in education and that the focus of citizenship education within this frame is on 'promoting trust and solidarity and creating "imagined communities"' (16).

In Canada, three versions of social cohesion have emerged in relation to discussions of diversity. One views social cohesion as built on common values and a sense of shared identity. A second, which draws heavily on the work of Putnam (2001), sees social cohesion as built on trust between the diverse groups and individuals in a society. In this view, it is less important to develop a shared sense of identity than to invest in creating bonds between individuals and bridges between different communities. The third view emphasizes civic participation and focuses on how citizens engage with each other. Even though all three have been part of the policy conversation in Canada, the first two have been most influential (Joshee and Sinfield 2010).

The common values approach draws on the neoconservative *we/they* discourse. The *we* in this case is the (Northern and Western) European group, which is constructed as always having shown tolerance and acceptance of others. The implication is that any problems or conflict, past or current, exist because *the others*, in the case of non-indigenous groups, were not or are not open, tolerant and accepting (for a more complete discussion see Joshee and Sinfield 2010). In the case of indigenous peoples, the *we*, or settlers, develop their sense of identity by either denying the existence of the *they*, indigenous peoples, or by constructing them as uncivilized and therefore incapable of being part of mainstream society (for further discussion, see Paquette et al. 2017; Neeganagwedgin 2014).

In the second version of social cohesion, which relates to Putnam's (1993) notion of social capital, the Policy Research Initiative (PRI) (2005) expressed a belief that 'people and groups with extensive social connections linking them to people with diverse resources tend to be more hired, housed, healthy, and happy' (1). This view focuses on investing in citizens to ensure they can participate in the economy as an important first step towards involvement in public life more generally. Moreover, participation in public life should be geared towards those phenomena that promote harmony, meaning that conflict or dissent of any kind is to be avoided. Thus, we see the emphasis on duty and responsibility in citizenship education for adult immigrants. These duties and responsibilities include obeying the law, getting a job, performing jury duty, voting in elections and volunteering in the community (Citizenship and Immigration Canada 2012).

The third version of social cohesion has elsewhere been called 'social inclusion' (Joshee and Sinfield 2010) or 'democratic social cohesion' (Bickmore 2006). With its focus on how people interact rather than on shared values or bonds of trust, some believe this version has the potential to support a justice-oriented approach to citizenship and multiculturalism (Bickmore 2006; Kymlicka 2013; Soroka, Johnston, and Banting 2006). In this view, 'Social cohesion requires economic and social equity, peace, security, inclusion and access. Diversity and differences are conducive to social cohesion because they contribute to a vibrant political and social life' (PRI 2002, 5). The definition of social cohesion that emerges from this perspective includes three components: (a) participation in political and civil society (including dissent), (b) bonds of trust between individuals, institutions and policies (like bilingualism and multiculturalism) that would bridge difference and promote mutual respect and (c) an inclusive society built on the principles of income distribution, equity and access for all (Joshee and Sinfield 2010). While this approach does allow for dissent and conflict, diversity remains something to be endured and bridged rather than an asset in and of itself. This leads to what Kymlicka (2013) has called 'neoliberal multiculturalism', noting, 'The goal of neoliberal multiculturalism is not a tolerant national citizen who is concerned for the disadvantaged in her own society but a cosmopolitan market actor who can compete effectively across state boundaries' (111). Clearly, none of these approaches to social cohesion will lead to the creation of a more socially just society.

The process through which the policy on social cohesion has developed involved government based policy workers in a cross-sector undertaking called the Policy Research Initiative (PRI) identifying social cohesion as a broad policy direction. From there PRI officials held conversations with key senior bureaucrats who 'agreed to launch a renewal of policy research in the area of social cohesion … and also to bring fresh insights to the task of setting the direction for future policy research in this area' (Canada, Department of Justice and Department of Canadian Heritage 2002, ii). Following this step, consultations were held with about 130 individuals described as 'experts and acknowledged leaders' (Canada, Department of Justice and Department of Canadian Heritage 2002, iii). In total, twenty-two of the people involved in the conversation were from a range of community-based organizations, twenty-nine were researchers and the remainder were federal civil servants. Significantly of the community-based groups involved in the consultations, none represented ethnocultural or indigenous communities.

Since the initial consultation, there has been a Senate Report on Social Inclusion and Social Cohesion which allowed for some 235 groups and individuals to present evidence related to the broad issue of social cohesion (Standing Senate Committee on Social Affairs, Science and Technology 2013). The term is currently used as an organizer for areas as diverse as seniors, health care, justice, art and culture, public safety, peace and security, immigration and democratic reform (Government of Canada 2016); however, no major public consultation has taken place since 2002.

Policy process for peace

From a Gandhian perspective, the means is as important as the ends. If we are interested in moving from the current social cohesion view(s) of diversity towards a framework of peace, then defining a policy process that is compatible with such a framework is at least as important as recommending content. I would argue that to this point diversity policy in Canada has been guided by traditional approaches to policy development. Morcol (2001) has argued that traditional policy processes are framed by a positivist understanding of policy analysis. Simply put, this means that policy development is guided by a belief that policies are best constructed following a neutral process of problem identification, research into alternatives and rational decision-making based on empirical evidence provided by the experts. The process tends to be guided by state-based actors who are seen as policy-makers. Johnson (2005) has criticized this process for its fundamental belief that there is a clear distinction between facts and values. DeSantis (2010) adds a further criticism noting the lack of attention to the basic issue of who is allowed and not allowed to be involved in policy development. As a result, policy decisions in the area of diversity have been, and are still made, by people from dominant groups with little or no attention to the perspectives of marginalized groups, who tend to be most affected by the policies.

In the past three decades, MacMillan (2010) asserts that governments have included public consultation as part of policy processes in an attempt to address the so-called 'democratic deficit' by creating opportunities for citizen participation in policy creation. In the preceding review of diversity policy, we see that such opportunities for consultation have been created. Importantly, Malacrida and Duguay (2009) draw a distinction between participation and consultation, noting that 'consultation operates by invitation only, provides limited exchanges of views, lacks accountability to citizens [and] reinforces passive models of decision-making' (21). Not surprisingly, there is considerable concern over whether community-based policy actors involved in consultations have any real influence in policy development (Culver and Howe 2004; Laforest and Orsini 2005; Malacrida and Duguay 2009). There is also some concern that when state actors control who is involved in a public consultation process that access is limited to those groups or individuals that the state deems as worthy (Lundberg 2013). Thus, as one federal official noted, 'what we call consultations are really insultations' (Jeff Bullard, personal communication, 1999). From a Gandhian perspective, the impetus to get involved in conversation about policy is laudable. Rather than being a pro forma exercise in consultation or a debate regarding the merits of different perspectives, it is important to think of public dialogues on policy as a place for people and ideas to meet rather than compete. As part of his discussion of ahimsa, Chapple (1993) noted, '[t]he most violent acts arise from the nonacceptance of another's viewpoint. The inability to expand or alter one's own opinions often brings about the objectification of those who do not cleave to that particular vision' (96). His solution to this is '[i]ntellectual nonviolence [which] requires a commitment to one's own belief system accompanied with an ability to tolerate and perhaps celebrate the positions of others' (97). Because this standpoint is grounded in a belief in ahimsa, to do no harm in thought, word or deed, the viewpoints expressed and the responses to them would need to be measured against the standard of harm. Thus dialogue is neither the kind of discussion that requires people to adopt an opinion and defend it at all costs nor is it a free- wheeling exchange where every opinion is as valid as every other is. For example, an opinion that does harm, such as demeaning a group or individual, is not compatible with this form of dialogue. Building from work in the area of participatory and democratic policy analysis (DeLeon 1997; Fine et al. 2012; Hogan et al. 2014; Tuck and Gorlewski 2016) and critical policy sociology (Diem et al. 2014; Gale 2001; Marshall et al. 2014; Thomson et al. 2010), I am proposing a model of policy dialogue for peace that I believe would lead to a robust peace policy inclusive of diversity and social justice. My interpretation of dialogue is informed by the understanding of slow peace my colleagues and I are developing (Joshee and Thomas 2017; Joshee et al. 2016) and draws on insights from Young (1990, 1997) and Mansbridge (1997), both of whom speak to the difficulties of involving members of dominant and marginalized groups in dialogue together. They focus our attention on the need to address power differentials and diversity in respectful ways that will enhance communication and understanding between members of historically dominant and minoritized groups. Young (1997), in particular, proposes an approach to dialogue based on what she calls 'asymmetrical reciprocity', which she explains in the following manner:

> This reciprocity of equal respect and acknowledgement of one another, however, entails an acknowledgement of *asymmetry* between subjects. While there may be many similarities and point of contact between them, each position and perspective transcends the others, goes beyond their possibility to share or imagine. Participants in communicative interaction are in a relation of approach. They meet across distance of time and space and can touch, share, overlap their interests. But each brings to the relationships a history and structured positioning that makes them different from one another, with their own shape, trajectory, and configuration of forces. (50)

The purpose of dialogue then is not necessarily to develop a common perspective. Rather, it is to do one's best to understand the differences between one's own position and that of others. At the same time, drawing from Mansbridge (1997), we must also acknowledge that certain positions and points of view have had more access to the public sphere. Indeed, as Nixon (2011) has demonstrated, certain people are never heard because they are not see as credible witnesses. Given this reality we must find ways to bring silenced and lesser-known perspectives to the fore.

Moving forward to Canadian peace policy

It is important that Canada has existing traditions of diversity and social justice policies. The work for a robust peace policy should build on the strengths and learn from the shortcomings of past policy initiatives. As we think of how to bring silenced and lesser-known perspectives to the fore, we must take into account that we cannot simply bring people into policy processes without any experience or preparation. We need to find respectful ways to engage that also include opportunities to share knowledge of existing policy and systems with those who we want to include in the conversation. For any of this to happen, we cannot simply view peace policy as the purview of the state and make recommendations we hope someone will take up. We must recognize that we are all policy actors and thus have a role to play in redefining policy processes. My own definition of policy is that at the best of times it is an ongoing conversation about the things that matter in society. Given the current state of the world and concerns about environmental degradation, gender inequality, the increasing concentration of wealth in the hands of a few, and armed conflict, just to name a few, there can be no doubt that we need to engage in a meaningful conversation about peace. I trust that the ideas I have advanced in this chapter will contribute to that conversation.

Notes

1   The latest issue of the Canadian Encyclopedia reports that 'peace, order and good government', which appears in Section 91 of the British North America Act, 'has come to be considered the Canadian counterpart to the United States' "life, liberty and the pursuit of happiness"', http://www.thecanadianencyclopedia.ca/en/article/peace-order-and-good-government/

2   Diversity policies cover a wide range of issues and aspects of social diversity in Canada and it is beyond the scope of this paper to try to do an overview of all of these policies. Instead, I will focus on cultural diversity policies as an illustrative example.

3   The addition of the suffix '-ji' to a person's name is a sign of respect. Because my
    mother knew and learned from Gandhiji, it has been the practice in my family to
    refer to him in this way.

References

Arbess, Saul and Ben Hoffman. 'Here's Why Canada Needs a Department of Peace'.
    Ottawa Citizen, 11 April 2017.

Badescu, Cristina G. 'National Security: Canada's Continuing Engagement with
    United Nations Peace Operations'. *Canadian Foreign Policy Journal* 16, no. 2
    (2010): 45–60.

Bickmore, Kathy. 'Democratic Social Cohesion (assimilation)? Representations of Social
    Conflict in Canadian Public School Curriculum'. *Canadian Journal of Education/
    Revue canadienne de l'éducation* 29, no. 2 (2006): 359–386.

Björkdahl, Annika. 'Urban Peacebuilding'. *Peacebuilding* 1, no. 2 (2013): 207–221.

Bohaker, Heidi and Franca Iacovetta. 'Making Aboriginal People 'Immigrants Too':
    A Comparison of Citizenship Programs for Newcomers and Indigenous Peoples
    in Postwar Canada, 1940s–1960s'. *Canadian Historical Review* 90, no. 3 (2009):
    427–462.

Bromley, Patricia. 'Multiculturalism and Human Rights in Civic Education: The Case of
    British Columbia, Canada'. *Educational Research* 53, no. 2 (2011): 151–164.

Burnaby, B. 'Language Policy and Education in Canada'. In *Encyclopedia of Language
    and Education*, 331–341. New York: Springer US, 2008.

Byrne, Sean and Cynthia Irvin. 'Economic Aid and Policy Making: Building the Peace
    Dividend in Northern Ireland'. *Policy & Politics* 29, no. 4 (2001): 413–429.

Canada. 'Department of Justice and Department of Canadian Heritage'. In *INCLUSION
    FOR ALL: A Canadian Roadmap to Social Cohesion*. Ottawa: Government of
    Canada, 2002. http://www.justice.gc.ca/eng/rp-pr/csj-sjc/jsp-sjp/tr01-rt01/tr01.pdf.

Canada. 'Government of Canada'. *Budget 2016*. Ottawa: Government of Canada, 2016.
    https://www.budget.gc.ca/2016/docs/plan/ch5-en.html?wbdisable=true.

Cardinal, Linda. 'The Impact of the Commission on Bilingualism and Biculturalism
    on Francophone Minority Communities in Canada'. *Canadian Issues* Fall (2013):
    18–22.

Chapple, Christopher. *Nonviolence to Animals, Earth, and Self in Asian Traditions*.
    Albany, NY: SUNY Press, 1993.

Citizenship and Immigration Canada. *Evaluation of Multiculturalism Program*. Ottawa:
    Government of Canada, 2012. http://www.cic.gc.ca/english/resources/evaluation/
    multi/index.asp.

Culver, Keith and Paul Howe. 'Calling all Citizens: The Challenges of Public
    Consultation'. *Canadian Public Administration* 47, no. 1 (2004): 52–75.

DeLeon, Peter. *Democracy and the Policy Sciences*. Albany, NY: SUNY Press, 1997.

DeSantis, Gloria. 'Voices from the Margins: Policy Advocacy and Marginalized Communities'. *Canadian Journal of Nonprofit and Social Economy Research* 1, no. 1 (2010): 23.

Diehl, Paul F. 'Exploring Peace: Looking beyond War and Negative Peace'. *International Studies Quarterly* 60, no. 1 (2016): 1–10.

Diem, Sarah, Michelle D. Young, Anjalé D. Welton, Katherine Cumings Mansfield, and Pei-Ling Lee. 'The Intellectual Landscape of Critical Policy Analysis'. *International Journal of Qualitative Studies in Education* 27, no. 9 (2014): 1068–1090.

Druick, Zoë. *Projecting Canada: Government Policy and Documentary Film at the National Film Board*, Vol. 1, Kingston, ON, and Canada: McGill-Queen's Press-MQUP, 2007.

Fine, Michelle, Jennifer Ayala, and Mayida Zaal. 'Public Science and Participatory Policy Development: Reclaiming Policy as a Democratic Project'. *Journal of Education Policy* 27, no. 5 (2012): 685–692.

Gale, Trevor. 'Critical Policy Sociology: Historiography, Archaeology and Genealogy as Methods of Policy Analysis'. *Journal of Education Policy* 16, no. 5 (2001): 379–393.

Galtung, Johan. 'Violence, Peace, and Peace Research'. *Journal of Peace Research* 6, no. 3 (1969): 167–191.

Galtung, Johan and Daisaku Ikeda. *Choose Peace*, trans. and ed. Richard Gage, 127. East Haven, CT: Pluto Press, 1995.

Hayday, Matthew. 'Canada's Bilingual Education Revolution: The B&B Commission And Official Languages in Education'. *Canadian Issues* (Fall 2013): 29–33.

Hogan, Lindsay, Enrique Garcia Bengoechea, Jon Salsberg, Judi Jacobs, Morrison King, and Ann C. Macaulay. 'Using a Participatory Approach to the Development of a School-based Physical Activity Policy in an Indigenous Community'. *Journal of School Health* 84, no. 12 (2014): 786–792.

Hughes, Andrew S., Alan M. Sears, and Gerald M. Clarke. 'Adapting Problem-based Learning to Social Studies Teacher Education'. *Theory & Research in Social Education* 26, no. 4 (1998): 531–548.

Imboden, Bahar Akman. 'Unpacking the Peacekeeping–Peacebuilding Nexus: A Human Security Proposal'. *Conflict Resolution Quarterly* 30, no. 2 (2012): 173–196.

Johnson, Genevieve Fuji. 'Taking Stock: the Normative Foundations of Positivist and Non-Positivist Policy *Analysis* And Ethical Implications of the Emergent Risk Society'. *Journal of Comparative Policy Analysis: Research and Practice* 7, no. 2 (2005): 137–153.

Joshee, Reva. 'An Historical Approach to Understanding Canadian Multicultural Policy'. In *Multicultural Education in a Changing Global Economy: Canada and the Netherlands*, edited by T. Wotherspoon and P. Jungbluth, 23–40. New York: Waxmann Munster, 1995.

Joshee, Reva. 'Citizenship and Multicultural Education in Canada: From Assimilation to Social Cohesion'. *Diversity and Citizenship Education: Global Perspectives* (2004): 127–156.

Joshee, Reva. 'Ahimsa and Teaching'. *Connections* 29, no. 1 (2006): 6–13.

Joshee, Reva. 'Challenging Neoliberalism Through Gandhian Trusteeship'. *Critical Studies in Education* 53, no. 1 (2012): 71–82.

Joshee, Reva, Margaret Shane, Simone Shirvell, and Monica Thomas. *Slow Peace: A Gandhian Inspired Approach to Education*, Invited talk presented at El Centro de Investigacion y Docencia, Chihuahua, Mexico, 27 May 2016.

Joshee, Reva and Ivor Sinfield. 'The Canadian Multicultural Education Policy Web: Lessons to Learn, Pitfalls to Avoid'. *Multicultural Education Review* 2, no. 1 (2010): 55–75.

Joshee, Reva and Monica Thomas. 'Multicultural and Citizenship Education in Canada: Slow Peace as an Alternative to Social Cohesion'. In *Citizenship Education and Global Migration: Implications for Theory, Research, and Teaching*, edited by James A. Banks, 91–106. Washington, DC: American Educational Research Association, 2017.

Kunz, Jean Lock and Stuart Sykes. *From Mosaic to Harmony: Multicultural Canada in the 21st Century*. Ottawa: Policy Research Initiative, 2007.

Kymlicka, Will. 'Neoliberal Multiculturalism'. In *Social Resilience in the Neoliberal Era*, edited by Peter A. Hall and Michèle Lamont, 99–125. Cambridge: Cambridge University Press, 2013.

Laforest, Rachel and Michael Orsini. 'Evidence-Based Engagement in the Voluntary Sector: Lessons from Canada'. *Social Policy & Administration* 39, no. 5 (2005): 481–497.

Lévesque, Stéphane. 'Becoming Citizens: High School Students and Citizenship in British Columbia and Québec'. *Encounters with Education* 4 (Fall 2003): 107–126.

Levin, David. 'Framing Peace Policies: The Competition for Resonant Themes'. *Political Communication* 22, no. 1 (2005): 83–108.

Lundberg, Erik. 'Does the Government Selection Process Promote or Hinder Pluralism? Exploring the Characteristics of Voluntary Organizations Invited to Public Consultations'. *Journal of Civil Society* 9, no. 1 (2013): 58–77.

MacMillan, C. Michael. 'Auditing Citizen Engagement in Heritage Planning: The Views of Citizens'. *Canadian Public Administration* 53, no. 1 (2010): 87–106.

Malacrida, Claudia and Stefanie Duguay. '"The AISH Review Is a Big Joke": Contradictions of Policy Participation and Consultation in a Neo-liberal Context'. *Disability & Society* 24, no. 1 (2009): 19–32.

Mansbridge, Jane. 'Taking Coercion Seriously'. *Constellations*, 3, no. 3 (1997): 407–416.

Marshall, Catherine, Keren Dalyot, and Stephanie Galloway. 'Sexual Harassment in Higher Education: Re-framing the Puzzle of Its Persistence'. *Journal of Policy Practice* 13, no. 4 (2014): 276–299.

McLean, Lorna R. 'Education, Identity, and Citizenship in Early Modern Canada'. *Journal of Canadian Studies* 41, no. 1 (2007): 5–30.

Morçöl, Göktuğ. 'Positivist Beliefs among Policy Professionals: An Empirical Investigation'. *Policy Sciences* 34, no. 3–4 (2001): 381–401.

Neeganagwedgin, Erica. '"They Can't Take Our Ancestors Out of Us": A Brief Historical Account of Canada's Residential School System, Incarceration,

Institutionalized Policies And Legislations against Indigenous Peoples'. *Canadian Issues* (Spring 2014): 31–36.

Nixon, Rob. *Slow Violence and the Environmentalism of the Poor*. Cambridge, MA: Harvard University Press, 2011.

Paquette, Jonathan, Devin Beauregard, and Christopher Gunter. 'Settler Colonialism and Cultural Policy: The Colonial Foundations and Refoundations of Canadian Cultural Policy'. *International Journal of Cultural Policy* 23, no. 3 (2017): 269–284.

Paulson, Julia and Michelle J. Bellino. 'Truth Commissions, Education, and Positive Peace: an Analysis of Truth Commission Final Reports (1980–2015)'. *Comparative Education* 53, no. 3 (2017): 351–378.

Policy Research Initiative (PRI). *Inclusion for All: A Canadian Roadmap to Social Cohesion. Insights from Structured Conversations*. Ottawa, ON: Government of Canada, 2002.

Policy Research Initiative. *Measurement of Social Capital*. Ottawa, ON: Government of Canada, 2005.

Price, John. 'Canada, White Supremacy, and the Twinning of Empires'. *International Journal* 68, no. 4 (2013): 628–638.

Putnam, Robert D. *Bowling Alone: The Collapse and Revival of American Community*. New York: Simon and Schuster, 2001.

Putnam, Robert D. 'The Prosperous Community'. *The American Prospect* 4, no. 13 (1993): 35–42.

Regehr, Ernie. 'Canada and Ballistic Missile Defence: An Interception Scenario'. *Peace Research* 36, no. 2 (2004): 115–122.

Schugurensky, Daniel. '"This Is Our School of Citizenship": Informal Learning in Local Democracy'. *Counterpoints* 249 (2006): 163–182.

Shuayb, Maha, eds. *Rethinking Education for Social Cohesion: International Case Studies*. New York: Palgrave Macmillan, 2012.

Smith, David and Terry Carson. *Education for a Peaceful Future*. Toronto, Ontario, Canada: Kagan and Woo, 1998.

Soroka, Stuart N., Richard Johnston, and Keith G. Banting. *Ties that Bind? Social Cohesion and Diversity in Canada*. Montreal, QC: Institute for Research on Public Policy, 2006.

Standing Senate Committee on Social Affairs, Science and Technology. *In from the Margins, Part II: Reducing Barriers to Social Inclusion and Social Cohesion*. Ottawa: Government of Canada, 2013. https://sencanada.ca/content/sen/Committee/411/soci/rep/rep26jun13-e.pdf.

Thomson, Pat, Christine Hall, and Ken Jones. 'Maggie's Day: A Small-Scale Analysis of English Education Policy'. *Journal of Education Policy* 25, no. 5 (2010): 639–656.

Toh, Swee-Hin and Virginia Floresca-Cawagas. 'Educating Towards A Culture Of Peace'. In *Weaving Connections: Educating for Peace, Social and Environmental Justice*, edited by Tara Goldstein and David Selby, 365–388. Toronto, ON: Canadian Scholars, 2000.

Truth, and Reconciliation Commission of Canada. *Canada's Residential Schools: The Final Report of the Truth and Reconciliation Commission of Canada*, Vol. 1, McGill-Queen's Press-MQUP, 2015.

Tuck, Eve and Julie Gorlewski. 'Racist Ordering, Settler Colonialism, and edTPA: A Participatory Policy Analysis'. *Educational Policy* 30, no. 1 (2016): 197–217.

Weaver, Sally M. 'The Joint Cabinet/National Indian Brotherhood Committee: A Unique Experiment in Pressure Group Relations'. *Canadian Public Administration* 25, no. 2 (1982): 211–239.

Young, Iris Marion. *Intersecting Voices: Dilemmas of Gender, Political Philosophy, and Policy*. Princeton, NJ: Princeton University Press, 1997.

Young, Iris Marion. *Justice and the Politics of Difference*. Princeton, NJ: Princeton University Press, 1990.

Zembylas, Michalinos, Constadina Charalambous, Panayiota Charalambous, and Panayiota Kendeou. 'Promoting Peaceful Coexistence in Conflict-ridden Cyprus: Teachers' Difficulties and Emotions towards a New Policy Initiative'. *Teaching and Teacher Education* 27, no. 2 (2011): 332–341.

Zimelis, Andris. 'Trust and Normative Democratic Peace Theory: Nexus between Citizens and Foreign Policies?' *International Journal of Sociology and Social Policy* 32, no. 1/2 (2012): 17–28.

6

The Democratization of Education Expertise: Examining Policy Shifts and Implications in the UK

Karen Edge

Chapter outline

- Introduction
- Global City Leaders Project
- Democratization in the English education system
- Teacher training: shifting from universities to schools
- The rise of social media use and educational activism
  - *ResearchED*
  - *WomenEd*
  - Other educator-led organizations
- Conclusions

Keywords: democracy, decentralization, educational governance, Global Cities, social media, education in England, educational activism

Introduction

In the early 2000s, a growing evidence base championed how key jurisdictions were successfully implementing school-level administrative and financial decentralization including Chicago (Bryk, Thum, Easton, and Luppenscu 1998; Hess 1999), New Zealand (Wylie 1996) and El Salvador (Jiminez and Sawada

1999). While the evidence of the influence of decentralization on student learning and achievement remains inconclusive, decentralization of decision-making and responsibility to the school level remains a popular policy choice in many jurisdictions around the world. It has seemingly become part of a global reform agenda, through circulation of a particular set of ideas and ideologies relating to educational governance.

Conversely, mounting evidence demonstrates that school-based management does not automatically lead to improved student outcomes (Leithwood and Menzies 1998). In North America, there remains consistent political and evidentiary support for the value of districts as a middle tier between national or state governments and schools. While imperfect, districts have been recognized as essential for educational improvement (Johnson and Crispeels 2010; Togneri and Anderson 2003), improving student outcomes (Leithwood 2010), instruction (Leithwood, Seashore, Anderson, and Walhstrom 2004), leadership development and capacity building (Mascall and Leithwood 2010).

In England, a completely different approach and attitude to the middle tier has evolved. Over the past several decades, successive governments have explicitly supported the rise of school-based management while deliberately weakening LAs. At the moment, system-wide improvement agenda in England is referred to as the Self-improving School System (SISS) (Hargreaves 2010, 2012). SISS is grounded by several key principles comprising: teachers and schools holding responsibility for improvement; learning between schools to share practice; system leaders working across the system to facilitate excellence and minimal government intervention (Greany 2015; Hargreaves 2012). This approach is radically different from that being taken in more centralized systems, such as Ontario, for example, where districts, or middle tiers, are both supported and expected to generate school improvement objectives.

While the overall pace of decentralization and school-based management research has slowed, the focus has consistently, and perhaps unsurprisingly, remained on the primary outcomes of decentralization – bringing policymaking closer to schools, financial and administrative efficiencies, and improving student outcomes (McGinn and Welsh 1999). At the same time, much of the research on school-based management and school districts has been conducted within one country or jurisdiction. While these patterns may not be surprising, recent research, upon which this chapter is based, prompts a reconsideration of the influence of both, within the context of transnational circulation of educational ideas. While we were studying Generation X (GenX) (born between 1966 and 1980) (Edge 2014), school leaders in London, New York City and Toronto, we observed interesting patterns – possibly symbolic – of the unintended influences of educational decentralization on the wider teaching profession. Without our comparative vantage point, we would surely have missed these nuances, thus demonstrating the inherent value of considering these issues simultaneously across multiple jurisdictions.

While the core focus of our research was on educational leadership, the influence of different structural and political approaches to managing the school system had an even greater influence than we had previously observed in the literature. An intensification of how England was shifting the structures, funding and responsibility for the system and school-level success to schools was, in our opinion, demonstrative of an attempt to create greater democratic engagement in educational and school-level policy and practice. We categorized the shifts in three ways: (1) a reinvigoration of the push to democratize school governance by giving schools more authority and local communities, in the form of governing bodies, a greater say over the running of the school; (2) a redefinition of the locus of educational knowledge and expertise in which the schools and individual teachers or leaders gain prominence, often away from universities, as the experts; and (3) a redistribution of educational voice and influence as the proliferation of social media presence increases the reach and influence of individual educators and activist associations. We strongly believe that the confluence of these patterns has a significant influence on the structure and future of the sector, perhaps decreasing the very democratic engagement that, at least in theory, underpins its design.

This chapter presents two specific instances of democratization that may create a shift in education policy and practice and examines how structural shifts in governance and social media may be intentionally and unintentionally influencing education. As these observations emerge from our recent GenX leadership study, the chapter begins with a brief introduction to our study and the observations that triggered our interest in the current state and possible influence of democratization of the English education system. We introduce our overall strategy for gathering, understanding and interpreting the evidence presented in the chapter. In turn, we focus more intently on two of the three aforementioned areas of interest: teacher training and the rise of social media as example of shifts in the locus and power of educational knowledge in the system. At the conclusion of the chapter, we will present some forward-looking research and policy questions to support others as they begin to explore how these conditions may enhance our current policy and practice understanding.

Global City Leaders Project

Our recent Economic and Social Research Council (UK)-funded research focused on leadership policy and practice in three global cities (Sassen 1991): London, New York City and Toronto, chosen for their English majority language, highly diverse populations and positions as centres of globally influential educational research, policy and practice (see Elmore 2004; Higham et al. 2007; Hutchings et al. 2012; Levin 2008).

Working across the three cities, with high-level policy and practice advisory groups guiding our work, we began the three-year study with robust policy and leadership development studies in each city. Throughout the project, we had the opportunity to learn with and from GenX school leaders in each of the cities. The study set out to understand more about the careers, work and lives of this new generation of school principals and vice principals via annual interviews with cohorts of a minimum of twenty leaders in each city and annual city-based networking focus group events. To frame our overall work, we first gathered information on the structural elements of the education systems in each city from publicly available sources. We began with developing cases of the overarching structures of the education systems including the roles of the top (e.g. department of education), middle tier (e.g. district) and local structures (e.g. networks, families of schools). Our structural profiles also included general student population, number/type of schools, leadership demographics (Armstrong, Edge, and Batlle 2013).

Throughout the study, we spent considerable time working to understand the trajectory and pace of policy changes in London (Armstrong, Edge, and Batlle 2013), New York City (Mejias, Edge, Armstrong, and Batlle 2013) and Toronto (Edge, Armstrong, and Batlle 2013). We observed striking differences in how leaders in the systems experience their lives and work which appear to be more deeply influenced by the greater education and social policy context. For example, there are stark contrasts between London and Toronto and, more widely, England and Ontario, in teacher and leader recruitment and retention (Edge 2017). Based on our early observations, we posit that these may be influenced by a set of conditions that get less research and policy attention than they deserve – namely, the level of decentralization and intentional democratization of the education system. This chapter is drawn from an early strand of inquiry examining the ten-year leadership-related policy trajectories in each city: policy development and enactment, the landscape of governmental and non-governmental policy actors, and the leadership development programmes.

Democratization in the English education system

In some policy jurisdictions, democratization of educational decision-making and responsibility takes place through the introduction of variations in school-based management and/or parent or governing councils. However, over the past decade in England, a more aggressive and invasive democratization process has been evolving. As part of a deliberate strategy to weaken the middle tier of educational governance, the LA, there has been a proliferation of new types of schools, with greater autonomy from LA control and restriction. This is one explicit example of how successive governments have attempted to create a more school-focused education system. The reduction of central funding allocated to LAs has been paralleled by reductions in LA control over schools. For many budget lines, resources flow directly to schools for head teachers and governors to allocate. This process, in my opinion, has prompted an emergent and growing layer of educational organizations, with consultants offering their services to schools. The renewed and accelerated marketization of the English education system, in the guise of more democratic and local control, has created a new set of challenges for the system as recruitment and retention of teachers and leaders worsens.

Teacher training: shifting from universities to schools

While the provision of teacher training remains central to many national and global education debates, there is consistent agreement that teacher quality remains the single most important factor attributed to high performing school systems (OECD 2005). Over the past two decades, the English education system began to diversify the number and type of routes to entry of the profession. Primarily in response to an increasing demand for teachers, paralleled by decreasing numbers of applicants, the diversification was intended to create more agile, responsive pathways for individuals seeking to qualify to teach. In parallel, a more formally and seemingly deliberate movement of teacher training from wholly university-driven to equally schools-led provision occurred. As alternate models of teacher training have emerged, so has the delivery of these models by non-university actors, including not-for-profits, individual and groups schools, and groups of schools. Among these new pathways, fast-track teacher training programmes including Teach First gained prominence and obtained government favour and funding. Schools also became more engaged in the process through graduate training programmes and School-Centred Initial Teacher Training (SCITT), where trainees spend the majority of learning time in schools with teacher mentors. While this shift has gradually occurred over the past fifteen years, it has taken place in a climate of government rhetoric about the negative influence of education academics within the sector that had reached fever pitch with left-leaning academics publicly and collectively labelled as 'the blob' by conservative politicians and ministers (Guardian 2013).

The development of the teaching profession, through teacher certification and professional standards, is relatively new, beginning in the first half of the twentieth century (Ravitch 2016). The history of state education has influenced this development, as access to education has increased across all phases from elementary to further and higher education (Robinson 2006). This evolution has influenced the development and delivery of initial teacher training (ITT). Robinson (2006) suggests that throughout the last several centuries, teacher training has, in fact, moved back and forth like a 'swinging pendulum' between 'a school-based/apprenticeship or a college or university-based model of training' (Robinson 2006, 20). The first model of school-based ITT began with the pupil–teachers model in the nineteenth century. The evolution of ITT into formalized credited training in higher education institutions (HEIs) initialized with the Cross Commission in 1888, which advocated for the development of education faculties in universities. The 1902 Education Act centralized control of teacher training with LEAs. The development of the field of education within HEIs increased in the post-war period, leading up to the James Report in 1972, which formalized teaching as an all-graduate profession (Robinson 2006).

The beginning of the twenty-first century was marked by a return to government-controlled school-based models, using a prescriptive approach, driven by a 'mandatory national curriculum for trainees and standards-driven model of assessment for the final award of qualified teacher status' (Robinson 2006, 24).

Robinson claims that the 1992 speech by Kenneth Clarke, then Minister of Education, emphasizing the importance of school-based training and arguing for 80 per cent of teacher training to be school based, was instrumental in shifting the balance of ITT away from what the government perceived as 'overly theoretical approaches to teacher training' … towards 'more relevant practical classroom skills and techniques, and more recently professional values' (Robinson 2006, 24). The transition was to be accompanied by formal partnerships between schools and universities shifting the distribution of funding to schools for providing teacher training programmes and mentors. Avalos cites Lovett et al. (2008); Nielsen, Barry, and Staab (2008); Nir and Bogler

(2008) showing increased teacher satisfaction in all professional development activities that were considered by teachers to be 'close to home and to their needs and expectations, and when they contributed to the improvement of curricular understanding and increased self-efficacy' (Avalos 2011, 13).

According to Robinson, among the major characteristics of the modernization of the teaching profession is the 'relocation of the serving teacher to the heart of the professional preparation of the next generation of teachers' (2006, 25). In 2012, the serving Education Secretary announced his intention to provide schools with greater control over both the recruitment and training of teachers in England, citing the ambition for over half of all teachers to receive school-led training by 2015 (UniversitiesUK 2014).

The dominant discourse in England, in my opinion, has been one that frames the need for shifts in teacher recruitment and development as linked to the need to remove bad teachers and replace them with new good ones. This is incredibly damaging to those in the system and is increasingly recognized as flawed. Wiliam (2013), in the article 'Love the One You're With: Improving Professional Development in Schools', argues that teacher quality is the most important factor in system-wide educational improvement and future economic prosperity. The article dismisses the option of getting rid of less effective teachers and argues against raising the bar for entry into teacher degrees, claiming that both options are costlier and more time consuming than they are effective on overall outcomes. However, the article asserts that the biggest impact on teacher quality will result from 'new kinds of teacher learning, new models of professional development, and new models of leadership' (2013, 1). This is not limited to ITT but extends to teacher development across their professional life course.

Challenges to a prioritization of school-based training include concerns that educational theory is being rejected as an essential element of teacher development and practice and more practically focused concerns regarding 'support, time, expertise, commitment and priorities' (Robinson 2006, 26) and 'sustainability' and 'teacher supply issues' (Campbell and Kane 1998; Furlong and Smith 1996; Hobson 2002; Maynard 2000). The Impact of Initial Teacher Training Reforms on English Higher Education Institutions report cites evidence from global high-performing school systems, including Finland, South Korea and Singapore, all of which rely heavily on university-based ITT (UniversitiesUK 2014). Despite the arguments proffered by researchers and higher education institutions, government policy seems to be strengthening school-based teacher training approaches through policy reforms including those heralded in the 2010 White Paper 'Importance of Teaching' (DfE 2010).

In response, universities are increasingly offering pathways into accredited teaching degrees designed to provide more experience, pedagogical instruction and implementation including Masters in Teaching programmes. Given the arguments that each generation of teachers will be required to share a different kind of knowledge with a new skill set from their predecessors, the debate continues about where the best place to train teachers is (Levine 2006). While the overall intention in England appears to be a continuous move away from university-focused delivery, the shift to democratize whose knowledge and expertise informs the development of the next generation of teachers will, more than likely, continue to inspire debate and discussion. While there is little evidence on the scale and influence of the rise of social media within this context, based on our observations in New York City and Toronto, London provides an interesting example of the rise of social media and individual and collective influence in the policy process.

The rise of social media use and educational activism

In recent years, overt government actions to decrease the role of academics and universities in the development of teachers have occurred against the backdrop of the rigorous policy shifts to increase school-level responsibility for overall management and teacher training. Simultaneously, the influence of social media-facilitated discussions of education policy and practice has increased. In this climate, individual teachers and leaders have harnessed the power of Twitter, specifically, to shape and build their individual profiles and followings. The confluence of this alongside the rise of social media has resulted in what I believe is a fundamental question in education policy and research: 'Whose knowledge counts?' While I have long been a supporter of ensuring the fusion of traditional academic research and the lived experience and wisdom of teachers and leaders, challenge is maintaining the balance between large-scale longitudinal peer-mediated research and local small studies and the battle for what constitutes research and evidence in educational discussions.

While there has been little research on the emergence of an educational twitterati in England, a small group of voices is often heard across social media and increasingly in government policy debates and discussions. Government ministers have cited blogs and tweets rather than research in speeches and announcements. Similarly, government advisory and expert panels are increasingly more often populated with school and system-level educators, educational companies and non-profit organization – especially those with large social media followings – than researchers or academics. Academics are now in the minority on expert panels. Inspired to tackle some of the greatest recent education challenges, social media-mediated movements have formed, built followings, received government funding and changed the professional development landscape in England. For example, the rise of educator activist organizations such as researchED and WomenEd has been possible in this climate of knowledge democratization.

Leading the pack of teachers creating a formidable presence in social media spaces is the Teacher Toolkit. Founded by Ross McGill, Teacher Toolkit specializes in classroom ideas, teacher training and school resources and advertises itself as 'the most influential education blog in the UK' (Teacher Toolkit 2018) and has 192,000 Twitter followers. In similar veins, a host of other now well-recognized teachers and leaders share their wisdom, expertise and recommendations widely and often. Again, little empirical evidence attests to the influence of these resources and recommendations, but their reach is substantial. Similarly, several powerful teacher- and leader-led movements have been founded during this period, notably researchED and WomenEd.

ResearchED

ResearchED was founded by Tom Bennett, a former teacher, who remains as its director. Bennett also writes a personal blog, has chaired the DfE Behaviour Management Group and serves as the DfE's behaviour advisor. Another teacher and teacher professional developer, Helene Galdin-O'Shea, serves as the researchED conference manager (researchED 2018). The initial conception for researchED was a conference for teachers to increase the use of evidence in teaching and schools (researchED 2018). The first conference was hosted in 2013. researchED describes their purpose as:

> researchED is a grassroots, teacher-led organization aimed at improving research literacy in educational communities, dismantling myths in education, getting the best research where it is needed most and providing a platform for educators, academics and all other parties to meet and discuss what does and doesn't work in the great project of raising our children. (researchED, https://files.eric.ed.gov/fulltext/ED574406.pdf)

The popularity of the event has led to subsequent international researchED events and numerous national and local English events throughout the year (Bennett 2016, 2017).

WomenEd

The emergence of WomenEd on the English national and international educational landscape is well encapsulated by blog posts by national WomenEd leaders: Vivienne Porritt (Porritt 2015), Jill Berry and Helena Marsh (Berry and Marsh 2018). After several online discussions, a group of women leaders came together to combat the gender inequality among educational leaders. According to its website (WomenEd 2015), 'WomenEd is a grassroots movement' which connects existing and aspiring leaders in education.' It further notes, 'Even though women dominate the workforce across all sectors of education there still remain gender inequalities, particularly at senior leadership level.'

According to Porritt, the ultimate aim is to support the leadership pipeline for women in education through promoting leadership development for women through developing a network (Porritt 2015). WomenEd's core activity has been an annual 'unconference' open-space conference (Berry and Marsh 2018) offering workshops, keynotes and meetings, which seek to promote connection, collaboration and strategizing to address challenges facing women in educational leadership roles. Regional networks throughout the UK have been developed, and international networks have also grown. Current national leaders for WomenEd are Sameena Choudry, Jules Daulby, Keziah Featherstone, Vivienne Porritt and Hannah Wilson.

The organization does have partnerships with Microsoft, Equitable Education and Staffrm, although it is unclear how much financial support is received from these partners. Conferences and gatherings are held, and a blog which discusses and promotes the same causes is maintained.

Other educator-led organizations

Within this landscape, other similar organizations or movements have formed, including Equitable Education, led by Sameena Choudry (Equitable Education 2018), a consultancy intending to reduce attainment gaps in gender and among English as an Additional Language, Black and Minority Ethnic, low-income and special needs students. Pedagoo, led by Helene Galdin-O'Shea (Pedagoo 2018), is a network of teachers who have meet-ups and discussions to share best educational practices. TeachMeet and online Twitter chats serve the purpose of convening teacher- and leader-led gatherings to share best practice.

Conclusions

The intentional creation of markets is often intended to give individuals more control of their choices and options. In the English educational landscape, the deliberate market creation has been couched in a governmental intention to improve school-level educational provision. Market acceleration occurred when resource for educational improvement was transferred to schools and LA became less influential in their school improvement and financial roles. At this point, head teachers and governors gained control and responsibility for improving schools and choosing how to deploy their resources to best suit their own developmental needs.

A second acceleration of the English educational marketplace occurred when the provision of teacher training began to transition, at least in part, from university-based provision towards school-level responsibility. In effect, by creating opportunities for the greatest number of individuals to actively engage in both processes, the government catalysed an unprecedented democratization of educational knowledge and expertise – away from universities and to teachers and leaders in schools. Accelerated by the rising presence of social media platforms and the opportunities for school- and system-level educators to shape the overall educational discourse, the English education system now finds itself at an interesting, if not unique, moment in time.

These shifts have led to a proliferation of new roles within the education system. This context has nurtured the growth in numbers of educational support, innovation and consulting organizations that exist beyond traditional university and state-funded entities. These organizations offer teachers the opportunity to extend their educational careers well beyond their classrooms. While empirical evidence on both these patterns remains scant, research and policy investigation into the implications of the blossoming educational third sector in England may offer insight, at least in part, and provide a new avenue of exploration into the current reasons for teacher and leader recruitment and retention challenges.

As global passion for education system comparison continues to grow, academics are increasing their calls for a greater focus on the overall social and education policy context within which the students, teachers and leaders work. Both the pace and shape of changes in where expertise rests and whose knowledge counts within education policy and practices discussions can greatly influence the overall direction of travel of an education system. As systems struggle to recruit and maintain healthy and skilled cadres of teachers, considering both the intended and unintended outcomes of structural policy decisions and the increasingly open spaces for educational policymaking will be increasingly important.

Echoing calls for greater funding and focus on robust and meaningful comparative education studies, without our work across the three cities, these patterns would not have become as acutely focused. The potential influence that decentralization policies and social media growth were potentially having on the educational workforce, system design and policy landscape would not have been as clear. The drastic differences in the number of non-governmental actors working to support schools in London and the influence of educators use of social media would not have been as sharply brought into focus. While the convergence in escalating access to school-based improvement resources has dovetailed with greater social media engagement, a less explicit and perhaps more ground up shift in educational debates and discussions has emerged. While, at first glance, the current educational expertise marketplace in England may appear to be more equitable and open, future research may indicate that a similarly narrow set of voices are influencing policy in an unprecedented manner.

Acknowledgement

The research was supported by an Economic and Social Research Council Grant [RES-061-24-0532] to the Young Global City Leaders Project. The research would not have been possible without the support and advocacy of our city-based advisory group members and our research participants.

References

Armstrong, Paul, Karen Edge, and N. Nuria Batlle. *School Leadership Policy Landscape: London, UK*. London: Institute of Education, University of London, 2013.

Armstrong, Paul, Karen Edge, and Nuria Batlle. *School Leader Responsibilities and Accountabilities in London, New York and Toronto*. London: Institute of Education, University of London, 2013.

Avalos, Beatrice. 'Teacher Professional Development in *Teaching and Teacher Education* over Ten Years'. *Teaching and Teacher Education* 27, no. 1 (2011): 10–20.

Bennett, Tom. *The School Research Lead*. London, UK: Education Development Trust, 2016.

Bennett, Tom. 'Tom Bennett's School Report'. 2017. Retrieved from Blogspot. http://behaviourguru.blogspot.co.uk/192017/08/false-profits-and-why-representation.html.

Bennett, Tom. 'Tom Bennett's School Report'. Retrieved from Blogspot, 20 January 2017. http://behaviourguru.blogspot.co.uk/2017/08/false-profits-and-why-representation.html.

Berry, J. and H. Marsh. 'The Development of #WomenEd.' ASCL blog. 2018. Accessed 14 September 2018. https://www.ascl.org.uk/news-and-views/blogs_detail. html?shorturl=the-development-of-womened.

Bryk, Anthony S., Yeow Meng Thum, John Q. Easton, and Stuart Luppescu. *Academic Productivity of Chicago Public Elementary Schools.* Chicago: Consortium on Chicago School Research, 1998.

Campbell, Anne and Ian Kane. *School-based Teacher Education: Telling Tales from a Fictional Primary School.* London: David Fulton, 1998.

Department for Education. *Importance of Teaching.* London, UK: Department for Education, 2010.

Edge, Karen. 'A Review of the Empirical Generations at Work Research: Implications for School Leaders and Future Research'. *School Leadership and Management* 2 (2014): 136–155.

Edge, Karen. *The Unintended Outcomes of Decentralisation: How the Middiel Tier May Be Influencing Teacher Recruitment and Retention.* Melbourne, Australia: Centre for Strategic Education, 2017.

Edge, Karen, Paul Armstrong, and Nuria Batlle. *School Leadership Policy Landscape: Toronto, Ontario.* London, UK: Institute of Education, University of London, 2013.

Elmore, Richard. *School Reform from the inside Out: Policy, Practice, and Performance.* Cambridge, MA: Harvard Education Press, 2004.

Equitable Education. 'Equitable Education'. Retrieved 20 January 2018. http://www. equitableeducation.co.uk/.

Furlong, John and Richard Smith, eds. *The Role of Higher Education Initial Teacher Training.* London: Kogan Page, 1996.

Greany, Toby. *The Self-improving School System in England: Review of the Evidence and Thinking.* England: ACSL, 2015.

Guardian. 'Why does Michael Gove keep referring to the Blob'. 2 October 2013. https://www. theguardian.com/politics/shortcuts/2013/oct/02/michael-gove-referring-to-the-blob.

Hargreaves, David. *A Self-improving School System: Towards Maturity.* Nottingham, UK: National College for School Leadership, 2012. Retrieved from: http://www. education.gov.uk/nationalcollege/docinfo?id=177472&filename=a-self-improving-school-system-towards-maturity.pdf.

Hargreaves, David. *Creating a Self-improving School System.* Nottingham, UK: National College for School Leadership, 2010.

Hess, Alfred G. 'Expectations, Opportunity, Capacity, and Will: The Four Essential Components of Chicago School Reform'. *Education Policy* 13, no. 4 (1999): 494–517. Doi: 10.1177/0895904899013004002.

Higham, Rob, David Hopkins, and Elpida Ahtaridou. *Improving School Leadership: Country Background Report for England.* Paris: OECD, 2007.

Hobson, Andrew. 'Student Teachers Perceptions of School-based Mentoring in Initial Teacher Training (ITT)'. *Mentoring and Tutoring* 10, no. 1 (2002): 5–20.

Hutchings, M., C. Greenwood, S. Hollingworth, A. Mansaray, and A. Rose, with S. Minty, and K. Glass. *Evaluation of the City Challenge Programme.* London, UK: DfE, 2012.

Jimenez, Emmanual and Yasuyki Sawada. 'Do Community-managed Schools Work? An Evaluation of El Salvador's EDUCO Program'. *World Bank Econ Rev.* 13, no. 3 (1999): 415–441. Doi: 10.1093/wber/13.3.415.

Johnson, Peggy and Janet Haggerman Chrispeels. 'Linking the Central Office and Its Schools for Reform'. *Educational Administration Quarterly* 46 (2010): 738–775. Doi: 10.1177/0013161X10377346.

Leithwood, Kenneth. 'Characteristics of School Districts That Are Exceptionally Effective in Closing the Acheivement Gap'. *Leadership and Policy in Schools* 9, no. 3 (2010): 245–291.

Leithwood, Kenneth, Karen Seashore Louis, Stephen Anderson, and Kyla Wahlstrom. *How Leadership Influences Student Learning. Review of Research.* New York: The Wallace Foundation, 2004.

Leithwood, Kenneth and Teresa Menzies. 'A Review of Research Concerning the Implementation of Site-based Management'. *School Effectiveness and School Improvement* 9, no. 3 (1998): 233–285.

Levine, Authur. *Education School Teachers.* Princeton, MA: Education School Project, 2006.

Levin, Benjamin. *How to Change 5000 Schools: A Practical and Positive Approach for Leading Educational Change at Every Level.* Cambridge, MA: Harvard Education Press, 2008.

Lovett, M. W., L. Lacerenza, M. De Palma, N. J. Benson, K. A. Steinbach, and J. C. Frijters. 'Preparing Teachers to Remediate Reading Disabilities in High School: What Is Needed for Effective Professional Development?' *Teaching and Teacher Education* 24, no. 4 (2008): 1083–1097.

Mascall, Blair and Kenneth Leithwood. 'Investing in Leadership: The District's Role in Managing Principal Turnover'. *Leadership and Policy in Schools* 9, no. 4 (2010): 367–383.

Maynard, Trisha. 'Leading to Teach or Learning to Manage Mentors? Experiences of School-based Teacher Training'. *Mentoring and Tutoring* 8, no. 1 (2000): 17–30.

McGinn, Noel F. and Thomas Welsh. *Decentralization of Education: Why, When, What And How?* Paris, France: UNESCO: International Institute for Educational Planning, 1999.

Mejias, Sam, Karen Edge, Paul Armstrong, and Nuria Batlle. *School Leadership Policy Landscape: New York City, USA.* London, UK: Institute of Education, University of London, 2013.

Nielsen, Diane, Barry Corcoran, Arlene Lundmark and Pam Trefz Staab. 'Teachers' Reflections of Professional Change during a Literacy-Reform Initiative'. *Teaching and Teacher Education: An International Journal of Research and Studies* 24, no. 5 (2008): 1288–1303.

Nir, Adam E. and Ronit Bogler. 'The Antecedents of Teacher Satisfaction with Professional Development Programs'. *Teacher and Teaching Education* 24, no. 2 (2008): 377–386.

OECD. *Teachers Matter: Attracting, Developing and Retaining Effective Teachers*. Paris: Organization for Economic Cooperation and Development, 2005.

'Pedagoo' Pedagoo. Accessed 20 January 2018. http://www.pedagoo.org/about-us/i.

Porritt, V. '*WomenEd – Supporting Female Leaders in Education*'. Published on SecEd 2015. http://www.sec-ed.co.uk/blog/womened-supporting-female-leaders-in-education.

Ravitch, D. *The Death and Life of the Great American School System: How Testing and Choice Are Undermining Education*. New York: Basic Books, 2016.

researchEd. *How does researchEd work?* Accessed on 7 June 2018. https://researched.org.uk/about/how-it-works/.

Robinson, Wendy. 'Teacher Training in England and Wales: Past, Present and Future Perspectives'. *Education Research and Perspectives* 33, no. 2 (2006): 19–36.

Sassen, Saskia. *The Global City: New York, London, Tokyo*. Princeton: Princeton University Press, 1991.

'Teacher Toolkit'. Teacher Toolkit. Accessed 2 March 2018. https://www.teachertoolkit.co.uk/.

Togneri, Wendy and Stephen Anderson. *Beyond Islands of Excellence: What Districts Can Do to Improve Instruction and Achievement in All Schools*. Washington, DC: The Learning First Alliance and the Association for Supervision and Curriculum Development, 2003.

UniversitiesUK. *The Funding Environment for Universities: An Assessment*. London, UK: UniversitiesUK, 2014.

Wiliam, Dylan. Love the One You're With: Improving Professional Development in Schools. Published in the *Guardian*. 1 July 2013. https://www.theguardian.com/teacher-network/teacher-blog/2013/jul/01/schools-improving- professional-development-teaching.

Wylie, Cathy. 'Finessing Site-based Management with Balancing Acts'. *Educational Leadership* 53, no. 4 (1996): 54–57.

Part Three

Transnational Perspectives on Citizenship and Education

7

Educating for Global Citizenship in Formal Schooling in Canada: Early Engagement with Complexity, Pedagogy and the Challenges of Implementation

Mark Evans

Chapter outline

- Introduction
- Educating for global dimensions of citizenship worldwide
  - Early characterizations
    - Learning goals
    - Teaching and learning practices
    - Divergent perspectives and orientations.
- Educating for global dimensions of citizenship in formal schooling in Canada
  - A wave of interest in educating for global citizenship
- Issues, challenges and concluding considerations
- Notes

Keywords: global citizenship education; democratic education; curriculum and pedagogy; formal schooling in Canada

Introduction

Characterizations of citizenship throughout the world today are heavily nuanced and reveal a wide range of contrasting perspectives, policy tendencies and on-the-ground practices, reflective of diverse historical influences and shifting contextual pressures. In recent times, various forces of change that transcend national boundaries have prompted heightened attention to global dimensions of citizenship. Not surprisingly, there has been increasing attention to and deliberation about the kind of education needed to meaningfully respond to these shifting global forces. Educating for global citizenship has emerged as a prominent line of inquiry and formal education systems worldwide are increasingly viewing this dimension of education as an important avenue through which to deepen global understanding and to assist youth to develop suitable capacities to actively engage in, and respond to, questions and issues of civic global interest and importance.

This chapter focuses on educating for global citizenship in formal schooling in Canada in today's evolving educational milieu. The section 'Educating for global dimensions of citizenship worldwide' illuminates the developing interest in and attention to global dimensions of citizenship in schooling contexts worldwide. Emerging understandings, policy tendencies and pedagogical practices are briefly considered. The section 'Educating for global dimensions of citizenship in formal schooling in Canada' explores early understandings and gradual steps towards educating for global citizenship in formal schooling contexts (K-12) in Canada. Examples of recent scholarly work, curriculum policy reform, resource development and teacher education activity across the Canadian educational landscape are introduced. The section 'Issues, challenges and concluding considerations' discusses, in the way of concluding considerations, some of the issues and challenges associated with introducing this dimension of education into formal schooling contexts in a quickly changing and increasingly globalized world. Lastly, an expanded reading list and sampling of online classroom resources are offered for further inquiry.

It is important to note at the outset that this chapter provides, at best, only an introductory sketch of this emerging area of educational study and practice in Canada. Much of the work presented is based on recent scholarly literature in this area of study and borrows from a range of collaborative research and curriculum and instructional development work that I have participated in with a number of collaborators over the past two decades, locally and internationally. These class presentations were intended primarily for graduate candidates, most of whom were either educators, curriculum developers or beginning educational researchers.

Educating for global dimensions of citizenship worldwide

Characterizations of citizenship in the 'west', often associated with liberal and civic republican traditions, have continued to shift, moving from rather narrow and exclusive understandings (associated with privilege) to those that feature broadened and more inclusive social, political, economic, cultural, religious and global considerations. Complex, interconnected and contested concepts (e.g. rights and freedoms, responsibilities and duties, identity and membership affiliations and allegiances, rule of law, civic literacy, equity and social justice, conflict, engagement and activism) underpin contemporary understandings of citizenship and are interpreted through different ideological and contextual lenses (Heater 2004; Ichilov 1998; Marshall 1950).

In recent times, forces that transcend national boundaries have prompted an expanding attentiveness to global dimensions of citizenship. While notions of citizenship that extend beyond the nation are not new, questions related to membership in the wider community of humanity, the deliberation of issues of transnational significance (e.g. a deepening of economic globalization and inequality, an intensification and misuse of information and communication technologies, concerns about environmental sustainability and climate change, the rise of populist nationalism, and global migration and the pursuit for equality among diverse groups), and the development of understandings and competencies to engage in a combination of public spheres from the local to the global, for example, are being given additional consideration in current conversations about citizenship (Dower and Williams 2002; Held, McGrew, Goldblatt, and Perraton 1999; Kymlicka 2003; Torres 2011).

Within this context, educational stakeholders worldwide are finding themselves recurrently, investigating, assessing and reimagining *what* learning goals ought to underpin a citizenship curriculum for the future, *how* learning and teaching experiences may be effectively constructed and *where* it ought to be located/situated in school curricula as characterizations of citizenship broaden and diversify. As might be expected, different conceptions of and orientations to educating for citizenship have emerged, revealing varying perspectives, learning intentions, practices and issues (Arthur, Davies, and Hahn 2008; Banks 2004, 2008, 2017; Kennedy, Lee and Grossman 2011; Westheimer 2015). Educating for global citizenship has emerged as an important focus in these deliberations, nudged by a growing recognition internationally that educational systems need to do more in both formal and non-formal educational contexts to deepen global understanding and assist youth to meaningfully engage in today's world.

Early characterizations

Educating for global citizenship in formal schooling contexts began to experience increased attention in the second half of the twentieth century, influenced by various educational movements (e.g. peace education, human rights education, education for sustainable development, development education, education for intercultural awareness) and efforts of various educational stakeholders worldwide. Work undertaken during this period developed gradually, resting mostly on 'western' ideas of citizenship and education. The blending of 'citizenship education' and 'global education', in particular, was instructive in framing early iterations of learning intentions and pedagogical processes associated with educating for global dimensions of citizenship (Davies and Pike 2009; Evans, Davies, Dean, and Waghid 2008). This blending, according to Davies (2006), offered something more than – or different to – previous conceptions, 'a confirmation of the direct concern with social justice and not just the more minimalist interpretations of global education ... about "international awareness" or being a more well-rounded person' (6).

As a relatively new area of educational research and practice at the time, a small group of us decided to investigate and attempt to map out how educating for global citizenship was being characterized in contemporary scholarly literature. A series of 'working' conceptual frameworks were developed in an effort to clarify some of the varied perspectives and complexities associated with emerging dimension of citizenship education. As might be expected, a contrasting range of learning intentions, pedagogical practices, and orientations surfaced, revealing an emerging complexity in theory and practice.

Learning goals. Literature reviewed, revealed a broad range of interrelated, learning goals (Evans, Ingram, MacDonald, and Weber 2009, 23–24). These included:

- Deepening understanding of global themes, structures and systems (e.g. interdependence, peace and conflict, sustainable development, geo-political systems)
- Exploring and reflecting upon one's identity and membership through a lens of world- mindedness (e.g. indigenous, local, national, cultural, religious)
- Examining diverse beliefs, values, and worldviews within and across varied contexts to guide civic thinking and action (e.g. cultural, religious, political)
- Learning about rights and responsibilities within the context of civil society and differing governance systems from the local to the global (e.g. human rights, rights of the child, corporate social responsibility)

- Deepening understanding of power, privilege, equity, and social justice within governing structures and processes (e.g. personal and global inequities, power relations and power sharing)
- Investigating global issues and ways to manage and deliberate conflict (e.g. health, ecological, human rights, and terrorism and security)
- Developing critical civic literacy capacities (e.g. critical inquiry, decision making, media literacy, conflict management)
- Learning about and engaging in informed and purposeful civic action (e.g. community involvement and service, involvement with non-governmental organizations, development of civic engagement capacities).[1]

Teaching and learning practices. The review also revealed a variety of teaching and learning practices to assist learners deepen their understandings of the world and think and act more critically and ethically about questions and issues of civic global interest and importance. Critical literacy was often acknowledged as an important underlying pedagogical feature, based on the assumption that all knowledge is partial and incomplete, constructed through our contexts, cultures and experiences (Evans, Ingram, MacDonald, and Weber 2009, 25–26). Figure 7.1 (below) gives a visual representation of highlighted teaching and learning practices: Teaching and learning practices highlighted included:

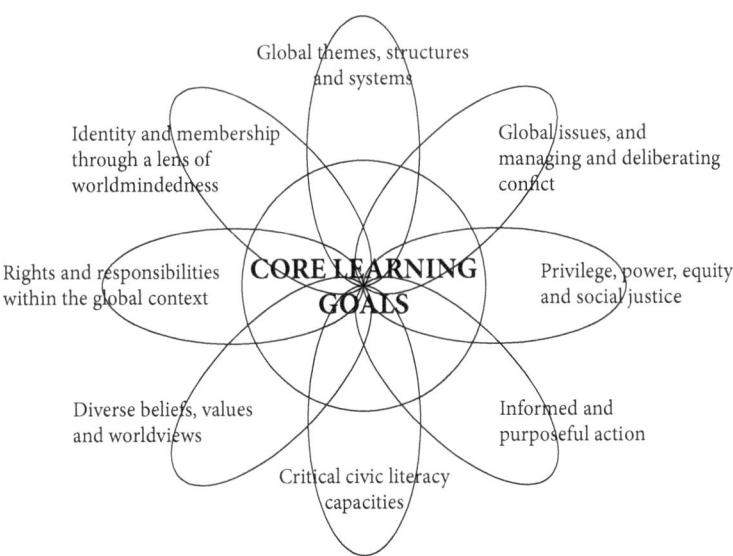

Figure 7.1 *Core Learning Goals* (Evans, Ingram, MacDonald, and Weber 2009, 23–24).

- Nurturing a respectful, inclusive, and interactive classroom and school ethos (e.g. shared understanding of classroom norms, student voice, seating arrangements, use of walls or visual spaces, global citizenship imagery).
- Infusing learner-centred and culturally responsive independent and interactive teaching and learning approaches that align with learning goals (e.g. independent and collaborative learning structures, deliberative dialogue, media literacy).
- Embedding authentic performance tasks (e.g. creating displays on children's rights, creating peace-building programmes, creating a student newspaper addressing global issues).
- Drawing on globally oriented learning resources that assist students in understanding a 'larger picture' of themselves in the world in relation to their local circumstances (e.g. a variety of sources and media, comparative and diverse perspectives).
- Making use of assessment and evaluation strategies that align with the learning goals and forms of instruction used to support learning (e.g. reflection and self-assessment, peer feedback, teacher assessment, journals, portfolios).
- Offering opportunities for students to experience learning in varied contexts, including the classroom, whole-school activities, and in their communities – from the local to the global (e.g. community participation, international exchanges, virtual communities).
- Recognizing the teacher as a role model (e.g. being up to date on current events, fostering community involvement, practicing environmental and equity standards).[2]

Divergent perspectives and orientations. Literature examined in this earlier study also signalled a range of divergent perspectives and orientations, that is, approaches reflecting particular learning intentions and practices in distinctive ways. Increasingly evident in these conceptions was an emphasis on criticality. Shultz (2007), for example, introduced three differing orientations to global citizenship education (e.g. the neoliberal global citizen, the radical global citizen and the transformational global citizen) and considered the implications for educational policy, from K-12 schooling to institutions of higher education, revealing conflicting understandings and agendas. Additional orientations evident in the literature at the time, included for example, learning for world-mindedness, fostering cosmopolitan understanding, preparation for the global marketplace, cultivating critical literacy and planetary responsibility, and encouraging deep understanding and civic action to redress global injustices (Evans, Ingram, MacDonald, and Weber 2009, 26–28). Intentions and practices foregrounded in these orientations ranged from neo-liberal approaches that foregrounded competencies required to be effective participants in the global marketplace to transformative approaches that highlighted the importance of deepening understanding of cultures, regions and issues of equity and social justice. These 'working' conceptual frameworks, while not exhaustive, provided early snapshots of a compelling, shifting and often contested, range of learning intentions, practices and orientations associated with developing characterizations of educating for global dimensions of citizenship at the time, revealing conceptual variation and a mixture of challenges facing its translation and application in formal classroom and schooling contexts.

More recent developments

In recent years, work connected to educating for global citizenship has continued to expand and deepen worldwide, moving well beyond earlier conceptual constructions. Work investigating and contrasting theoretical orientations, curriculum policy tendencies and pedagogical practices related to schooling contexts are contributing to a rapidly growing body of scholarly literature (Davies, Li-Ching, Kiwan, Peck, Peterson, Sant, and Waghid 2018; Harshman, Augustine, and Merryfield 2015; Oxley and Morris 2013; Reid, Gill, and Sears 2010). Efforts to construct universal conceptions have also become more apparent (UNESCO 2014). UNESCO's recent work, *Global Citizenship Education: Topics and Learning Objectives* (UNESCO 2015), for example, was developed as a resource for educators, curriculum developers, teacher educators and policymakers 'to clarify the conceptual underpinnings of global citizenship education and provide policy and programmatic directions … in response to the needs of Member States for overall guidance on integrating global citizenship education in their education systems' (7).

Three key learning attributes are identified in this resource:

Informed and critically literate: Knowledge of global governance systems, structures and issues; understanding the interdependence and connections between global and local concerns; knowledge and skills required for civic literacy, such as critical inquiry and analysis, with an emphasis on active engagement in learning.

Socially connected and respectful of diversity: Understanding of identities, relationships and belonging; understanding of shared values and common humanity; developing an appreciation of, and respect for, difference and diversity; and understanding the complex relationship between diversity and commonality.

Ethically responsible and engaged: Based on human rights approaches and including attitudes and values of caring for others and the environment; personal and social responsibility and transformation; and developing skills for participating in the community and contributing to a better world through informed, ethical and peaceful action. (23, 24)

In addition, a sampling of adaptable practices and resources is provided, drawing on various understandings of and approaches to global citizenship education from different parts of the world and recognizing that there is no 'one size fits all' model.

There has been continuing attention to approaches to delivery and the nuances of pedagogical practice as attention to educating for global dimensions of citizenship become more evident in schooling contexts (Banks 2017; Organization for Economic Organization and Development and Asia Society 2018; Rapoport 2015; Shulsky, Baker, Chvala, and Willis 2017). Similarly, as understandings and practices deepen and diversify, a variety of issues have surfaced in relation to the manner and degree to which educating for global citizenship is being enacted. In one recent study, *Global Citizenship Concepts in Curriculum Guidelines of 10 Countries: Comparative Analysis* (Asia-Pacific Centre of Education for International Understanding (APCEIU) and the International Bureau of Education (IBE-UNESCO) 2016), for example, the presence of concepts associated with global citizenship education were compared in history and social sciences, and civics and moral education curricula of both primary and secondary education in the national school curricula across ten countries with distinctly different cultures and levels of development across different regions of the world (Africa, Asia, Europe, Latin America and Southeast Asia). Results revealed that certain themes associated with global citizenship education were present in all ten countries, but that only 'two countries' in Southeast Asia provided consistent and comprehensive curricular coverage (3). Results also showed variation in terms of the learning goals preferred, suggesting more attention to goals related to themes of identity and diversity and less attention to themes related to the study of global issues or civic engagement (22), what learning goals are to be given what priority and what depth of coverage is expected.

Educating for global dimensions of citizenship in formal schooling in Canada

Educating for citizenship in Canadian public education has been recognized as an important curricular theme for over a century. Early characterizations of educating for citizenship in the late nineteenth and early twentieth century were often associated with social and political initiation and nation-building, with a 'pro-British assimilationist bent'. Educating for citizenship in schools was addressed largely through social studies and history curricula and focused mostly on structures and processes of local and national governments and attributes like loyalty and responsibility. Teaching practices were often emphasized recitation, memorization and largely passive learning (McLeod 1989, 11). Implementation was inconsistent and not everyone accepted the dominant citizenship narrative. Difference among Canada's varied populations was often suppressed with detrimental consequences. For Aboriginal peoples, for example, the effect of the Canadian assimilationist project was particularly harmful. A state-sponsored and a church-run residential school system sought to eradicate indigenous languages and customs.

A variety of developments arising during and following the Second World War (e.g. the Quiet Revolution in Quebec, shifting immigration patterns, First Nations land claims, an increasing American dominance of the Canadian economy, Canada's growing military involvement in peacekeeping initiatives) kindled a re-examination of citizenship education's purposes and practices. Hodgetts' study of civic education in Canada (1968) advanced a renewed vision of citizenship education that stressed an increasing multidimensionality of Canadian civic identity, its diverse cultural and pluralistic nature, its conflictual character and an emerging global dimension. The Canadian government's introduction of the Multiculturalism Policy (1971) and the Canadian Charter of Rights and Freedoms (1982) signalled further shifts in official understandings of Canadian national identity and citizenship. Citizenship education became more apparent in provincial educational policy reform initiatives. New Canadian Studies curricula, developed during this period, created more opportunities for teachers and students to explore Canada's expanding cultural diversity, the complex dynamics of French–English relations and Canadian–American relations, and Canada's emerging role in a global community. Demands for more effective schools at the time led to increased attention to pedagogical practices (e.g. local inquiries, critical thinking, and civic engagement and action projects) that were more congruent with citizenship education's shifting vision. It became widely accepted by the 1980s that understandings of citizenship education were broadening, becoming more participatory in scope, signifying what Osborne (1994, 52) referred to as 'a new conception of citizenship education'.

Consideration of global themes and issues in the early decades of the twentieth century was mostly evident through non-formal avenues of education such as church groups, adult education and international organizations like the 4H

Club and Red Cross rather than through formal education (Christie 1983). Developments within Canada and worldwide in the second half of the twentieth century, however, prompted a growing interest in global themes and issues in formal schooling contexts in Canada. Efforts of educators, researchers, international development government agencies, charities, development education centres and various educational movements during the 1980s and 1990s contributed to a range of ideas for promoting global understanding and teaching about questions and issues of civic global interest, influencing to a certain extent educational guidelines and priorities of Canadian Ministries of Education, School Boards and Canadian Faculties of Education (e.g. Clark and Case 1999b; Lyons 1992; Pike 2000; Pike and Selby 1988; Sears 1996). The Canadian Council of Ministers' Report, *Education for Peace, Human Rights, Democracy, International Understanding and Tolerance* (South House Exchange 2001), in particular, described various ways that themes of citizenship and global understanding were being included in the curricula across Canada during the 1980s and 1990s, illuminating how Canadian curricula was expanding understandings of citizenship to include global dimensions. Implementation of this renewed vision of citizenship education in Canadian schools, however, was slow and uneven and continued to foreground more long-established learning intentions and pedagogical practices.

A wave of interest in educating for global citizenship

Nonetheless, citizenship education continued to widen and deepen in schools across Canada into the twenty-first century. Various researchers have proposed new and contrasting theoretical constructs for citizenship education and have continued to investigate its more distinctive facets such as democratic engagement with conflict, movement towards deep diversity, issues of social justice and equity and youth engagement and activism.[3] Connections among citizenship education, indigeneity education and work emerging from the Truth and Reconciliation Commission of Canada (established in 2008), in particular, have received increasing consideration (Orr and Ronayne 2009; Tupper 2014; Tupper and Cappello 2008, 2012). Provincial policy related to citizenship education curriculum reflects steady, incremental reform. Themes such as identity in various communities, democratic governance structures and processes, diversity and multiple perspectives, equity and inclusion, active and responsible participation, regional and global interconnections, and the development of civic literacy skills, for example, have been increasingly evident in the rhetoric of most provincial curricula, largely through a liberal/

civic republican lens (Bickmore 2006, 2014; Hughes and Sears 2008). Educators continued to develop a range of promising teaching practices and resources (e.g. case analysis, public issue inquiry projects, peace-building programmes, public information exhibits, community participation activities, youth forums) that encourage students to become informed, think critically and reflectively about various aspects of citizenship, examine a range of current civic themes and issues, and build capacities for active involvement (Evans 2008; Sears 2004).

Educating for global citizenship has experienced a significant wave of interest and activity within this broader context. Scholarly work focusing on global citizenship education has expanded steadily among a number of Canadian academics during this period, revealing a heightened sense of criticality.[4] The focus of these inquiries has been wide-ranging, focusing on varying theoretical understandings, issues of diversity and equity, postcolonial and anti-racist considerations, ideological tensions between the national and the global, environmental sustainability, human rights, peace and conflict education, learning experiences and pedagogical insights, multilingualism, teacher education, challenges and persisting issues, and so on.

Curriculum policy reforms, administered through education departments in provincial and territorial governments operating within a federal system in Canada, exhibit increased attention to different international and global themes and issues across the curriculum in particular subject areas, cross-curricular documents and school-wide initiatives (Evans and Kiwan 2017; Mundy and Manion 2008). These reforms, from British Columbia to the Atlantic provinces, reveal not only increasing rhetoric of global and international themes within curriculum guidelines but also regional nuances and increased consideration of pedagogical considerations. Ample opportunities for and expectations of educators to infuse global themes, issues and perspectives associated with global citizenship education throughout K-12 curricula are provided (Evans, Ingram, MacDonald, and Weber 2013).

At the same time, educators across Canada have been exploring and developing classroom, school-wide and district-wide teaching and learning resources that accommodate the varied learning goals associated with global dimensions of citizenship. A host of teaching and learning resources and new websites have also been developed by a range of educational stakeholders (e.g. teacher federations, provincial subject councils, NGOs, education divisions of local and national media organizations, and various education and other government departments, locally, provincially and nationally) to inform and guide teachers' work in various aspects of global citizenship curriculum and instruction.[5]

Increasing attention to global dimensions of citizenship has also been evident in initial teacher education programmes and through continuing professional learning initiatives (Gaudelli 2016; Guo 2013, 2014; Larsen and Fadden 2008; McLean, Cook, and Crowe 2006, 2008; McLean and Ng-A-Fook 2013; Montemurro, Gambhir, Evans, and Broad 2014; Rathburn and Lexier 2016). Different initial teacher education programmes at Faculties of Education across the country have created curricular space for global citizenship education (e.g. University of Ottawa, University of Toronto, University of British Columbia, University of Prince Edward Island, Queens' University, University of Alberta). A number of organizations (e.g. the Centre for Global Citizenship Education and Research at the University of Alberta, the Canadian Commission for UNESCO (CCUNESCO), the Citizenship Education Research Network (CERN)), for example, provide additional support for researchers, policymakers and educational practitioners interested in exploring the complex interplay among theory, practice and context in relation to educating for global dimensions of citizenship.

Issues, challenges and concluding considerations

While many have been encouraged by these recent developments both within and outside of Canada in recent years, there has also been increasing recognition of a variety of issues and challenges associated with these early steps forward, complicating the manner and degree to which implementation is taking place in schooling contexts. A brief sampling of these issues and challenges is discussed below.

Conceptual complexity, for example, is presenting challenges for educators attempting to determine what learning goals are to be given what priority, what depth of coverage is expected, and how these intentions may suitably be translated into meaningful learning experiences in schooling contexts. Different inquiries in Canada have revealed provincial and regional variations and a reluctance to address learning goals that encourage critical awareness or civic engagement, that investigate issues of global conflict or controversy, or consider questions of equity (Bickmore 2006, 2014; Evans 2006; Evans, MacDonald, Ingram, and Weber 2013; MacDonald-Vemic, Evans, Ingram, and Weber 2015; Tupper and Cappello 2008). Many have suggested that learning goals need to be much more substantive and critical, raising questions about the inherent dangers involved in reinforcing privilege and uninformed action (Pashby and

Andreotti 2015; Peck and Pashby 2018; Pike 2008; Shultz 2007). Abdi (2014) has urged, for example, that 'learners must be given the tools to examine the thick and connected threads of systematically oppressive processes – mainly those of colonialism, racism and the denial of other knowledge systems – to understand why the majority of the world's populations are without basic rights and cannot meet their needs and fulfill their expectations' (20).

There is an increasing acknowledgement of the need for more learning experiences and sophisticated forms of pedagogy that are congruent with and address the wide-ranging and intricate learning goals associated with educating for global citizenship. Pedagogical practices associated with certain critical goals (e.g. controversial global issues, equity and social justice themes, participatory activities) are complicated and often under-addressed and/or avoided. While examples of promising classroom, school-wide and community-based teaching and learning practices – underscoring participatory, inclusive, experiential, inquiry-based, and online experiences – are more and more evident in different parts of the world, considerable variability continues, raising questions about what types of learning are being experienced and what types of learning experiences count (Banks 2017; Evans and Kiwan 2017). Within Canadian schooling contexts, concerns about the challenges of suitable pedagogical practice are similarly being expressed (Abdi, Shultz, and Pillay 2015; Andreotti 2015; Bickmore 2014; Eidoo, Ingram, MacDonald, Nabavi, Pashby, and Stille 2011). Dei (2014), for example, has argued that learning environments need to be constructed in ways that allow for critical engagement in ways that, for example, 'confront the conditions and unequal power relations that have created unequal advantage and privilege among nations' and 'seriously acknowledge the contribution of all to global humanity'. Concerns regarding variability across learning experiences for students in Canadian schools have also been noted (Llewellyn, Cook, Westheimer, Giron, and Suurtamm 2007), particularly for 'those from less privileged backgrounds who have few opportunities to practice democratically relevant citizenship learning in school' (Bickmore 2014, 258). Coupled with these challenges have been concerns about teacher preparation (both initial and continuing) and the types of professional learning support required to suitably address the conceptual and instructional complexities associated with the learning intentions associated with educating for global dimensions of citizenship (Cook 2014; Guo 2013, 2014; Larsen and Faden 2008; McLean, Cook and Crowe 2006; McLean and Ng-A-Fook 2013).

More broadly, educating for global citizenship faces the challenge of being introduced in contexts where citizenship has been most often linked to the nation-state, legally and operationally. Understandings of citizenship are inextricably linked to national governance systems, laws and norms of behaviour, holding people accountable in ways that global infrastructures do not. 'Global citizenship ... is virtual. It does not exist in any legal sense or constitutional sense and, in view of opponents, is open to a plethora of abuses and misinterpretations' (Davies and Pike 2009, 66).

Official orientations to citizenship education emphasizing global dimensions – whether deriving from provincial and/or national governance contexts – tend to involve the presentation of global themes as a matter of national self-interest. In Canada, concerns have been raised that official orientations to educating for global citizenship are often conceptualized through a narrow lens, explicitly prioritizing the Canadian nation-state and its economic interests in a global context rather than taking on a broader global perspective (Pike 2000; Reid, Gill, and Sears 2010; Richardson 2004; Richardson and Abbott 2009).

Lastly, implementing new curricula in long-established schooling contexts poses its own set of complications. Not surprisingly, implementation has been slow and fragmented in schooling contexts worldwide. A variety of factors (e.g. a crowded curriculum and competing priorities, lack of funding and commitment by senior management, low status, workload, school cultures that are not supportive of learning goals associated with global citizenship education) can facilitate and/or inhibit implementation. In a recent study of Canadian K-12 classroom teachers' understandings and practices of global dimensions of citizenship working in public schools in three culturally diverse metropolitan regions (Halifax, Toronto and Vancouver), a variety of factors were highlighted. The most significant facilitating factor driving implementation, according to the respondents, was teachers' personal interest in the area. Other facilitating factors included student enthusiasm, supportive administration and collegial support. The most common factor identified inhibiting teachers' efforts to educate for global citizenship were challenges associated with accessing resources and time constraints. Additional hindrances included the challenges of teaching controversial issues, competition with other school priorities (e.g. literacy and numeracy), and recognition of the increasing complexity of teaching in recent years (Evans, Ingram, MacDonald, and Weber 2013).

Notwithstanding these issues and challenges, educating for global citizenship continues to gain attention worldwide as an important dimension of education through which to enhance global understanding and assist youth learn grapple with questions and issues of civic global interest and importance. Various curriculum initiatives, policy reforms and research studies are currently underway in an expanding range of contexts as academics, policymakers and educators attempt to better understand its curricular and pedagogical intent and location in formal schooling, in ways that are relevant and responsive to a quickly changing and increasingly globalized world.

Notes

1   References investigated at the time relating to learning goals included: Andreotti 2006; Banks 2004, 2008; Boulding 1988; Davies 2006; Davies, Evans, and Reid 2005; Harber and Yamashita 2004; Heater 1996, 2002; Hicks and Holden 2007; Joshee 2004; Kymlicka 1998; Lee and Leung 2006, 2003; Merryfield 1998; Mundy and Manion 2008; Osler and Starkey 2003, 2006; Peters, Britton, and Blee 2008; Richardson 2004; Schattle 2008; Selby and Pike 1988, 2000.

2   References investigated at the time relating to teaching and learning practices included Banks 2004; Bickmore 2006, 2007; Boyd 2009; Claire and Holden 2007; Davies 2006; Davies and Issitt 2005; Evans 2005, 2008; Evans and Reynolds 2005; Holden and Hicks 2007; Ibrahim 2005; Ikeno 2005; Larsen 2008; Lee and Leung 2006; Merryfield 1998; Nelson and Kerr 2006; Osborne 1994, 2001; Oxfam 2006; Parker 1996; Pike and Selby 1988, 2000.

3   Questions linking democratic engagement with conflict, movement towards deep diversity, social class, issues of social justice and equity, youth engagement and activism with broader constructs of citizenship education have, for example, received heightened attention from Canadian scholars such as Bickmore 2014; Broom, 2016; Kennelly and Llewellyn 2011; Llewellyn Cook and Molina 2010; McLean, Bergen, Thruong-White, Rottmann, and Glithero 2017; Peck, Thompson, Chareka, Joshee, and Sears 2010; Tupper, Cappello, and Sevigny 2010.

4   Examples of recent scholarly work in Canada includes, for example: Abdi and Shultz 2008; Abdi, Shultz, and Pillay 2015; Bickmore 2007, 2009, 2014; Dei 2014; Eidoo, Ingram, MacDonald, Nabavi, Pashby, and Stille 2011; Evans, Ingram, MacDonald, and Weber 2009, 2013; Evans and Kiwan 2017; Guo 2012, 2013, 2014; Kymlick, 1998, 2003; Larsen and Faden 2008; McLean, Cook and Crowe, 2006, 2008; Mundy and Manion 2008; O'Sullivan and Pashby 2008; Pashby and Andreotti 2015; Peck and Pashby 2018; Pike, 2000, 2008; Richardson 2004; Richardson and Abbott 2009; Selby and Pike 2000; Shultz 2007; Tarc 2015.

5   Below is a sampling of online resources developed by educations across Canada: *Natural curiosity: Building children's understanding of the world through environmental inquiry/A resource for teachers*, written by Lorraine Chiarotto, Toronto: The Laboratory School at The Dr. Eric Jackman Institute of Child

Study, OISE, University of Toronto, 2011; *Educating for Global Citizenship in a Changing World: A Teacher's Resource Handbook*, edited by Mark Evans and Cecilia Reynolds, Toronto: OISE, University of Toronto, 2004; *The ETFO Curriculum Development Inquiry Initiative Global Education WebBook*, edited by Anne Rodrigue, Toronto: Elementary Teachers' Federation of Ontario, Fédération des enseignantes et des enseignants de l'élémentaire de l'Ontario, 2010; *ACT! Active Citizens Today: Global Citizenship for Local School*, written by Marianne Larsen, London, University of Western Ontario, 2008; Saskatchewan Council for International Cooperation, Global Citizenship Education Modules; UNICEF Canada's Rights Respecting Schools Project; University of Alberta, Centre for Global Citizenship Education and Research.

References

Abdi, Ali A. 'Reflecting on Global Dimensions of Contemporary Education'. In *Inquiry into Practice: Learning and Teaching Global Matters in Local Classrooms*, edited by David Montemurro, Mira Gambhir, Mark Evans, and Kathy Broad, 19–21. Toronto: Ontario Institute for Studies in Education, 2014.

Abdi, Ali A. and Lynette Shultz, eds. *Educating for Human Rights and Global Citizenship*. New York: SUNY Press, 2008.

Abdi, Ali A., Lynette Shultz, and Thashika Pillay, eds. *Decolonizing Global Citizenship Education*. Rotterdam: Sense Publishers, 2015.

Andreotti, Vanessa. 'Global Citizenship Education Otherwise'. In *Decolonizing Global Citizenship Education*, edited by Ali A. Abdi, Lynette Shultz, and Thashika Pillay, 221–230. Rotterdam: Sense Publishers, 2015.

Andreotti, Vanessa. 'Soft versus Critical Global Citizenship Education'. *Policy and Practice: A Development Education Review* 3, autumn (2006): 40–51.

Arthur, James, Ian Davies, and Carole Hahn, eds. *The Sage Handbook of Education for Citizenship and Democracy*. Los Angeles: Sage, 2008.

Banks, James A. 'Diversity, Group Identity, and Citizenship Education in a Global Age'. *Educational researcher* 37, no. 3 (2008): 129–139.

Banks, James A., ed. *Diversity and Citizenship Education: Global Perspectives*. San Francisco: Jossey-Bass, 2004.

Banks, James A. 'Failed Citizenship and Transformative Civic Education'. *Educational Researcher* 46, no. 7 (2017): 366–377.

Bickmore, Kathy. 'Citizenship Education in Canada: "Democratic" Engagement with Differences, Conflicts and Equity Issues?'. *Citizenship Teaching and Learning* 9, no. 3 (2014): 257–278.

Bickmore, Kathy. 'Democratic Social Cohesion (Assimilation)? Representations of Social Conflict in Canadian Public School Curriculum'. *Canadian Journal of Education* 29, no. 2 (2006): 359–386.

Bickmore, Kathy. 'Global Education to Build Peace'. In *Visions in Global Education: The Globalization of Curriculum and Pedagogy in Teacher Education and Schools: Perspectives from Canada, Russia, and the United States*, edited by Toni Fuss Kirkwood-Tucker, 270–285. New York: Peter Lang, 2009.

Bickmore, Kathy. 'Linking Global with Local: Cross-Cultural Conflict Education in Urban Canadian Schools'. In *Education, Conflict and Reconciliation: International Perspectives*, edited by Fiona E. Leach and Máiréad Dunne, 237–252. Oxford: Peter Lang, 2007.

Boulding, Elise. *Building a Global Civic Culture: Education for an Interdependent World*. New York: Teachers College Press, 1988.

Broom, Catherine A. 'Exploring Youth Civic Engagement and Disengagement in Canada'. *Journal of International Social Studies* 6, no. 1 (2016): 4–22.

Centre for Global Citizenship and Research University of Alberta. *The National Youth White Paper on Global Citizenship*, 2015.

Christie, Jean. 'A Critical History of Development Education in Canada'. *Canadian and International Education* 12, no. 3 (1983): 8–20.

Claire, Hilary and Cathie Holden, eds. *The Challenge of Teaching Controversial Issues*. Stoke on Trent: Trentham Books, 2007.

Clark, Penney and Roland Case. 'Four Purposes of Citizenship Education'. In *The Canadian Anthology of Social Studies: Issues and Strategies for Teachers Studies*, edited by Penney Clark and Roland Case, 17–27. Vancouver: Simon Fraser University Press, 1999a.

Clark, Penney and Roland Case. 'Global Education: It's Largely a Matter of Perspective'. In *The Canadian Anthology of Social Studies: Issues and Strategies for Teachers Studies*, edited by Penney Clark and Roland Case. Vancouver: Simon Fraser University Press, 1999b.

Cook, Sharon Anne. 'Reflections of a Peace Educator: The Power and Challenges of Peace Education with Pre- Service Teachers'. *Curriculum Inquiry* 44, no. 4 (2014): 489–507.

Cox, Cristian. *Global Citizenship Concepts in Curriculum Guidelines of 10 Countries: Comparative Analysis*. Geneva: International Bureau of Education (IBE-UNESCO) and Asia-Pacific Centre of Education for International Understanding (APCEIU), 2016.

Davies, Ian, Mark Evans, and Alan Reid. 'Globalizing Citizenship Education? A Critique of "Global Education" and "Citizenship Education"'. *British Journal of Educational Studies* 53, no. 1 (2005): 66–89.

Davies, Ian and John Issitt. 'Reflections on Citizenship Education in Australia, Canada and England'. *Comparative Education* 41, no. 4 (2005): 389–410.

Davies, Ian, Ho Li-Ching, Carla L. Dina Kiwan, Andrew Peterson Peck, Edda Sant, and Yusef Waghid, eds. *The Palgrave Handbook of Global Citizenship and Education*. London: Palgrave Macmillan, 2018.

Davies, Ian and Graham Pike. 'Global Citizenship Education: Challenges and Possibilities'. In *The Handbook of Practice and Research in Study Abroad: Higher*

Education and the Quest for Global Citizenship, edited by Ross Lewin, 61–76. New York: Routledge, 2009.

Davies, Lynn. 'Global Citizenship: Abstraction or Framework for Action?' *Educational review* 58, no. 1 (2006): 5–25.

Dei, George. 'Reflecting on Global Dimensions of Contemporary Education'. In *Inquiry into Practice: Learning and Teaching Global Matters in Local Classrooms*, edited by David Montemurro, Mira Gambhir, Mark Evans, and Kathy Broad, 9–11. Toronto: Ontario Institute for Studies in Education, 2014.

Dower, Nigel and John Williams. *Global Citizenship: A Critical Reader*. New York: Routledge, 2002.

Eidoo, Sameena, Leigh-Anne Ingram, Angela MacDonald, Maryam Nabavi, Karen Pashby, and Saskia Stille. '"Through the Kaleidoscope": Intersections between Theoretical Perspectives and Classroom Implications in Critical Global Citizenship Education'. *Canadian Journal of Education* 34, no. 4 (2011): 59–85.

Evans, Mark. 'Citizenship Education, Pedagogy, and School Contexts'. In *The Sage Handbook of Education for Citizenship and Democracy*, edited by James Arthur, Ian Davies, and Carole Hahn, 519–532. Los Angeles: Sage, 2008.

Evans, Mark. 'Educating for Citizenship: What Teachers Say and What Teachers Do'. *Canadian Journal of Education* 29, no. 2 (2006): 410–435.

Evans, Mark and Cecilia Reynolds, eds. *Educating for Global Citizenship in a Changing World: A Teacher's Resource Handbook*. Toronto: OISE/UT, 2005.

Evans, Mark, Ian Davies, Bernadette Dean, and Yusef Waghid. 'Educating for Global Citizenship in Schools: Emerging Understandings'. In *Comparative and International Education: Issues for Teachers*, edited by Karen Mundy, Kathy Bickmore, Ruth Hayhoe, Meggan Madden, and Katherine Madjidi, 273–298. Toronto: Canadian Scholars Press, 2008.

Evans, Mark, Leigh-Anne Ingram, Angela MacDonald, and Nadya Weber. *Educating for the Global Dimension of Citizenship in Schools in Canada: A Study in Three Metropolitan Regions*. Toronto: Social Sciences and Humanities Research Council of Canada (SSHRC) Report, 2013.

Evans, Mark, Leigh Anne Ingram, Angela MacDonald, and Nadya Weber. 'Mapping the "Global Dimension" of Citizenship Education in Canada: The Complex Interplay of Theory, Practice and Context'. *Citizenship Teaching and Learning* 5, no. 2 (2009): 17–34.

Evans, Mark and Dina Kiwan. 'Comparing Global Citizenship Education in Schools: Evolving Understandings, Constructing Practices'. In *Comparative and International Education: Issues for Teachers*, edited by Kathy Bickmore, Ruth Hayhoe, Caroline Manion, Karen Mundy, and Robyn Read. Toronto: Canadian Scholars Press, 2017.

Freire, Paulo. *Pedagogy of the Oppressed*. New York: Continuum, 1970.

Gaudelli, William. *Global Citizenship Education: Everyday Transcendence*. New York: Routledge, 2016.

Guo, Linyuan. 'Globalization: A Shifting Context for the Canadian Education Landscape'. *Canadian Journal of Education* 35, no. 3 (2012): 1.

Guo, Linyuan. 'Preparing Teachers to Educate for 21st Century Global Citizenship: Envisioning and Enacting'. *Journal of Global Citizenship & Equity Education* 4, no. 1 (2014): 1–23.

Guo, Linyuan. 'Translating Global Citizenship Education into Pedagogic Actions in Classroom Settings'. *Education Review* 3, no. 2 (2013): 8–9.

Harshman, Jason, Tami Augustine, and Merry M. Merryfield, eds. *Research in Global Citizenship Education*. Charlotte: Information Age Publishing, 2015.

Heater, Derek. *A Brief History of Citizenship*. New York: New York University Press, 2004.

Heater, Derek. *World Citizenship and Government: Cosmopolitan Ideas in the History of Western Political Thought*. New York: St. Martin's Press, 1996.

Held, David, Anthony McGrew, David Goldblatt, and Jonathan Perraton. *Global Transformations: Politics, Economics, and Culture*. Cambridge: Polity Press, 1999.

Hicks, David and Cathie Holden. *Teaching the Global Dimension: Key Principles and Effective Practice*. London: Routledge, 2007.

Hodgetts, A. Bernie. *What Culture? What Heritage? A Study of Civic Education in Canada*. Toronto: Ontario Institute for Studies in Education, 1968.

Hughes, Andrew and Alan Sears. 'The Struggle for Citizenship Education in Canada: The Centre Cannot Hold'. In *The Sage Handbook of Education for Citizenship and Democracy*, edited by James Arthur, Ian Davies, and Carol Hahn, 124–139. London: Sage, 2008.

Ibrahim, Tasneem. 'Global Citizenship Education: Mainstreaming the Curriculum?' *Cambridge Journal of Education* 35, no. 2 (2005): 177–194.

Ichilov, Orit. 'Patterns of Citizenship in a Changing World'. In *Citizenship and Citizenship Education in a Changing World*, edited by Orit Ichilov, 11–27. London: The Woburn Press, 1998.

Ikeno, Norio. 'Citizenship Education in Japan after World War II'. *Citizenship Teaching and Learning* 1, no. 2 (2005): 93–98.

Joshee, Reva. 'Citizenship and Multicultural Education in Canada: From Assimilation to Social Cohesion'. In *Diversity and Citizenship Education: Global Perspectives*, edited by James A. Banks, 127–158. San Francisco: Jossey-Bass, 2004.

Kennedy, Kerry J., Wing On Lee, and David L. Grossman, eds. *Citizenship Pedagogies in Asia and the Pacific*. New York: Springer, 2011.

Kennelly, Jacqueline and Kristina R. Llewellyn. 'Educating for Active Compliance: Discursive Constructions in Citizenship Education'. *Citizenship Studies* 15, no. 6–7 (2011): 897–914.

Kymlicka, Will. 'Multicultural Citizenship'. In *The Citizenship Debates: A Reader*, edited by Gershon Shafir, 167–188. Minneapolis: University of Minnesota Press, 1998.

Kymlicka, Will. 'Multicultural States and Intercultural Citizens'. *School Field* 1, no. 2 (2003): 147–169.

Larsen, Marianne and Lisa Faden. 'Supporting the Growth of Global Citizenship Educators'. *Brock Education Journal* 17, no. 1 (2008): 71–86.

Lee, Wing On and Sai Wing Leung. 'Global Citizenship Education in Hong Kong and Shanghai Secondary Schools: Ideals, Realities and Expectations'. *Citizenship Teaching and Learning* 2, no. 2 (2006): 68–84.

Llewellyn, Kristina R., Sharon Anne Cook, and Alison Molina. 'Civic Learning: Moving from the Apolitical to the Socially Just'. *Journal of Curriculum Studies* 42, no. 6 (2010): 791–812.

Llewellyn, Kristina R., Sharon Anne Cook, Joel Westheimer, Luz Alison Giron, and Karen Suurtamm. 'The State and Potential of Civic Learning in Canada: Charting the Course of Youth Civic and Political Participation'. Canadian Policy Research Networks Report, 2007.

Lyons, Tom. 'Education for a Global Perspective'. *Orbit* 3, no. 1 (1992): 10–12.

MacDonald-Vemic, Angela, Mark Evans, Leigh-Anne Ingram, and Nadya Weber. 'A Question of How: A Report on Teachers' Instructional Practices When Educating for Global Citizenship in Canada'. In *Research in Global Citizenship Education*, edited by Jason Harshman, Tami Augustine, and Merry M. Merryfield, 83–118. Charlotte: Information Age Publishing, 2015.

Marshall, Thomas H. *Citizenship and Social Class and Other Essays*. Cambridge: Cambridge University Press, 1950.

McLean, Lorna R., Jennifer K. Bergen, Hoa Truong-White, Jenn Rottmann, and Lisa Glithero. 'Far from Apathetic: Canadian Youth Identify the Supports They Need to Speak about and Act on Issues'. *Citizenship Teaching and Learning* 12, no. 1 (2017): 91–108.

McLean, Lorna R., Sharon Anne Cook, and Tracy Crowe. 'Educating the Next Generation of Global Citizens through Teacher Education: One New Teacher at a Time'. *Canadian Social Studies* 40, no. 1 (2006): 1–7.

McLean, Lorna R., Sharon A. Cook, and Tracy Crowe. 'Imagining Global Citizens: Teaching Peace and Global Education in a Teacher-Education Programme'. *Citizenship Teaching and Learning* 4, no. 1 (2008): 50–64.

McLean, Lorna R. and Nicholas Ng-A-Fook. 'Developing a Global Perspective for Educators'. *Education Review* 3, no. 2 (2013): 1.

McLeod, Keith A. *Exploring Citizenship Education: Education for Citizenship in Canada and Citizenship Education*. Toronto: Canadian Education Association, 1989.

Merryfield, Merry M. 'Pedagogy for Global Perspectives in Education: Studies of Teachers' Thinking and Practice'. *Theory & Research in Social Education* 26, no. 3 (1998): 342–379.

Montemurro, David, Mira Gambhir, Mark Evans, and Kathy Broad, eds. *Inquiry into Practice: Learning and Teaching Global Matters in Local Classrooms*. Toronto: Ontario Institute for Studies in Education, 2014.

Mundy, Karen and Caroline Manion. 'Global Education in Canadian Elementary Schools: An Exploratory Study'. *Canadian Journal of Education* 31, no. 4 (2008): 941–974.

Nelson, J. and David Kerr. Active Citizenship in INCA Countries: Definitions, Policies, Practices and Outcomes (Final Report). Slough, UK: National Foundation for Educational Research in England and Wales, 2006.

OXFAM. *What Is Global Citizenship?* Oxford, UK: OXFAM, 2006. Accessed 18 May 2018. https://www.oxfam.org.uk/education/who-we-are/what-is-global-citizenship.

Organization for Economic Organization and Development and Asia Society, Centre for Global Education. *Teaching for Global Competence in a Rapidly Changing World.* Organization for Economic Organization and Development, 2018.

Orr, Jeff and Robyn Ronayne. 'Indigeneity Education as Canadian First Nations Citizenship Education'. *Citizenship Teaching and Learning* 5, no. 2 (2009): 35–49.

Osborne, Ken. 'Democracy, Democratic Citizenship, and Education'. In *The Erosion of Democracy in Education: Critique to Possibilities*, edited by John P. Portelli and Patrick P. Solomon, 29–61. Calgary: Detselig Enterprises, 2001.

Osborne, Ken. 'Teaching for Democratic Citizenship: Democracy, Citizenship, and Education'. In *Sociology of Education in Canada: Critical Perspectives on Theory, Research, and Practice*, edited by Lorna Erwin and David R. MacLennan, 417–442. Toronto: Copp Clark Longman, 1994.

Osler, Audrey and Hugh Starkey. *Cosmopolitan Citizenship, Changing Citizenship: Democracy and Inclusion in Education.* Maidenhead: Open University Press, 2006.

Osler, Audrey and Hugh Starkey. 'Learning for Cosmopolitan Citizenship: Theoretical Debates and Young People's Experiences'. *Educational Review* 55, no. 3 (2003): 243–254.

O'Sullivan, Michael and Karen Pashby. *Citizenship Education in the Era of Globalization: Canadian Perspectives.* Rotterdam: Sense Publishers, 2008.

Oxley, Laura and Paul Morris. 'Global Citizenship: A Typology for Distinguishing Its Multiple Conceptions'. *British Journal of Educational Studies* 61, no. 3 (2013): 301–325.

Parker, Walter, ed. *Educating the Democratic Mind.* Albany: SUNY Press, 1996.

Pashby, Karen and Vanessa Andreotti. 'Critical Global Citizenship in Theory and Practice: Rationales and Approaches for an Emerging Agenda'. In *Research in Global Citizenship Education*, edited by Jason Harshman, Tami Augustine, and Merry M. Merryfield, 9–34. Charlotte: Information Age Publishing, 2015.

Peck, Carla L. and Karen Pashby. 'Global Citizenship in North America'. In *The Palgrave Handbook of Global Citizenship and Education*, edited by Ian Davies, Ho Li-Ching, Carla L. Dina Kiwan, Andrew Peterson Peck, Edda Sant, and Yusef Waghid, 51–65. London: Palgrave Macmillan, 2018.

Peck, Carla L. Laura A. Thompson, Ottilia Chareka, Reva Joshee, and Alan Sears. 'From Getting along to Democratic Engagement: Moving toward Deep Diversity in Citizenship Education'. *Citizenship Teaching and Learning* 6, no. 1 (2010): 61–75.

Peters, Michael A., Alan Britton, and Harry Blee, eds. *Global Citizenship Education: Philosophy, Theory and Pedagogy.* Rotterdam: Sense Publishers, 2008.

Pike, Graham. 'Global Education and National Identity: In Pursuit of Meaning'. *Theory into Practice* 39, no. 2 (2000): 64–73.

Pike, Graham. 'Reconstructing the Legend: Educating for Global Citizenship'. In *Educating for Human Rights and Global Citizenship*, edited by Ali A. Abdi and Lynette Shultz, 223–237. New York: SUNY Press, 2008.

Pike, Graham and David Selby. *In the Global Classroom 2*. Toronto: Pippin, 2000.

Pike, Graham and David Selby. *Global Teacher, Global Learner*. London: Hodder and Stoughton, 1988.

Rathbun, Melanie and Roberta Lexier. 'Global Citizenship in Canadian Universities: A New Framework'. *Journal of Global Citizenship & Equity Education* 5, no. 1 (2016): 1–24.

Rapoport, Anatoli. 'Global Citizenship Education: Classroom Teachers' Perspectives and Approaches'. In *Research in Global Citizenship Education*, edited by Jason Harshman, Tami Augustine, and Merry M. Merryfield, 119–136. Charlotte: Information Age Publishing, 2015.

Reid, Alan, Judith Gill, and Alan Sears. 'The Forming of Citizens in a Globalizing World'. In *Globalization, the Nation-State and the Citizen: Dilemmas and Directions for Civics and Citizenship Education*, edited by Alan Reid, Judith Gill, and Alan Sears, 3–16. New York: Routledge, 2010.

Richardson, George H. 'Global Education and the Challenge of Globalization'. In *Challenges and Prospects for Canadian Social Studies*, edited by Alan Sears and Ian Wright, 138–149. Vancouver: Pacific Education Press, 2004.

Richardson, George H. and Laurence Abbott. 'Between the National and the Global: Exploring Tensions in Canadian Citizenship Education'. *Studies in Ethnicity and Nationalism* 9, no. 3 (2009): 377–394.

Roberts, Boyd (2009). *Educating for Global Citizenship: A Practical Guide for Schools*. Cardiff: International Baccalaureate, 2009.

Schattle, Hans. *The Practices of Global Citizenship*. Lanham: Rowman & Littlefield, 2008.

Sears, Alan. 'In Search of Good Citizens: Citizenship Education and Social Studies in Canada'. In *Challenges and Prospects for Canadian Social Studies*, edited by Alan Sears and Ian Wright, 90–106. Vancouver: Pacific Education Press, 2004.

Sears, Alan. '"Something Different to Everyone": Conceptions of Citizenship and Citizenship Education'. *Canadian and International Education* 25, no. 2 (1996): 1–15.

Selby, David and Graham Pike. 'Global Education: Relevant Learning for the Twenty-first Century'. *Convergence* 33, no. 1 (2000): 138–149.

Shulsky, Debra D., Sheila F. Baker, Terry Chvala, and Jana M. Willis. 'Cultivating Layered Literacies: Developing the Global Child to Become Tomorrow's Global Citizen'. *International Journal of Development Education and Global Learning* 9, no. 1 (2017): 49–63.

Shultz, Lynette. 'Educating for Global Citizenship: Conflicting Agendas and Understandings'. *Alberta Journal of Educational Research* 53, no. 3 (2007): 248.

South House Exchange. *Education for Peace, Human Rights, Democracy, International Understanding, and Tolerance*. Ottawa: Council of Ministers of Education and Canadian Commission of UNESCO, 2001.

Tarc, Paul. 'What Is the Active in 21st Century Calls to Develop "Active Global Citizens"? Justice-oriented Desires, Active Learning, Neoliberal Times'. In *Research in Global Citizenship Education*, edited by Jason Harshman, Tami Augustine, and Merry M. Merryfield, 35–58. Charlotte: Information Age Publishing, 2015.

Torres, Carlos A. 'Education, Power and the State: Dilemmas of Citizenship in Multicultural Societies'. In *Citizenship, Education and Social Conflict: Israeli Political Education in Global Perspective*, edited by Hanan A. Alexander, Halleli Pinson, and Yossi Yonah, 61–82. New York: Routledge, 2011.

Tupper, Jennifer. 'Social Media and the Idle No More Movement: Citizenship, Activism and Dissent in Canada'. *Journal of Social Science Education* 13, no. 4 (2014): 87–94.

Tupper, Jennifer A. and Michael P. Cappello. '(Re)creating Citizenship: Saskatchewan High School Students' Understandings of the "Good" Citizen'. *Journal of Curriculum Studies* 44, no. 1 (2012): 37–59.

Tupper, Jennifer A. and Michael Cappello. 'Teaching Treaties as (Un)usual Narratives: Disrupting the Curricular Commonsense'. *Curriculum Inquiry* 38, no. 5 (2008): 559–578.

Tupper, Jennifer A., Michael P. Cappello, and Phillip R. Sevigny. 'Locating Citizenship: Curriculum, Social Class, and the "Good" Citizen'. *Theory & Research in Social Education* 38, no. 3 (2010): 336–365.

UNESCO. *Global Citizenship Education: Preparing Learners for the Challenges of the 21st Century*. Paris: Author, 2014.

UNESCO. *Global Citizenship Education: Topics and Learning Objectives*. Paris: Author, 2015.

Westheimer, Joel. *What Kind of Citizen? Educating Our Children for the Common Good*. New York: Teachers College Press, 2015.

8

Citizenship Education on the World Stage: Curriculum for Cosmopolitanism

Julie McLeod

Chapter outline

- Introduction
- Internationalism and changing the world through educational means
- Pedagogies of internationalism
  - The League as School Prefect
- Local enactments and public opinion
- History curriculum and the figure of the internationally minded student
- Conclusion: Cosmopolitan student-citizens and the global order
- Notes

Keywords: Citizenship, Curriculum, Internationalization, Cosmopolitanism, Youth, League of Nations, International Bureau of Education

---

Introduction

In the early decades of the twenty-first century, national and supra-national educational organizations forthrightly promote the responsibilities of schools to foster students in possession of global outlooks. International sensibilities are applauded, often implicitly pitted against the risks and limitations associated with a blinkered nationalism indifferent to the dynamic interconnectedness of the contemporary world. So pervasive is the commitment of education systems to the ideals of global citizenship that it barely warrants justification beyond the expression of in-principle statements, as evidenced in mission statements from local schools through to system-level strategic goals. UNESCO's programme for Global Citizenship Education 'aims to instil in learners the values, attitudes and behaviours that support responsible global citizenship: creativity, innovation, and commitment to peace, human rights and sustainable development' (UNESCO 2018). The ideal of global citizenship is clearly value-laden, calling forth particular social and ethical stances, not simply referencing an outward-looking attitude. Looking to case of Australia, the *Melbourne Declaration on Educational Goals for Young Australians* (MCEETYA 2008) documents the high-level principles underpinning national and state-based educational programmes, giving priority to the provision of education that has a goal of creating Australians who become 'active and informed citizens' and 'responsible local and global citizens' (9). This focus is linked to an awareness of transforming social and economic contexts. As noted in the Preamble: 'Global integration and international mobility have increased rapidly in the past decade …. This heightens the need to nurture an appreciation of and respect for social, cultural and religious diversity, and a sense of global citizenship' (5).

Such hopeful flourishes immediately invite scrutiny of how aspirations for global citizenship have been translated into pedagogical and curricular practices in diverse national and local settings. Of interest here, however, is unpacking some of the longer history of contestation over the role of education systems in cultivating global citizenship and the shifting rationales and contexts framing this work. This chapter considers how education has been variously regarded as a means to promote international understanding in service of agendas beyond schoolrooms. The overall argument is that critical attention to the history and changing constructions of the 'global citizen' offers a valuable context for understanding the specificity of contemporary educational discourses on globalization, youth citizenship and associated international agendas for education. In other words, the idea of the global youth citizen is not an invention of the contemporary era but enters social and policy discourse with a longer history of cultural referents and educational effects. Understanding some of the character of this is important for recognizing the reach of educational practices and imagined subjectivities called forth in current international agendas. Moreover, an historical angle helps to reveal the contingent role of education in mediating shifting dynamics of global and national allegiances and the significance of educational practices in translating popular and democratizing aspects of internationalism, beyond elite circles and networks, into the everyday worlds of teachers and students.

It is thus useful to begin with a brief comment on how citizenship is understood here. Following Osler and Starkey, citizenship is taken to have 'three essential and complementary dimensions: It is a status, a feeling and a practice' (Osler and Starkey 2005, 11). The current discussion gives most critical attention to the affective or 'feeling' dimension and to pedagogical practices that are imagined to foster dispositions towards world-mindedness and global citizenship. Conceptually, this aligns with Engin Isin's genealogical approach to citizenship which, he proposes, 'questions the universal idea of citizenship … [and] opens up ways of seeing the specificity of contemporary boundaries, acts and struggles of citizenship' (Isin 1997, 130). As such, citizenship is analysed in terms of acts and practices. Shifting from a concern with legal rights and principles to a focus on practices, Isin and Nielsen's key questions are: 'Under what conditions do subjects act as citizens?' (Isin and Nielsen 2007, 18) and 'what are the habits of the everyday through which subjects become citizens'? (17). Further, they argue that these acts of citizenship are relational, that is, one claims and is constituted as a citizen through a dynamic process of differentiation from others, which is also open to change and variation across time and place (Isin 2002); one aim of their genealogies is to examine the different ways in which citizenship is constituted and practised.

Accordingly, I frame interventions into the making of internationally minded young people, the citizens of tomorrow, as instances of the affective and relational practices of citizenship. In the examples examined here, these practices are normatively defined through an assemblage of techniques and aspirations that express the inherent value of cosmopolitan world views and worldly understanding and cooperation. In doing so, I implicitly touch on the shadow side of this construction of citizenship – invoking the non-internationally minded student-subject, positioned beyond the metropolitan gaze and predominantly European world views (Fuchs 2004), an imagined subject that also points to the colonial and racial dimensions of the idealized community of cooperation. Querying whether interwar internationalism and, specifically, the activities of the League of Nations can be accurately characterized as cosmopolitan, Daniel Laqua has suggested that many 'protagonists of intellectual co-operation view global order as a dialogue between "civilizations"'. As such, 'intellectual co-operation was subject to inherent limitations, exemplified by an attachment to categories of civilization, race, empire, and nationhood' (Laqua 2011, 229). I return to these important arguments in the concluding comments.

The chapter begins by examining debates among international organizations in the interwar years of the twentieth century that looked to schools and education systems to forge internationally minded students who would greet the world with cosmopolitan outlooks and a commitment to uphold world peace. It focusses on the initiatives of the Geneva-based League of Nations (1919–1946), with reference to intersecting activities of the International Bureau of Education (IBE, 1925) – one of the antecedent organizations to UNESCO. Both sought to influence the school curriculum of member nations through concerted efforts to review and revise national curriculum and textbooks (Hofstetter and Schneuwly 2013; Klerides 2018; Osborne 2016) and, in the case of the League, to disseminate advice on how to instruct young people in the aims and spirit of the League of Nations. It then offers a reading of these matters in relation to education for citizenship and civics curriculum in Australia during the same period. It presents, as illustration, responses in Australia to the League's call to disseminate its aims (Ellis 1922) and promote an understanding of and, indeed, a natural affection for the ambitions of the League within young people. I now turn to situate these matters in relation to the aspirations of interwar internationalism, before offering a glimpse of the League's aims for reforming curriculum and shaping the hearts and minds of the young.

Internationalism and changing the world through educational means

Historians of internationalism describe the early twentieth century as marking a significant shift in practices of international relations, one which strengthened in the aftermath of the Great War and the devastating legacies of nationalism (Sluga and Clavin 2016). A new spirit of internationalism, influentially characterized by Akira Iriye (Iriye 1997) as cultural internationalism, was evident in the optimistic embrace of greater communication across borders with hopes for better understanding between nations – the path to international peace was imagined to lie in enhanced opportunities for cultural exchange and collaboration to enable a sense of shared values.[1] This represented a break with earlier expressions of internationalism that predominantly addressed political relations between sovereign states (Sluga 2013). According to Iriye, 'there was a vigorous engagement with cultural, as against political, internationalism since the late [nineteenth] century, and a large number of national as well as international organizations, both public and private, played their roles' (Iriye 2013, 16).

The language of cooperation, Joyce Goodman argues, 'linked local and global communities without denying constitutional sovereignty or demanding further centralization of power' (Goodman 2012, 359). Moreover, it gave expression to the idea that 'peace could be fostered through the engagement of elites with cultural, intellectual and psychological aspects of the international order and by shaping public opinion via popular culture' (Goodman 2012, 359). In this regard, education was a crucial force, embodying the promise of international understanding based on cooperation and the exchange of ideas. In the work of teachers, the curriculum of schools and the activities and attitudes of students, education offered a forum to guide present-day interactions and conduct while also embedding such internationalist sentiments in generations to come. The temporal logics of education – as both securing aspirations in the present and looking to their realization in the future – were reflected in the reforming missions of international organizations.

The spread of initiatives to support the cultivation of world-minded citizens was both aided by and part of what Eckhardt Fuchs describes as a process of 'institutionalised internationalisation', which, in relation to education, included 'the international exchange of teachers and students, international educational exhibitions, international congresses, transnational institutions, multilateral standardization and international journals' (Fuchs 2004, 757). Beginning in the late nineteenth century, and reflected in events such as World Fairs, this process flourished during the interwar years, mobilized through institutional networks, of which the League and the IBE were especially important for education, as well as through the collaborations of individual experts, including educators, social scientists and government administrators (McLeod and Paisley 2016). The exchange of ideas was enhanced by the popularity of international congresses, including those supported by the UK-based and influential New Education Fellowship (NEF) (Brehony 2004; Campbell and Sherington 2006; Fuchs 2007; Godfrey 2004). Philanthropic organizations, notably the Carnegie Corporation of New York (CCNY), were crucial supporters of these transnational events (Lawn 2004; McLeod and Wright 2013; White 1997) and these, in turn, invariably endorsed the pivotal role of education in achieving broader political and cultural agendas.

The Geneva-based League of Nations was established in 1919, following a recommendation of the Treaty of Versailles, as a forum to resolve international disputes. It was disbanded in 1946 at the close of the Second World War, amid the stark evidence of its 'failure' to prevent large-scale wars. Its founding purpose was to maintain universal peace: 'to develop cooperation [among nations], and to guarantee them peace and security' (United Nations 2018). The Covenant of the League provided its charter and outlined three main objectives: 'to ensure collective security, to assure functional cooperation, and to execute the mandates of peace treaties'.[2] In addition, the articles of the Covenant spelled out the social and political obligations of member nations to promote international cooperation, with the scope of the League extending from disarmament to health, slavery, trade, transport, the struggle against drugs and trafficking in women and children, refugees and the youth question (Brown 2008; United Nations 2018). In 1922, the League established the Intellectual Cooperation Committee (ICC), which was crucial in advancing the League's educational reach and was to become part of the genesis of UNESCO (Kolasa 1962). Underpinning these various agendas was a concern with moral disarmament, a notion that obviously played on the pressing call for disarmament in the sense of militarization, weapons and warfare. This was accompanied by a shift in mentality away from nationalist interests towards shared international values and the striving for peace and greater understanding through cooperation. As Goodman observes, a connection was drawn between material and moral disarmament, with intellectual cooperation a central, if not essential, pre-cursor to this ethical and political position (Goodman 2012, 361).

In such work, the League was pre-eminently concerned with influencing and managing public opinion (Brown 2008) and, as Nicholas Brown has suggested, exploring the League's work through this lens can help reveal how it opened up and spoke to a new constituency.[3] Education was fundamentally important to realizing the imagined new worlds that fuelled the League's machinations – through its many Council and Assembly debates and resolutions and in its voluminous correspondence with member states urging them to spread the spirit of the League. However, the nature of the League's interest in education – the school curriculum, the work of teachers and the dispositions and knowledge of students – was not unique. It intersected with a range of contemporaneous networks and organizations, such as the Geneva-based IBE and UK-based New Education Fellowship (NEF). Both organizations were concerned with the future of education in a self-conscious new era and promoted critical review of the purposes of education. Such matters were widely debated at the time among a range of educational progressives, with schools positioned as a kind of social laboratory for forming particular types of citizen that would better serve, enact and, indeed, embody internationalist ambitions, promising a new type of rational, world-minded citizen of the future (McLeod 2012).

The IBE was officially established as a private, non-governmental organization at the end of 1925. Its first director, Pierre Bovet, was from the Institute of

J.J. Rousseau in Geneva, which was supported by funds from the Rockefeller Foundation (Hofstetter and Schneuwly 2013; Rosselló n.d.). By the late 1920s, the IBE had re-organized itself on a governmental basis, with a new director, Jean Piaget (1929), who, with assistant director Pedro Rosselló, went on to lead the IBE for the next forty years. In 1999, the IBE became the 'UNESCO institute responsible for educational content, methods and teaching/learning strategies through curriculum development' (IBE 2015). The IBE had its own initiatives and committees promoting intellectual cooperation and eagerly advocated the value of exchanging educational ideas via international congresses – teacher exchange, conferences on the moral purposes of education and, especially, the scope and focus of history curriculum (Hofstetter and Schneuwly 2013; Osborne 2016; Rosselló n.d.). Much like the League, as further discussed below, the IBE saw intellectual cooperation affording ways of working against the nationalist sentiments then seen to be pervading school curriculum and pedagogy. It undertook, for example, an extensive international review of history teaching in the early years of its establishment, with a view to showing the significance of history curriculum in moral and citizenship education.

A further context for understanding the League's educational mission is the people and politics of new or progressive education during the interwar years (Howlett 2013), notably that of the NEF – an organization established in the UK in 1921, with far-ranging international affiliations and outposts. While a proper account of these interconnections is beyond the scope of this chapter (but see Brehony 2004 and Watras 2011), it is important to note intersecting agendas as part of the more widespread hopefulness attached to internationalizing reforms of education. In the case of New Education in particular, this brought together psychological understandings of child-centred education – the creativity and preciousness of the inner life of the child – with an outward orientation towards world-mindedness and the child's formation as a cosmopolitan citizen. NEF described itself as a 'rallying point for people of all countries who felt that a radical reform of education, based on a proper understanding of childhood and of the unity in diversity of mankind, was essential if ever world peace was to be assured'.[4] Its philosophy was underpinned by egalitarian and democratic principles and an optimistic view of the emancipatory promise of education (Abbis 1998; Jenkins 2000; McLeod 2012; Middleton 2013). It saw itself in service of international friendship and cooperation and of 'carrying into effect a conception of education worthy of and adequate to the democratic way of life'.[5] As NEF's founder, Beatrice Ensor, opined: 'We can train our children to be citizens of democracy by helping them to react co-operatively instead of individually … new education is primarily a thing of spirit … new relationships between child and teacher ... new attitudes towards learning, towards authority, and one might also say between life itself' (Ensor 1938, 96–97).

In this context, the League's activities in this domain can be understood as part of an assemblage of expertise and administrative practices directed to reforming education and better managing the 'youth question'. Tamson Pietsch's (2013) work on the nature of networks among settler academics in establishing universities offers helpful insight here. She argues that 'experiences of study and travel, and the strong personal connections academics forged during them, created shifting social landscapes of intellectual production and exchange' (120).[6] Similar kinds of networks and affective connections characterized the movement of educational progressivism and internationalism during the League years.

I now turn to consider in more detail the League's guidance for curriculum and associated arts of persuasion, looking at their activities to disseminate the ethos and work of the League through strategies to instruct young people in the aims of the League and promote textbook revision, particularly history textbooks in schools. I think of these as pedagogic translations and enactments of internationalism. In doing so, I examine how the League's spirit, advocacy of education for peace and worldly understanding were mobilized and materialized in classrooms, in teacher's professional knowledge, in young people's activities and in civics and history curriculum. In other words, I argue that it is important to explore the aspirational, along with the mundane, ways in which the spirit of the League was to become part of teachers' working knowledge and to enter into the life and habits of the child.

Pedagogies of internationalism

The League's activities directed to influencing educational practices took a number of paths. Initiatives under the auspices of the International Committee for Intellectual Co-operation (Goodman 2012; Sluga 2013, chapter 2) included support for teacher exchange and summer schools and concerns with school curriculum. Such initiatives were in support of an overarching aim to foster 'a general mentality among the peoples of the world more appropriate to co-operation than the nationalistic mentality of the past' (cited in Laqua 2011, 224). The League's Committee for Intellectual Co-operation maintained, as Glenda Sluga notes, a 'focus on the cultural and social role of intellectuals moving themselves and ideas across national borders in aid of the development of a

"League of Minds" and a "universal conscience"' (Sluga 2013, 62). To become internationally minded, as Osborne suggests, did not 'require renouncing one's sense of national identity and patriotism but rather tempering them with the realization that other peoples had their own equally legitimate claims to identity and distinctiveness'. The key message, however, was that such acceptance of difference 'must be combined with the recognition that all nations have no choice but to work together peacefully as one global community' (Osborne 2016, 219).

Of direct interest here is advice to member states on how to disseminate the spirit of the League and instruct young people in the aims of the League of Nations. This work comprised a combination of governmental, administrative and pedagogic injunctions seeking to influence national educational jurisdictions to implement internationalist agendas. It included a concentrated focus on curriculum, specifically the review and revision of history textbooks to ensure that messages in support of world-mindedness were not subordinated to national pre-occupations. Here, the practical and ethical purposes of education were to the forefront, with curriculum not only encompassing formal content but also embracing the formation of worldly orientations – in the language of today, dispositions towards global citizenship.

In her account of British engagement with the League, Helen McCarthy observes that 'the campaign to internationalise the curriculum was amongst the most successful interwar ventures of the League movement' (McCarthy 2011, 104). It sought to counter and curb nationalist tendencies that were seen to characterize state education systems, believing that this, in turn, would help pave the way for greater interest in and knowledge about international affairs. 'League supporters', McCarthy continues, 'conceived of their task as one of inculcating "world citizenship" and "enlightened patriotism", terms which captured the imagination of thousands of teachers, academics and educational reformers, particularly within the discipline of history wherein, it was believed, lay the richest possibilities for internationalising the story of humanity's past and future progress' (McCarthy 2011, 104). Education was thus a key forum in which the temporal logics of the League's vision were mediated, representing a break with the (nationalistic) past and a kind of future insurance that its aspirations would be embedded in future generations, ensuring an enduring impact and legacy.

The League as school prefect

In 1926, the League established a sub-committee of experts to investigate how best to promote *Instruction of Youth in the Aims of the League of Nations*.[7] The committee prepared a list of recommendations distributed to member nations and requested reports from governments on the 'measures they had found possible to take in order to carry out the recommendations'.[8] An accompanying booklet *How to Make the League of Nations Known and Develop the Spirit of International Cooperation* (1927) was widely disseminated.[9] The recommendations included ensuring all children were given age-appropriate instruction in the Covenant of the League, its aims and achievements. Such instruction comprised relevant questions included in examinations; essay competitions on the topic; advice for teaching across all schools (vocational, agricultural, primary and secondary); the need for libraries equipped with sufficient resources, including slides and films; and teachers themselves to receive appropriate education in these matters, especially during their initial teacher training, and having opportunities to participate in international exchange. Of note is the special role accorded to women: Recommendation 1 for schools advised that 'In view of the important part played by women in forming the character of the young, care should be taken in those countries where the education of boys and girls is different to see that this instruction is given to girls as well as boys'.[10] Recognition of national diversity – and implicitly cultural and religious differences – is accommodated, but only to the extent that the overall ambitions for international harmony are not put at risk. Maternalist and civilizational discourses were constitutive of and embedded in this strand of cosmopolitan education.

The Committee of Experts received correspondence and reports from governments on their progress against these recommendations: a report from a 1930 meeting of the sub-committee found that their work had received 'the most encouraging reception from the public' and that, indeed, in 'many countries, Governments, the major international associations, national associations, professional bodies of teachers and professors have effectively helped to spread a knowledge of the League among young people'.[11] Reports from the Union of South Africa (6 January 1928), for example, noted that the aims of the League were now included in the syllabus of Teacher Training colleges in the Transvaal and Natal Education Departments. Further, in the Orange Free State, schools received a quarterly circular on the work of the League and 'inspectors of schools [were] requested to test the pupils' knowledge in this respect when making their regular school visits'.[12]

Turning to Australia, a member nation, similar types of educational activities were undertaken.[13] In February 1928, the Western Australian Premier's Department responded to the League recommendations (via the Prime Minister and External Affairs), advising that they were receiving 'sympathetic consideration' and that 'instruction on the subject is already being given to children in both primary and secondary schools. All students passing through the Teachers Training College will also receive such instruction. Literature on the subject is included in the Teachers' Library'. However, there were some constraints on international exchange due to Australia's 'isolated position' which 'prevents the adoption of proposals for interchange of children for International holiday camps, etc. Tours for young Australian boys are arranged from time to time, and exchanges of teachers are regularly made'.[14] Reports from other Australian states had a similarly generic tone, with somewhat formulaic assurances of the commitment to embrace the League's injunctions.

In 1928, the Commonwealth Department of External Affairs compiled a summary of activities undertaken by each of the Australian states as a basis for reporting back to the Committee for Intellectual Co-operation. Common themes included the work of local branches of the League of Nations Union, the inclusion of the aims in teacher college curriculum, essay competitions, articles in school magazines and the provisions of relevant library materials. The state of Victoria reported that: 'The school paper, which circulates throughout elementary and higher elementary schools, contains articles from time to time dealing with the League of Nations, international peace, etc'. Essay competitions were held and a book, *Australia and the League of Nations*, by A.D. Ellis (1922), 'formerly a teacher of the Victorian Educational Department, is prescribed for use in schools'.[15] In the following section, I give a small taste of public and pedagogic discussions on the place of the League in Australian schools, taking account of debates and deliberations beyond formal governmental responses to the League.

Local enactments and public opinion

Helen McCarthy's account of the League focuses on the reception of its educational injunctions in Britain (McCarthy 2011). Similar responses and concerns were evident in Australia, as noted above. There was among educators a ready, if perhaps rhetorical, embrace of a happy internationalism and fraternalism. This included deliberations on the practicalities of what was involved in complying with the League's instructions, with concerns to ensure that this went beyond a simple activity such as League of Nations day so that the 'spirit' of the League's mission was properly insinuated into the being of children. There were, as well, worries about the risks of indoctrination and propaganda that their politically directed modes of instruction might engender. This drew corresponding attention to the need for critical judgement, for students to cultivate an independence of mind – for world-mindedness to be matched with reason (McLeod 2012).

A 1935 report in the Melbourne *Age* on League of Nations Day in schools observed that: 'There will be broadcast addresses by speakers specially equipped to outline general principles and to fill in interesting details. There is, however, reason to believe that today's message will only supplement what many children are already hearing in their homes'. The League's message had been widely disseminated via essay competitions and school magazines, such that knowledge of the work League was now thought to be well embedded in everyday understandings: 'Recent experiments with school essays ... spontaneously disclosed that the first thing each youthful essayist would do, if invested with sufficient power, would be to abolish war'. Such responses suggested that the 'seeds of thought sown on this League of Nations day seems certain, therefore, to fall into receptive soil' (*Age* 1935).

In South Australia, considerable support was expressed in parliament in 1925 for '(1) The preparation of special text books and pamphlets concerning the League of Nations and international cooperation; (2) the remodelling of history books so as to make them conform to more recent ideas on international relations; and (3) lectures, conferences, and special classes' (*Register* 1925). Similar sentiments were articulated across the other states. In Victoria, news in 1933 that revisions to school curriculum were underway was greeted with much enthusiasm. The *Age* reported that the new teaching methods offered more 'than simply rote learning' and that the 'work of the League of Nations and other similar bodies would be given greater attention so that the rising generation would have an enlightened outlook on world affairs'. Of particular note was revision to the history curriculum which 'had in the past devolved itself into the glorification of one particular nation's deeds. While still adhering to the principle that patriotism was a cardinal virtue, it was hoped to strike an international note in this study' (*Age* 1933). At a conference held in 1929 in West Australia 'called to discuss methods of stimulating public interest in the League', there was strong support for the introduction of information on the League into primary schools through to Adult Education classes. A general opinion was expressed 'that no satisfactory course in history could be given in secondary schools that did not include teaching on the subject of the League of Nations ... and include a study of the ideals, activities and accomplishments of the League' (*Daily News* 1929).

Public advocacy organizations also had their say. In March 1927, the Council of Public Education in Victoria forwarded to the Committee on International

Co-operation, the following resolution in support of the League's work: 'That in view of the importance of the League of Nations as the great hope of the world for ending war and realizing the ideal of human brotherhood, it is desirable to enlist the enthusiastic support of the younger generation in the work and aims of the League. The Council therefore recommends that opportunity should often be taken to interest the pupils of our schools in the doings of the League … giving of addresses … to the boys and girls, well-informed articles in the School Papers and the offer of prizes for essays on the League.'[16]

A report prepared in 1930 for the League's magazine, the *Educational Survey*, on 'League of Nations Teaching in Australia' (by R. Watts) mapped a range of initiatives, from articles published in school magazines with a focus on peace, to stories about children from other lands in the school newspapers, to the work of the League of Nations Union. An example was given of the Victorian Branch of the League of Nations Union which had its own school committee 'to organise and promote its activities in the primary, secondary, public, private and catholic schools' and was establishing a Junior League of Nations.[17] Teacher Training Colleges were seen as the 'strategic centre for developing most quickly interest in international affairs'. It was the new generation of teachers who could give the most impartial sense of a new world order. In NSW, study of the League was required in Teacher Colleges, including examination questions on its aims. And, at one College in 1927, a study circle was held dealing with the League as part of the course on Modern Political Institutions.[18]

There was, then, quite widespread engagement at formal levels of reporting and education systems with the aims of the League, but it is not immediately clear the extent to which such commitments actually permeated into the hearts and minds of students. R. Watts' report to the League made clear that Australian educational interest in League was on the basis of the 'most liberal traditions of the British commonwealth of nations'.[19] Others were more hesitant about elevating the League without also attending to wider aspects of international relations, with the Minister for Public Instruction declaring in 1927 that it was 'more important to bring about a desire for friendly relations between nations than merely to give facts about the League'.[20] Australia's place in the British world was never far from the surface, with Australian children first and foremost positioned as members of the British race: reporting on the 1935 League of Nations day, it was noted by the *Age* that, among school children, there should be a 'blend of idealism and of wise caution which ever characterise the British race in the presence or prospect of serious problems. On League of Nations day Victoria's school children should be abundantly encouraged to develop these two qualities. They need not be in the slightest degree incompatible with any vital part of the League's propaganda' (*Age* 1935). The international ambitions of the League in relation to questions of empire and race – and the circumscribed view of who was and was not embraced as internationally minded – are returned to below, following a brief discussion of the League's enthusiasm for the revision of national history curriculum.

History curriculum and the figure of the internationally minded student

The League's interest in history textbooks and teaching arose in the context of concerns among national and educational groups dating from at least the late nineteenth century regarding the perceived role of this curriculum area, not only in promoting nationalistic narratives but also in generating 'misunderstanding among nations' (Klerides 2018, 226). Revision of text books thus addressed the 'elimination of factual errors and the avoidance of defamatory generalizations' (Klerides 2018, 226) as a means to work against intolerance of other nations (see too Osborne 2016, 228). In 1926, the League adopted the Cesares resolution (named after the Spanish representative, Julio Cesares) that national committees be established to review the content of history textbooks, a decision that prompted a considerable volume of correspondence and reports and, for a few years from 1929, the publication by the League of *The Educational Survey*.[21] Edited by Alfred Zimmern, a British international relations expert, influential League supporter and deputy director of the League's International Institute for Intellectual Cooperation (Osborne 2016), the *Educational Survey* brought together extended national reports on progress to revise history and related curriculum, examples of model approaches that could be emulated as well as more philosophical and political reflections on the state and purpose of school curriculum.

The editorial of the first issue of the *Survey* (vol. 1, July 1929) reflected on the discovery that the challenges lay not only in teaching about the League in 'different ways in different countries' but the realization, 'if one may so express it, [that] the League of Nations itself is not the same from country to country'.[22] In part, this conveys a familiar tension across the League's deliberations in navigating national and international interests, with the specificity and sovereignty of nations often set against the more expansive ambitions held by the League. But it also conveys an apprehension of the political and historical circumstances shaping the reception as well as the perception and workings of the League. For some in the League, this gave rise to calls for 'greater uniformity in educational systems and curricula', even the production, 'for general use in the schools of all the world, of standard textbooks in history and relative subjects'. The editorial view of the *Educational Survey*, however, was that:

> such abstract uniformity is not only practically unattainable but would represent a backward step in educational practice. Children in New Zealand and Japan can never look upon the work done at Geneva with quite the same eyes as their fellows in France, Germany, Italy or Switzerland itself. But even if the difficulty of perspective, due to the fact that the visible centre of the League is in a city of Western Europe, could be overcome, there would still remain the great variety of traditions and habits of mind, so clearly revealed in the [national] reports.[23]

The editor was not indifferent to the Euro-centric range of national reports submitted to the *Educational Survey*, reflecting on the difficulties the League of Nations Educational Information Centre faced in providing comprehensive inclusion beyond 'predominantly European countries'. This was largely due, he felt, to limited opportunities to build relationships that might allow for personal visits to 'secure satisfactory material from non-European countries'. Hopes were that this disproportional representation would be addressed in future issues, because until that time, the Educational Information Centre 'will never be completely equal to its task'; and nor would it be able to meet the 'comparative standards which are essential for an adequate survey'.[24]

These reflections capture some of the dilemmas that also beset contemporary discussions about globalizing policy agendas and education, where questions of standardization and uniformity vie with claims on and for national and local specificity. The historical circumstances are significantly different, in relation to, for example, mobility of peoples (forced and voluntary) decolonization movements, global flows of capital and knowledge and the space-time compression afforded by digital technologies. Such changes arguably intensify the above dilemmas; on the one hand, blurring distinctions between global and local and, on the other, accelerating a politics attuned to geo-social differentiation (Mitchell and Kallio 2017). The figure of the global (youth) citizen embodies and mediates many of these tensions. This is so not simply in the physical and material experience of mobility and of traversing the globe, but also in imaginatively adopting sensibilities that anticipate or valorize the global, while being anchored to varying degrees, in particular communities and educational settings. While hopes for internationally minded students were linked to agendas for peace, national cooperation and social harmony, the attributes of the global youth citizen of today arguably promise an individual competitive edge on the world market, while also paying lip service to intercultural understanding and tolerance of diversity. Here too, the ideal of being a global youth citizen, mobile and networked, is shot through with class, gender, regional and ethno-political differences. This points to the dividing practices of that ideal and the need to address the situated and local ways in which the meanings of being a global citizen take root.

The topic of interwar history curriculum revision and navigation of national and international interests (and of empire and colony) warrants considerably more critical attention than is possible to give in this chapter. Important related work has been undertaken by Osborne (2016) on the League's endeavours in this area (with examples drawn from the Canadian response), as well as by Klerides (2018), who also considers history curriculum revision in light of changing conceptualizations of 'homo nationalis' and 'homo interculturalis'; and Fuchs (2010) has provided a valuable historical analysis of practices of textbook revision in the context of historicizing the disciplines. Yet, there remains more work to be undertaken on the translations and contextual enactments of these knowledge-building activities, which were also directly concerned with repositioning national and international sensibilities and constructions of citizenship and identity. Such an analysis could yield further valuable insights into how these matters were navigated in specific settings, for example, in dominions such as Australia, where relations with the British Empire, a history of colonization of Indigenous peoples and responsibilities under the League towards its mandated territories formed part of the context in which the history textbooks represented national narratives and looked to new internationalist possibilities.

To take one example: the popular school textbook, Alice Hoy's *Civics in Australia*, underwent a number of editions from the early 1920s to the late 1930s (Meabank 1988). In the 1937 edition, explanations of Australia's place in the world centred not only on her relation to Britain but also on her relations to a wider international community, although the question of empire continued to be addressed in a dedicated chapter. The final chapters of the 1937 edition focused on Australia and the world, the role of international law and international agencies, yet as Hoy (1937) illuminates, returned to the responsibility of Australia's citizens to uphold the values of obedience to the law and loyalty to the 'British race' (132): in a multi-racial empire, however, only some could claim belonging to the British race.

In specific reference to the League, in the 1937 edition attention is drawn to the Mandates system and Australia's governing role in relation to New Guinea (a Class C mandate); Hoy (1937) explains to her readers that 'every year, Mandatories send in reports on the progress of the weaker countries, since the main object of the Mandates is the civilizing of backward nations' (130). The League of Nations, Hoy advises, 'has placed backward countries belonging before the Great War to Germany or her allies under the control of more civilized ones' (130). The implied paternalism of the League is overlooked in the more laudatory treatment of Australia as part of the government of empire and not a colony to be governed by empire. The League's internationalism serves to bestow a new national significance to Australia, a special part of the British world, but not only or entirely subjected to it. Looking at both elevated rhetoric and the more technical and everyday aspects of education and curriculum, I have offered a snapshot of some of the ways in which education was a key site for constructing understandings of the international and the national. I now draw together the threads of this chapter by raising some questions about the dominance and effects of contemporary educational discourses on global youth citizenship.

Conclusion: Cosmopolitan student-citizens and the global order

In my opening remarks, I noted the rise and reach of agendas for global youth citizenship, and the pervasiveness of this discourse across educational sectors and systems. I argued that it was important to have a grasp of the historical antecedents and contexts for these agendas, and not only because this helps to shed light on the specificities of contemporary educational practices and policy reforms. It is also important because it helps to reveal the invention and effects of particular tropes, such as that of the global youth citizen, which has some resonances with earlier calls for internationally minded youth, but what is conjured is not the same figure. That is, looking to earlier national and supranational attempts to mould international youth citizenship is not a simple warrant to understand present-day policy agendas as a natural and linear outcome of that past. Rather, it is a warrant to untangle how current agendas, while part of a longer history of education policy aspirations and contestation over the space and identity of the 'international', also represent quite distinct claims, possibilities and dangers.

I want to conclude with two observations that bring these discussions back to concerns with citizenship education in an era of globalization and specifically to questions of inclusion and exclusion. Much of the language of the interwar period as canvassed here dwelt on the possibilities of education to promote a new era of cooperation and greater understanding. While acknowledging limitations and risks in their current practices, education systems were nevertheless looked upon optimistically as transformative agents in achieving a new world, with interwar progressivism and the educational activities of the League representing a kind of apotheosis of cosmopolitan sensibilities in education. Even so, or perhaps precisely because of this expansive embrace, a very particular type of citizen and international mindset was called forth.

Laqua (2011) has argued that the League's commitment to collaboration and international understanding drew on ideas of civilization as a 'building block of global order', which means, he suggests, that 'the term "cosmopolitanism" – often understood as an embrace of diversity and difference – does not capture the nature of cultural internationalism in the interwar years' (Laqua 2011, 232). Moreover, he argues, this was underlined by the 'ambiguous role of race in intellectual cooperation' (232), such that while League 'sought to address issues of global order in its references to "civilizations" but – at least in semi-official settings – [it] rarely tackled the more delicate issues of race and empire' (233). Observations from the editor of the *Educational Survey*, noted above, implicitly pointed to some of these dilemmas in referencing the dominance of European reports, but this was represented as a matter resolved through improved communication, not as a matter to do with race and colonialism.

It is not possible to pursue Laqua's important analysis here, suffice to note that it underscores the paradoxes and categorical and political blind spots in constructions of international collaboration and world-mindedness. In so doing, it draws our attention to parallel critiques that might apply to ideals of the contemporary global youth citizen, giving us pause to consider the racialized lines and boundaries – the local, the global, the north/south, the metropole and the other that accompany this particular claim for achieving cosmopolitan ambitions. What kind of inclusions and affiliations are privileged, and what are the unremarked upon exclusions and their effects? In closing, this chapter has offered an historical lens onto current educational policy aspirations to cultivate students with global sensibilities; it has attempted to show some of the antecedents of these concerns while also pointing to significant differences in context and effect as well as resonances in the paradoxes and erasures when debating the international in education.

Acknowledgement

Research for this chapter was supported by funding from the Australian Research Council, Future Fellowship, 'Youth Identity and Educational Change in Australia since 1950: Digital Archiving, Re-using Qualitative Data and Histories of the Present' (FT110100646) Julie McLeod.

A version of this chapter is appearing in a special issue of the *Journal of Australian Studies* (2019): '"Are We Internationally Minded?" Everyday Cultures of Australian Internationalism in the Mid Twentieth Century'.

Notes

1 See Frances Fukyama's review of Iriye's book, *Cultural Internationalism and World Order*: 'Iriye argues that the traditional understanding of international relations as competition for power and wealth, and the consequent shunting aside of cultural issues as a matter for woolly headed idealists, needs to be rethought. His history of cultural internationalism – that is, the attempt to build cultural understanding, cooperation, and a sense of shared values across national borders through student exchanges, lectures, and the like – shows that it has been a constant feature of twentieth-century international relations' (Fukuyama 2009).

2 For details on membership of the League and the articles of the Covenant, see Pedersen 2015; United Nations 2018.

3 Nicholas Brown's (ANU) comments in plenary session at symposium, 'League of Nations: histories, legacies and impact', 10–11 December 2015, University of Melbourne.

4 Brochure for conference: 'Education for International Understanding' held in Australia, 1946. Australia, Archives of the World Education Fellowship, Institute of Education Library, University of London, WEF/A/111/201.

5 Ibid.

6 While it is not possible to develop this analysis in the current chapter, it is important to note Pietsch's further clarification that: 'Extending along the routes of empire, yet not to all its parts and places, it was in this limited yet expansive space of connection that academic ideas were also made'.

7 'Documents presented to and discussed at the 3rd session of the sub-Committee of Experts for Instruction of Young People in the Aims of the League of Nations, League of Nations, Secretariat, Registry Files 1928–1932', Section 5, Subsection 5C, Youth Questions, Box R2267, 1001/1902, General & Miscellaneous Report by the Secretary General to the Assembly, 1928.

8	Correspondence and general reports, League of Nations, Secretariat, Registry Files 1928–1932, Section 5, Subsection 5C Youth Questions Box R2267, 6895/1902: General & Miscellaneous Report by the Secretary General to the Assembly, 13 August 1928, p.xii.

9	Instruction of Youth in the Aims of the League, Booklet, National Archives of Australia, A981, League Ins 2.

10	Instruction of Youth in the Aims of the League, Booklet, p.11. National Archives of Australia, A981, League Ins 2.

11	Minutes and reports, 1930, League of Nations, Secretariat, Registry Files 1928–1932, Section 5, Subsection 5C Youth Questions Box R2268_21183/2422, Youth Committee, 3rd Session July 3–5 1930 Report.

12	General & Miscellaneous Report by the Secretary General to the Assembly, August 1928, Annex 1, report from Union of South Africa, (lodged 6 Jan 1928), p.2. League of Nations; Secretariat Registry Files 1928–1932, Section 5, Subsection 5C Youth Questions Box R2267 6895/1902.

13	Instruction of Youth in the Aims of the League [correspondence]. National Archives of Australia, A981 League Ins 1.

14	Letter from Premier of WA, [Philip Collier] to the Acting Prime Minister of the Commonwealth of Australia, 1 Feb 1927: National Archives of Australia, A981, League Ins 1, Instruction of Youth in the Aims of the League [correspondence].

15	Instruction of Young people in the Aims of the League of Nations – Action by State Authorities, External Affairs, 12th March 1928. National Archives of Australia, A981, League Ins 1, Instruction of Youth in the Aims of the League [correspondence].

16	Letter from Department of Education, Victoria, to the Committee on Intellectual Co-operation of the League of Nations, 1st March 1927, reporting advice from the Council of Public Education, Victoria, National Archives of Australia, A981, League Ins 1, Instruction of Youth in the Aims of the League [correspondence].

17	R. Watts, 'League of Nations Teaching in Australia', ms copy to be sent to the Educational Survey, League of Nations, in Papers and publications collected by Ken Cunningham on various matters, 1919–1942, Australian Council for Educational Research [ACER], Series 53, vol. 4, Box 5096.

18	R.Watts, Ibid.

19	R.Watts, Ibid.

20	R. Watts, Ibid.

21	Correspondence on the development and publication of the Educational Survey: Preparation of the Two 1930 Issues, 1929–1930. League of Nations, Secretariat, Registry Files 1928–1932, Section 5C Youth Questions, Box R2271,15424/4888, Educational Survey.

22	*Educational Survey*, Vol 1 No 1 1929, p.7. League of Nations Secretariat, Registry Files 1928–1932, Section 5C Youth Questions, Box R2271 13849/4888 Educational Survey, Text of First Issue Vol 1 No 1 & Circular Letter 212, 1929–1930.

23 Ibid, p.7.
24 Ibid, p.8.

References

Abbis, Jane. 'The "New Education Fellowship" in New Zealand: Its Activity and Influence in the 1930s and 1940s'. *New Zealand Journal of Educational Studies* 33, no. 1 (1998): 81–93.

Age (Melbourne, Vic.: 1854–1954). 'Modern Education'. 12 June 1933.

Age (Melbourne, Vic.: 1854–1954). 'League of Nations Day'. 9 August 1935.

Brehony, Kevin. 'A New Education for a New Era: The Contribution of the Conferences of the New Education Fellowship to the Disciplinary Field of Education 1921–1938'. *Paedagogica Historica* 40, no. 5 (2004): 733–755.

Brown, Nicholas. 2008. 'Enacting the International: R. G. Watt and the League of Nations Union'. In *Transnational Ties: Australian Lives in the World*, edited by Desley Deacon, Penny Russell, and Angela Woollacott, 75–94. Canberra, A.C.T: ANU E Press, 2008. Retrieved from http://press-files.anu.edu.au/downloads/press/p20951/mobile/ch05.html#d0e2529.

Campbell, Craig and Geoffrey Sherington. 'A Genealogy of an Australian System of Comprehensive High Schools: The Contribution of Educational Progressivism to the One Best Form of Universal Secondary Education, 1900–1940'. *Paedagogica Historica* 42, no. 1–2 (2006): 191–210.

Daily News (Perth, WA: 1882–1950). 1929. 'League of Nations'. 3 July 1929.

Ellis, Alexander D. *Australia and the League of Nations*. London: Macmillan & Co., 1922.

Ensor, Beatrice. 'A New World in the Making'. In *Education for Complete Living: The Challenge of to-Day, the Proceedings of the New Education Fellowship Conference held in Australia, August 1 to September 20, 1937 Australia*, edited by K. S. Cunningham, 96–97. Melbourne: Australian Council for Educational Research, 1938.

Fuchs, Eckhardt. 'Educational Sciences, Morality and Politics: International Educational Congresses in the Early Twentieth Century'. *Paedagogica Historica* 40, no. 6 (2004): 257–284.

Fuchs, Eckhardt. 'The Creation of New International Networks in Education: The League of Nations and Educational Organizations in the 1920s'. *Paedagogica Historica* 43, no. 2 (2007): 199–209. https://doi.org/10.1080/00309230701248305.

Fuchs, Eckhardt. 'Introduction: Contextualising Textbook Revision'. *Journal of Educational Media, Memory and Society* 2, no. 2 (2010): 1–12.

Fukuyama, Francis. 'Cultural Internationalism and World Order'. *Foreign Affairs*, 28 January 2009. Retrieved from https://www.foreignaffairs.com/reviews/capsule-review/1997-11-01/cultural-internationalism-and-world-order.

Godfrey, John. "'Perhaps the Most Important, and Certainly the Most Exciting Event in the Whole History of Education in Australia": The 1937 New Education Fellowship Conference and New South Wales Examination Reform'. *History of Education Review* 33, no. 2 (2004): 45–58.

Goodman, Joyce. 'Women and International Intellectual Co-Operation'. *Paedagogica Historica* 48, no. 3 (2012): 357–368.

Hofstetter, Rita and Bernard Schneuwly. 'The International Bureau of Education (1925–1968): A Platform for Designing a "Chart of Word Aspirations for Education"'. *European Educational Research Journal* 12, no. 2 (2013): 215–230.

Howlett, John. *Progressive Education: A Critical Introduction*. London: Bloomsbury Academic, 2013.

Hoy, Alice. *Civics for Australian Schools*. Melbourne: Lothian, 1937.

IBE. 'History'. Text. International Bureau of Education. 12 May 2015. Retrieved from http://www.ibe.unesco.org/en/who-we-are/history.

Iriye, Akira. *Cultural Internationalism and World Order*. Baltimore: Johns Hopkins University Press, 1997.

Iriye, Akira. *Global and Transnational History: The Past, Present, and Future*. Palgrave Pivot. Basingstoke: Palgrave Macmillan, 2013.

Isin, Engin F. 'Who Is the New Citizen? Towards a Genealogy'. *Citizenship Studies* 1 (1997): 115–132.

Isin, Engin F. *Being Political: Genealogies of Citizenship*. Minneapolis: University of Minnesota Press, 2002.

Isin, Engin F. and Greg M. Nielsen. *Acts of Citizenship*. London: Zed Books, 2007.

Jenkins, Celia. 'New Education and Its Emancipatory Interests (1920–1950)'. *History of Education* 29 (2000): 139–151.

Klerides, Eleftherios. 'History Education, Identity Formation and International Relations'. In *Uneven Space-Times of Education: Historical Sociologies of Concepts, Methods and Practices*, edited by Julie McLeod, Terri Seddon, and Noah W. Sobe, 220–239. World Yearbook. London; New York: Routledge, 2018.

Kolasa, Jan. *International Intellectual Cooperation (The League Experience and the Beginnings of UNESCO)*. Seria A. NR 81. Wrocklaw: Travaux de la Société des Sciences et des Letrres de Wrocklaw, 1962.

Laqua, Daniel. 'Transnational Intellectual Cooperation, the League of Nations, and the Problem of Order'. *Journal of Global History* 6 (2011): 223–247.

Lawn, Martin. 'The Institute as Network: The Scottish Council for Research in Education as a Local and International Phenomenon in the 1930s'. *Paedagogica Historica* 40, no. 5 and 6 (2004): 719–732.

McCarthy, Helen. *The British People and the League of Nations: Democracy, Citizenship and Internationalism, c.1918–45*. Manchester: Manchester University Press, 2011.

MCEETYA. 'Melbourne Declaration Educational Goals for Australians'. Melbourne, Vic.: Ministerial Council on Education, Employment, Training and Youth Affairs, 2008. Retrieved from https://nextlearning.com.au/2014/03/26/melbourne-declaration/.

McLeod, Julie. 'Educating for "World-Mindedness": Cosmopolitanism, Localism and Schooling the Adolescent Citizen in Interwar Australia'. *Journal of Educational Administration and History* 44, no. 4 (2012): 339–359.

McLeod, Julie and Fiona Paisley. 'The Modernization of Colonialism and the Educability of the "Native": Transpacific Knowledge Networks and Education in the Interwar Years'. *History of Education Quarterly* 56, no. 3 (2016): 473–502.

McLeod, Julie and Katie Wright. 'Education for Citizenship: Transnational Expertise, Curriculum Reform and Psychological Knowledge in 1930s Australia'. *History of Education Review* 42, no. 2 (2013): 170–184.

Meabank, Julann. 'A Contract with Education: Alice Hoy, 1893–1976'. Master of Education. Melbourne: University of Melbourne, 1988.

Middleton, Sue. 'Clare Soper's Hat: New Education Fellowship Correspondence between Bloomsbury and New Zealand'. *History of Education* 42, no. 1 (2013): 92–114.

Mitchell, Katharyne and Kirsi Kallio Pauliina. 'Spaces of the Geosocial: Exploring Transnational Topologies'. *Geopolitics* 22, no. 1 (2017): 1–14. https://doi.org/10.1080/14650045.2016.1226809.

Osborne, Ken. 'Creating the "International Mind": The League of Nations Attempts to Reform History Teaching, 1920–1939'. *History of Education Quarterly* 56, no. 2 (2016): 213–240.

Osler, Audrey and Hugh Starkey. *Changing Citizenship: Democracy and Inclusion in Education*. Maidenhead, UK: Open University Press, 2005.

Pedersen, Susan. *The Guardians: The League of Nations and the Crisis of Empire*. New York: Oxford University Press, 2015.

Pietsch, Tamson. *Empire of Scholars: Universities, Networks and the British Academic World 1850–1939*. Manchester: Manchester University Press, 2013.

Register (Adelaide, SA: 1901–1929). 1925. 'League of Nations'. 5 November 1925.

Rosselló, Pedro. 'Historical Note-Introduction'. In *C1963*, xi–xxii. Geneva: International Bureau of Education, n.d.

Sluga, Glenda. *Internationalism in the Age of Nationalism*, 1st edn. Pennsylvania Studies in Human Rights. Philadelphia: University of Pennsylvania Press, 2013.

Sluga, Glenda and Patricia Clavin, eds. *Internationalisms: A Twentieth-Century History*. Cambridge, United Kingdom New York: Cambridge University Press, 2016.

UNESCO. 'Global Citizenship Education'. UNESCO. 9 January 2018. Retrieved from https://en.unesco.org/themes/gced.

United Nations. 'The League of Nations (1919–1946)'. 2018. Retrieved from https://www.unog.ch/80256EDD006AC19C/(httpPages)/17C8E6BCE10E3F4F80256EF300 37D733? OpenDocument.

Watras, Joseph. 'The New Education Fellowship and UNESCO's Programme of Fundamental Education'. *Paedagogica Historica* 47, no. 1–2 (2011): 191–205.

White, Michael. 'Carnegie Philanthropy in Australia in the Nineteen Thirties – A Re-Assessment'. *History of Education Review* 26, no. 1 (1997): 1–24.

9

Learning to Live Together:
Children's Rights, Identities and Citizenship

Hugh Starkey

Chapter outline

- Learning to Live Together
- Utopia and human rights
- National and cosmopolitan citizenship: developing identities
- Citizenship education
- UN Convention on the Rights of the Child (CRC 1989)
- Rights Respecting Schools
- Identities and citizenship
- Conclusion
- Note

Keywords: Children's rights; human rights; utopia; citizenship; identities; globalization

---

Learning to live together

The early twenty-first century has seen increasing migration across the world and a consequent recognition of globalization as an irreversible phenomenon. This period has also witnessed numerous terrorist attacks often on civilian gatherings and these have been linked in political discourse to lax migration controls (Castles 2017). Responses to terrorism have included profound changes to urban infrastructures and greatly increased security apparatuses. The concrete barriers erected in cities are reminders of the current and persistent threats to liberal values and democracy from terrorism. However, the physical obstacles are only part of a solution to ensuring that citizens can freely engage in cultural activities. It is now widely recognized that education has a vital role to play in ensuring that human societies flourish at a time when they are rapidly changing in response to globalization and migration. Flourishing human communities are the context in which individuals can live free from fear and want (European Commission 2015; Group of Eminent Persons 2011).

This chapter takes its cue from a widely cited from a UNESCO Commission report that identified four pillars of education in the twenty-first century. It emphasizes 'learning to live together' as the most important challenge for education (Delors 1996). I argue that such learning requires both teachers and students to understand of citizenship as a key concept. Citizens recognize that human beings are vulnerable and require the support and solidarity of others, feeling part of a society in which they have rights and reciprocally responsibilities. I also argue that children are citizens rather than simply citizens in waiting. Learning to live together involves developing identities as citizens. This entails recognizing the diversity of cultures and identities of which even the apparently most homogeneous societies are made up.

Drawing on legal, philosophical and political theory, as well as empirical research, the chapter explores ways in which understandings of children's rights and citizenship inform a pedagogy of living together. It outlines the basic principles of international law and policy that inform the values that, when implemented in schools and classrooms, enable living together in contexts of diversity (Banks et al. 2005). While formal citizenship education tends to encourage national values and identities, the realities of migration and globalization suggest that educators should also promote cosmopolitan perspectives (Appiah 2006; Osler and Starkey 2005; Sen 2006). I illustrate this approach by reference to a relatively large-scale project in the UK known as the Rights Respecting Schools Award.

The UNESCO-sponsored report of the International Commission on Education for the twenty-first century presents an analysis of educational aims intended to be of universal application. The report identified four pillars, namely aims or broad purposes that provide the foundation for education: learning to know; learning to do; learning to be; and learning to live together. Of these, the priority aim is learning to live together which includes:

> developing an understanding of others and their history, traditions and spiritual values and, on this basis, creating a new spirit which, guided by recognition of our growing interdependence and a common analysis of the risks and challenges of the future, would induce people to implement common projects or to manage the inevitable conflicts in an intelligent and peaceful way. (Delors 1996, 20)

This definition eschews a narrowly nationalist curriculum. It makes no reference to national identities but rather there is an assumed 'us' that is left entirely open as to how this identity is defined. This open and malleable grouping is assumed to have a sense of 'history, traditions and spiritual values' that differs from that of 'others'. The Commission envisages students learning about the cultures of others and coming to a realization of the interdependence of individuals and groups faced with 'the risks and challenges of the future' that require action in the present. This action should lead to 'common projects', in other words working together, as the best means to manage conflicts and promote peace.

Building on the UNESCO report, recommendations from an international consensus panel convened by the prestigious Center for Multicultural Education at the University of Washington included an elaboration of learning to live together. The emphasis is on learning about interdependence in the face of global challenges:

> Students should learn about the ways in which people in their community, nation, and region are increasingly interdependent with other people around the world and are connected to the economic, political, cultural, environmental, and technological changes taking place across the planet. (Banks et al. 2005)

When faced with a specific terrorist attack in France on the journalists of the satirical weekly *Charlie Hebdo*, European ministers of education declared their intention to reinforce educational provision:

> Ensuring inclusive education for all children and young people which combats racism and discrimination on any ground, promotes citizenship and teaches them to understand and to accept differences of opinion, of conviction, of belief and of lifestyle, while respecting the rule of law, diversity and gender equality. (European Union Ministers of Education 2015)

This declaration focuses on education for promoting citizenship. In this context, citizenship is a useful shorthand term encapsulating a commitment to act to combat destructive forces in society such as racism and discrimination. In that sense, it is essentially about learning to live together. Citizenship education in this perspective includes accepting differences and respecting the rule of law and equalities whilst recognizing and valuing diversity.

Utopia and human rights

The question raised powerfully at the end of the twentieth century in the Delors report for UNESCO (1996) and a best-selling work of French sociology was whether we can live together as equals respecting difference (Touraine [1997]/2000). Learning to live together in multicultural societies requires the acceptance of the legitimacy of multiple points of view. Rather than being premised on 'them and us' nationalist narratives, education can take inspiration from a vision of a peaceful and harmonious world. Delors characterizes such a vision as a 'necessary utopia'.

Utopia can be an inspiration and a driving force motivating humans to exercise agency and shape history (Mannheim [1929, 1936]/1991). However, Nazism, Soviet Communism and Maoism were based on utopian visions of a better society. These 'failed utopias' (Klug 2000, 189) are based on assertions of the superiority of a race, class, or nationality. These murderous utopias are based on strict adherence to a party line that outlaw's alternative perspectives and minority voices. Authoritarian utopias use propaganda to promote 'the single story' (Adichie 2009). They respond to the challenge of living together by eliminating from the discourse of 'us' those individuals and groups that challenge the authority of the single story vision. Those offering alternative narratives become enemies of the regime, denied the protection of the law and vulnerable to arbitrary arrest, detention, exile and genocide.

The necessary utopia of the Delors report is grounded in 'the ideals of peace, freedom, and social justice'. These are the values and principles that underlie the international human rights regime. A human rights perspective on living together emphasizes that all must be included in the 'us', and it is this vision that drives the political action. Learning to live together in a society based on peace, freedom and social justice requires an understanding that citizenship in such a context is informed by human rights (Mejias and Starkey 2012). The University of Washington consensus panel argued that the teaching of human rights should underpin citizenship education courses and programmes in multicultural nation-states (Banks et al. 2005).

Human rights were formally codified in the 1940s. At the end of the Second World the United Nations (UN) was established as an international organization committed to justice and peace in the world. The Charter of the UN was signed in 1945 and proclaims that world peace can only prevail when there is respect for human rights. An international Human Rights Commission drafted the Universal Declaration of Human Rights (UDHR), which was proclaimed by the General Assembly of the UN on 10 December 1948.

The principles that underpin human rights are set out in the preamble to the UDHR which begins: 'Whereas recognition of the inherent dignity and of the equal and inalienable rights of all members of the human family is the foundation of freedom, justice and peace in the world … '. The key concepts in this formulation are the inherent dignity of all human beings and the entitlement of all human beings to equal rights. UDHR introduces a *universal* entitlement to rights applying to all 'members of the human family'. This is a major conceptual change from previous understandings that nation-states offered rights to their citizens and could also withdraw or withhold them. In other words, before the creation of the UN, national sovereignty could be invoked when states enacted discriminatory legislation or allowed their agents freedom to undertake extra-judicial killings or torture. The founding of the United Nations meant that moral pressure to uphold human rights standards could be applied since governments voluntarily commit themselves to the UDHR. Subsequently, a legal dimension has developed as human rights form the basis of international law.

The preamble to the UDHR also sets out a vision of a possible future that can be seen as a utopia, asserting that 'the advent of a world in which human beings shall enjoy freedom of speech and belief and freedom from fear and want has been proclaimed as the highest aspiration of the common people'. This section has its origins in a speech by US President Franklin J. Roosevelt in 1941. The UDHR preamble incorporates his idea of four freedoms that come as two pairs. The first pair is freedom of speech and belief. These are sometimes described as negative freedoms since it is argued that they should not be constrained by government. The freedoms of speech and belief are among the civil and political rights essential for any form of democracy and political activity. In fact, freedom of speech can be threatened by censorship and by intimidation. Its protection requires policing and courts and the active intervention of governments.

The two other freedoms are freedoms 'from'. The first is the psychological freedom from fear. This is the right of citizens and others living in the state to security, guaranteed through a system of policing and laws. Freedom from want is the right of access to basic standards of nutrition, health care, income and shelter. Without these, human beings are deprived of their capacity to develop their capabilities and thus effectively robbed of their dignity and personal liberty (Sen 2009).

The preamble to UDHR is an expression of cosmopolitanism. This Enlightenment concept, associated notably with Immanuel Kant, is based on a conception of human beings as a single community expressed as 'all members of the human family'. The cosmopolitan perspective has been defined as an ideal that combines: 'a commitment to humanist principles and norms, an assumption of human equality, with a recognition of difference, and indeed a celebration of diversity' (Kaldor 2003, 19).

Human rights are essentially humanist principles and norms, though norms that are also found in all major faith traditions. They are set out in UDHR in thirty articles. Cassin, one of the drafting committee, summarized the content as:

- personal rights (life, freedom, security, justice) in Articles 2–11;
- rights regulating relationship between people (freedom of movement, rights to found a family, asylum, nationality, property) in Articles 12–17;
- public freedoms and political rights (thought, religion, conscience, opinion, assembly, participation, democracy) in Articles 18–21;
- economic, social and cultural rights (social security, work, equal wages, trade unions, rest and leisure, adequate standard of living, education, cultural life) in Articles 22–27 (see Osler and Starkey 2010).

The argument that knowledge and understanding of human rights should underpin citizenship education is based on two premises. First, although national perspectives, traditions and constitutional and legal arrangements are important, they are not the only way of seeing the world. Citizens need to have knowledge and understandings of those universal principles and standards by which they can evaluate the actions and inactions of their governments.

A second consideration is that human rights are the basis of the regime of international law that underpins globalization. The political and economic superstructural elements of globalization, particularly trade deals and the World Trade Organisation, require and interact with a philosophical, moral and legal superstructure. Globalization requires the rule of law and the rule of law requires a philosophical justification based on moral purpose (Bingham 2011; Spring 2015).

Human rights, then, provide a way of looking at the world. The definition of human rights is determined by the rights that are set out formally and definitively in international human rights instruments. Human rights education includes knowledge of human rights instruments and developing a capacity to use the discourse of human rights in struggles for justice.

National and cosmopolitan citizenship: Developing identities

Citizenship education, as noted above, is one response to the questions of living together and preserving and promoting democratic values. It has gained currency in many parts of the world, particularly in response to migration and demographic diversity. National governments, usually controlling publicly funded education, are inclined to develop citizenship education as education for national identity. This is a conception of citizenship education that has its roots in the state formation era of the nineteenth century (Green 2013).

Indeed, as the great American educational philosopher John Dewey warned early in the twentieth century, national education systems have been based on promoting nationalist agendas at the expense of cosmopolitan perspectives. He noted that at the end of the nineteenth century, education 'became a civic function and the civic function was identified with the realization of the ideal of the national state'. The state 'was substituted for humanity; cosmopolitanism gave way to nationalism' (Dewey 1916/2002, 108).

Although nationalist education is the education of citizens, it aims to transmit a particular view of national identity and culture, rather than enabling reflection on plural identities. This model is often known as civic education and is based on education for assimilation into a given national culture. It survives in many contexts in the twenty-first century (Hahn 1998, 2005; Kymlicka 2001; Torney-Purta et al. 1999). However, in a globalizing world of demographic diversity in schools, a nationally focussed citizenship education may be inadequate. A more appropriate formulation incorporating a wider vision based on human rights has been proposed as education for *cosmopolitan* citizenship (Osler and Starkey 2005).

Education for cosmopolitan citizenship is a response to tensions common across the world and identified in the UNESCO report. First is:

> The tension between the global and the local: people need gradually to become world citizens without losing their roots and while continuing to play an active part in the life of their nation and their local community. (Delors 1996, 15)

The tension may be resolved by defining citizenship to include nationality as part of a citizenship identity, but not insisting that nationality determines that identity. Nationality, as Gutmann (2003) points out, is a group identity. However, individuals have numerous group identities associated with, among others, gender, profession, family, ethnicity all of which may extend beyond national boundaries.

Citizenship is a way of understanding one's associations with and connections to others. It can be characterized as having three dimensions: feeling, status and practice (Osler and Starkey 2005). The first element of this definition of citizenship is that it is based on a feeling of belonging or identity: citizens feel that they belong to a community or, more usually, to various communities.

Secondly, citizenship is a status. It can be legal, as a national, and also a moral status as a person entitled to dignity and human rights. Nationality is in the gift of governments that may be tempted on occasions to withhold or rescind it. Yet nationality may be simply an instrumental citizenship. In other words, it may be useful to have access to the passport of a particular country without necessarily feeling much affiliation with it. Moreover, many dual nationals may have affective ties to, and patriotic feelings for, more than one country.

Citizenship is also, thirdly, a practice. The practice of democratic citizenship centres on intervention. Citizens have a sense that they are entitled and empowered to act in the world, in order to defend their own rights or the rights of others. This sense of agency derives from their identity as a citizen. It does not have to be associated with nationality.

In a globalizing world, citizenship education that privileges promoting a national identity often defined by a dominant majority is challenged by sociological realities of many citizens having affective associations with more than one nation. In approving the British census categories for 2011, for instance, the UK government invites those who identify as British Asians to choose an ethnic group identity based on nationality, namely: Indian, Pakistani, Bangladeshi and Chinese (Richards 2016). In other words, since there is an official expectation that citizens may define themselves as British and Indian, for example, the myth of a single salient national identity collapses. More elaborated descriptions of children's identities embracing three continents were recorded by researchers exploring students' understandings of identity and citizenship in a multicultural city (Osler and Starkey 2005). Cosmopolitan citizenship, recognizing the diplomatic realities of national borders but not being constrained within a single national identity, is a status that describes the feelings of many young people in schools (Appiah 2006; Nussbaum and Cohen 1996).

Citizenship education

Citizenship education provides a conceptual framework that logically embraces human rights, global perspectives and equalities issues. The Council of Europe, an inter-governmental organization of forty-seven member states focusing on human rights and cultural policy, has been at the forefront of developing guidance on Education for Democratic Citizenship/Human Rights Education (EDC/HRE). The aims and purposes of citizenship education, as defined collectively by European states, focus on counteracting political forces that attempt to undermine the democratic basis of citizenship. In the early twenty-first-century, European Ministers of Education are concerned by:

> the growing levels of political and civic apathy and lack of confidence in democratic institutions, and by the increased cases of corruption, racism,

xenophobia, aggressive nationalism, intolerance of minorities, discrimination and social exclusion, all of which are major threats to the security, stability and growth of democratic societies. (Council of Europe 2002)

This formulation is very significant since it appears to recognize that, contrary to narratives widely repeated in the popular press, minorities that are not the problem for European states, but rather the inability of majority populations (the dominant communities) and traditional structures to adapt to diversity. It is not the minorities who are major threats; what is undermining democracy and security is, rather, the attitudes and behaviours of the dominant communities within these countries, including corruption, racism, xenophobia, aggressive nationalism, intolerance of minorities.

Another European report confirms that there is an issue with the behaviour and attitudes of majority populations, as it highlights obstacles to living together:

> Discrimination and intolerance are widespread in Europe today, particularly against Roma and immigrants, as well as people of recent migrant background, who are often treated as foreigners even in countries where they are both natives and citizens. (Group of Eminent Persons 2011, 5)

Hostility to immigrants and foreigners stems from a feeling of entitlement reserved for a national community. In other words, a nationalist myth based on privileging a national consciousness that excludes people perceived to be less entitled to national status has gained substantial currency.

Such understandings and attitudes are learned and so citizenship education based on commitments to human rights is recommended as an antidote. The basis for this form of citizenship education is set out in the Council of Europe *Charter on Education for Democratic Citizenship and Human Rights Education* (2010).

Education for citizenship encourages the development of citizenship as an identity. The educational process helps learners to see themselves as citizens. While all human beings have the capacity to be citizens, they only become citizens when they are able to recognize themselves as such. In other words, they need to name the feeling of identity with a social and political community of others as citizenship. When this feeling of identity extends beyond a national framework, and when it acknowledges the importance of human rights, learners may be able to feel and understand themselves as cosmopolitan citizens.

The pedagogical process of developing awareness of one's identity as citizen has been theorized by Hudson (2005), drawing on Bradley (1996), identifying three levels of social identity. The first is a passive or potential identity. All human beings have the capacity to be citizens, but unless they know the word and understand the concept they will not identify as citizen. It is a latent identity. Once they are able to identify themselves as citizens – a process that can be facilitated by citizenship education, learners can move from a passive or potential identity as a citizen to an active and conscious one. At this level, there is a burgeoning sense of agency as they become aware that citizenship is an identity that enables them to challenge injustices and work for change. The third level is characterized as a politicized identity. Building on the sense of agency attached to an identity as active citizen, some people start to view the world through a lens of citizenship. Every relationship, every political decision, every pronouncement is subject to critical appraisal on the basis of the extent of conformity to human rights principles and standards. At this level, citizens have a strong sense of agency and develop skills to become effective participants in change (Osler and Starkey 2005).

UN Convention on the Rights of the Child (CRC 1989)

Many educators have recognized the great significance of the UN Convention on the Rights of the Child (CRC) for their professional activity (Alderson 1999; Howe and Covell 2005; Lansdown 2007; Morrow 1999;). This chapter has introduced general principles relating to human rights, identities and citizenship using the Universal Declaration of Human Rights (UDHR) as the central point of reference. Although UDHR is not, in itself, a convention, in the sense of a binding treaty obligation, its principles underpin subsequent human rights instruments that are recognized formally in international law. The CRC has the status of a convention in international law, and it is the most widely ratified of all human rights treaties. It may be considered as setting out universally agreed norms and standards (Freeman 1996).

When opened for signature in 1989, the CRC reflected changing perspectives on childhood. It introduced a consensus that children (young people under eighteen years) have agency and that their views must be taken into consideration in all decisions that affect them. The rights in the CRC predictably address the specific vulnerability of children and propose standards of provision (e.g. the right to free education) and protection (e.g. a ban on exploitative labour and military service). The great innovation of the convention was its codification of participation rights, such as the right to express views and to have the views taken into consideration. The CRC helped to change the focus from children as needy and helpless to children as citizens with agency. Of course, children exercise agency more or less effectively depending among other issues on their maturity. Nonetheless, they can no longer be considered merely as citizens in waiting (Verhellen 2000). Children are citizens if they feel themselves to be citizens, if they have the status of rights holders and if they act as citizens. Since 1989 the CRC children are citizens and this has implications for relationships in schools and for pedagogy (Osler 2016; Osler and Starkey 2005, 2010).

Rights respecting schools

The legal justification for promoting children's rights through education is found in Articles 28 and 29 of the CRC, which address education and schooling directly. However, other CRC rights are also highly relevant to education since the CRC requires governments, and schools as government funded and controlled institutions, to recognize education as a key human right for all children and to provide education for human rights, and respect the rights of children (Lansdown 2007). This is sometimes expressed as the right to education, rights in education and rights through education (Verhellen 2000) or education about, for and through human rights (Lister 1984). These pedagogical principles are also elaborated in the European and global guidelines on human rights education (Council of Europe 2010; United Nations General Assembly 2011).

Education *about* human rights means providing basic information to develop knowledge and understanding of human rights. This may be considered as part of the right *to* education, which includes the right to human rights education. Education *for* human rights entails developing skills for recognizing and taking action on human rights issues. This is equivalent to the notion of rights *through* education, that is, education as the means to promote human rights. The formulation 'rights in education' is similar to education *through* human rights. It involves experiencing a school climate where the respect of rights is the basis for all activities.

Concrete experiments in developing school structures and education systems that embody the concepts of respect, justice and democracy have a distinguished history. Dewey's laboratory school at the University of Chicago at the end of the nineteenth century provided the basis for his theories of education based on democratic dialogue and shared values (1916/2002). Democracy, in this sense, is not just a system of government, but rather a way of interacting that respects the rights of all to be involved. As former secretary-general of the UN Boutros Boutros-Ghali observed at the time of the World Conference on Human Rights in 1993, democracy is not 'a model to copy from certain States, but a goal to be achieved by all peoples' (quoted in Rivière 2009, 239). Viewed in this way, the focus shifts from the integration of minorities to the development of political systems that ensure the representation and recognition of many voices that have traditionally been marginalized.

Since 2006, the implications of adopting the norms and standards of the CRC to inform whole school policy have been thoroughly explored and evaluated through the UNICEF UK initiative the Rights Respecting Schools Award (RRSA). UNICEF UK is a voluntary association set up to promote the aims of UNICEF and is not a part of the United Nations structure. The scale of the initiative makes it worthy of attention since some 4,000 schools educating 1.5 million students had, by 2017, voluntarily committed to participate in the programme. Schools engage in self-assessment and are subject to external evaluation. The criteria are based on the extent to which child rights are embedded in the school's practice and ethos.[1]

Schools receive the RRSA award when they can demonstrate that the CRC is known and understood by their leadership and integrated into management, curriculum and classroom climate. Pupil participation in decision-making is also a criterion for the award. Schools can work towards either a Level One or a Level Two award depending on how well integrated rights are within the school. Level One is awarded when they can demonstrate that they have shown good progress in four dimensions, namely:

- Rights-respecting values underpin leadership and management
- The whole school community learns about the CRC
- The school has a rights-respecting ethos
- Children and young people are empowered to become active citizens and learners

Level Two is achieved when schools can demonstrate that they have 'fully embedded' the principles and values of the CRC.

The first three years of RRSA (2006–2009), a pilot phase funded by the UK's Labour government in five areas of England, was evaluated with a focus on the impact of the RRSA specifically on the well-being and progress of children in participating schools (Sebba and Robinson 2009, 2010). Well-being of children was of particular concern for the government since a 2007 UNICEF study on child well-being in rich countries placed the UK last out of twenty-one countries overall and seventeen out of twenty-one for educational well-being (UNICEF 2007).

All schools involved in the evaluation study claimed that RRSA provided a framework that made other policies more coherent. Participation in the scheme also increased pupils', staff and parents' sense of well-being and belonging. There was evidence of improved engagement and behaviour and the scheme encouraged positive relationships and supported children to make a contribution locally, nationally and globally (Sebba and Robinson 2009).

The final report noted that in all thirty-one schools surveyed, relationships and behaviour were considered to have improved and could be attributed to:

> an improved understanding by pupils and staff of how to respect rights and greater control exercised by pupils over their own behaviour. In particular, it was noted that there was little or no shouting in school and conflicts between pupils escalated far less frequently than they had done before the schools developed an RRSA approach. (Sebba and Robinson 2010, 18)

These impressive claims may account for some of the increase in take up of the RRSA project. Heads and parents are likely to welcome any scheme that promotes good behaviour.

Other claims perhaps need to be treated with caution (Trivers and Starkey 2012). For example, the claim that pupils became more actively involved in upholding or defending the rights of others might have been better evidenced. The reports reference school projects on global issues, such as school linking with Brazil, Columbia and Ghana and encouragement to purchase fair-trade products or fundraise for a clean water project. However, it is not clear that such projects address inequalities and imbalances in the power relationship in such school to school links. In fact, teachers in three schools suggested that their work supporting pupils to fundraise for projects in partner schools may simply be tokenistic, providing 'a strong feel-good factor by those involved, but no greater understanding of the effect of their actions' (Sebba and Robinson 2009, 10). The evaluators also noted a perhaps somewhat patronizing sense that pupils 'felt sorry for people in poorer countries' (Sebba and Robinson 2010, 26).

Identities and citizenship

The final evaluation report on RRSA provides evidence that children in the programme were likely to acquire identities as citizens. Heads and teachers in all the schools confidently asserted that children and young people learnt to make informed decisions and had experience of being active citizens. Once students recognized their dual identities as learners and citizens, staff reported that it changed and improved the relationships between students and between students and their teachers. Teachers attributed this to the fact that an awareness of their rights led them to an awareness of the rights of others and hence a sense of responsibility (Sebba and Robinson 2010).

Over half the schools in the sample involved students in major decisions such as being represented on the governing body; participating in the interview process when new staff members were hired; providing constructive feedback on teaching and learning processes. In all schools, students were involved in collective decisions and these often concerned aspects of the school environment such as playground equipment, lunchtime arrangements and toilets. Such issues can make a great difference to a sense of well-being in school. Students were also reported as becoming confident, as citizens, to discuss issues of rights, global citizenship and sustainability. Consideration of rights gave them a moral perspective and the possibility of a sense of perspective.

One of UNICEF-UK's aims for the RRSA programme was to promote positive attitudes to diversity. The evaluators found strong evidence with respect to including students and staff with disabilities and those with behavioural or emotional challenges. Students from minoritized backgrounds reported feelings of inclusion and belonging in their RRSA schools, and the evaluators recorded many examples from interviews of students challenging stereotypes and ascribed identities.

The CRC was particularly appreciated in multi-ethnic schools as providing a coherent set of common principles to inform the proclaimed values of the school. Human rights principles were reflected in the school ethos which consequently focused on inclusion and celebrated religious and cultural diversity. Such an ethos sometimes challenged less accepting attitudes that students may bring from their homes and neighbourhoods.

Conclusion

This chapter argues that there is a widespread consensus, exemplified in guidance and policy documents from global and regional transnational organizations, such as UNESCO and the Council of Europe, that learning to live together is the greatest challenge for education in the context of the tensions and turbulence created by globalization. There is a further consensus that human rights education has a central role to play in addressing tensions within societies. The chapter highlights the Convention on the Rights of the Child as being a particularly relevant and powerful basis for human rights education at school level. Human rights education logically finds a place within the curriculum as part of civic or citizenship education.

Citizenship education, when promoted too forcefully as education for national citizenship, may exacerbate rather than mitigate antagonisms and prejudices in multicultural societies by defining national characteristics in a way that excludes some sections of the population. Where citizenship education is based on commitments to universal human rights, it takes on a cosmopolitan as well as a national perspective.

Education for cosmopolitan citizenship recognizes that feelings of identity may be associated with numerous co-existing group identities. It puts into perspective the frequently assumed salience of a national identity.

The Convention on the Rights of the Child provides common, universal, standards and principles to inform the school curriculum in the widest sense of everything that happens in schools. These principles provide the basis for the assertion that children are citizens. The Rights Respecting Schools Award initiative in the UK provides evidence of the benefits to school communities and wider society of drawing inspiration from the utopian vision expressed in human rights instruments.

Learning to live together requires commitment to common standards. These can be invoked when attempting to address tensions. Communities of citizens of all ages that strive for the common good share these common standards and recognize the need to protect the rights of others within and beyond national boundaries. Education for cosmopolitan citizenship inducts young people into a principled view of communities at all levels from the local to the global. It helps young people identify as citizens with agency and a commitment to justice and peace in the world.

Note

1   https://www.unicef.org.uk/rights-respecting-schools/about-the-award/awarded-schools/

References

Adichie, Chimamanda Ngozi. 'The Danger of a Single Story'. 2009. http://www.ted.com/talks/chimamanda_adichie_the_danger_of_a_single_story/transcript?language=en. Transcript available at:http://b.3cdn.net/ascend/2029fab7aa68da3f31_jqm6bn6lz.pdf.

Alderson, Priscilla. 'Human Rights and Democracy in Schools Do They Mean More Than "Picking up Litter and Not Killing Whales"?' *International Journal of Children's Rights* 7 (1999): 185–205.

Appiah, Kwame Anthony. *Cosmopolitanism: Ethics in a World of Strangers*. London: Allen Lane (Penguin), 2006.

Banks, James A., Cherry A. McGee Banks, Carlos E. Cortes, Carole Hahn, Merry Merryfield, Kogila A. Moodley, Stephen Murphy-Shigematsu, Audrey Osler, Caryn Park, and Walter C. Parker. *Democracy and Diversity: Principles and Concepts for Educating Citizens in a Global Age*. Seattle, WA: Center for Multicultural Education, University of Washington, 2005.

Bingham, Tom. *The Rule of Law*. London: Penguin, 2011.

Bradley, Harriet. *Fractured Identities: Changing Patterns of Inequality*. Cambridge: Polity, 1996.

Castles, Stephen. 'The Challenges of International Migration in the 21st Century'. In *Citizenship Education and Global Migration: Implications for Theory, Research and Teaching*, edited by James A. Banks, 3–22. Washington, DC: AERA, 2017.

Council of Europe. 'Recommendation by the Committee of Ministers of Education R (2002)12 on Education for Democratic Citizenship'. Strasbourg: Council of Europe, 2002.

Council of Europe. *Charter on Education for Democratic Citizenship and Human Rights Education Recommendation Cm/Rec (2010)7 and Explanatory Memorandum*. Strasbourg: Council of Europe, 2010.

Delors, Jacques. *Learning: The Treasure Within*. Paris: UNESCO, 1996.

Dewey, John. 'Democracy and Education: An Introduction to the Philosophy of Education'. In *John Dewey and American Education*, Vol. 3, edited by S. J. Maxcy. Bristol: Thoemmes, 2002. Original work published in 1916.

European Commission. 'European Commission – Fact Sheet: European Agenda on Security – State of Play 17 November 2015'. Brussels: European Commission Press Release Database, 2015.

European Union Ministers of Education. *Declaration on Promoting Citizenship and the Common Values of Freedom, Tolerance and Non-Discrimination through Education (Paris Declaration)*. Paris: European Council, 2015.

Freeman, Michael, eds. *Children's Rights: A Comparative Perspective*. Aldershot: Ashgate, 1996.

Green, Andy. *Education and State Formation: Europe, East Asia and the USA* (2nd edition). Basingstoke: Palgrave Macmillan, 2013.

Group of Eminent Persons. *Living Together: Combining Diversity and Freedom in 21st-Century Europe*. Strasbourg: Council of Europe, 2011.

Gutmann, Amy. *Identity in Democracy*. Woodstock, UK: Princeton University Press, 2003.

Hahn, Carole. *Becoming Political: Comparative Perspectives on Citizenship Education*. Albany: State University of New York Press, 1998.

Hahn, Carole. 'Diversity and Human Rights Learning in England and the United States'. In *Teachers, Human Rights and Diversity: Educating Citizens in Multicultural Societies*, edited by Audrey Osler, 23–40. Stoke on Trent: Trentham, 2005.

Howe, Brian and Katherine Covell. *Empowering Children: Children's Rights Education as a Pathway to Citizenship*. Toronto: University of Toronto Press, 2005.

Hudson, Anne. 'Citizenship Education and Students' Identities: A School-based Action Research Project'. In *Teachers, Human Rights and Diversity: Educating Citizens in Multicultural Societies*, edited by Audrey Osler, 115–132. Stoke on Trent: Trentham, 2005.

Kaldor, Mary. 'American Power: From "Compellance" to Cosmopolitanism?' *International Affairs* 79, no. 1 (2003): 1–22.

Klug, Francesca. *Values for a Godless Age: The Story of the UK's New Bill of Rights*. Harmondsworth: Penguin, 2000.

Kymlicka, Will. *Politics in the Vernacular: Nationalism, Multiculturalism and Citizenship*. Oxford: Oxford University Press, 2001.

Lansdown, Gerison. *A Human Rights-Based Approach to Education for All*. New York and Paris: UNICEF and UNESCO, 2007.

Lister, Ian. *Teaching and Learning about Human Rights*. Strasbourg: Council of Europe, 1984.

Mannheim, Karl. *Ideology and Utopia: An Introduction to the Sociology of Knowledge*. London: Routledge, 1991. Original work published in 1929 and 1936.

Mejias, Sam and Hugh Starkey. 'Critical Citizens or Neoliberal Consumers? Utopian Visions and Pragmatic Uses of Human Rights Education in a Secondary School in England'. In *Politics, Participation and Power Relations: Transdisciplinary Approaches to Critical Citizenship in the Classroom and Community*, edited by Richard C. Mitchell and Shannon A. Moore, 119–136. Rotterdam: Sense, 2012.

Morrow, Virginia. '"We Are People Too": Children's and Young People's Perspectives on Children's Rights and Decision-Making in England'. *International Journal of Children's Rights* 7 (1999): 149–170.

Nussbaum, Martha Craven and Joshua Cohen. *For Love of Country: Debating the Limits of Patriotism*. Boston: Beacon Press, 1996.

Osler, Audrey. *Human Rights and Schooling: An Ethical Framework for Teaching Social Justice*. New York NY: Teachers College Press, 2016.

Osler, Audrey and Hugh Starkey. *Changing Citizenship: Democracy and Inclusion in Education*. Maidenhead: Open University Press, 2005.

Osler, Audrey and Hugh Starkey. *Teachers and Human Rights Education*. Stoke-on-Trent: Trentham, 2010.

Richards, Raphael. 'Not in My Image: Ethnic Diversity in the Classroom'. In *Key Issues for Teaching Assistants:Working in Diverse and Inclusive Classrooms* (2nd edition), edited by Gill Richards and Felicity Armstrong, 31–41. Abingdon: Routledge, 2016.

Rivière, Françoise, ed. *UNESCO World Report. Investing in Cultural Diversity and Intercultural Dialogue*. Paris: UNESCO, 2009.

Sebba, Judy and Carol Robinson. *Evaluation of UNICEF UK's Rights Respecting Schools Award – Interim Report at the End of Year Two*. London: UNICEF UK, 2009.

Sebba, Judy and Carol Robinson. *Evaluation of UNICEF UK's Rights Respecting Schools Award. Final Report*. London: UNICEF UK, 2010.

Sen, Amartya. *Identity and Violence. The Illusion of Destiny*. London: Allen Lane, 2006.

Sen, Amartya. *The Idea of Justice*. London: Allen Lane, 2009.

Spring, Joel. *Globalization of Education: An Introduction*. New York: Routledge, 2015.

Torney-Purta, Judith, J. Schwille, and J. Amadeo. *Civic Education across Countries: Twenty-Four National Case Studies from the IEA Civic Education Project*. Amsterdam: Eburon/International Association for the Evaluation of Educational Achievement (IEA), 1999.

Touraine, Alain. *Can We Live Together? Equality and Difference*. Cambridge: Polity, [1997] 2000.

Trivers, Helen and Hugh Starkey. 'The Politics of Critical Citizenship Education: Human Rights for Conformity or Emancipation?' In *Politics, Participation and Power Relations: Transdisciplinary Approaches to Critical Citizenship in the Classroom and Community*, edited by Richard C. Mitchell and Shannon A. Moore, 137–152. Rotterdam: Sense, 2012.

UNICEF. *Child Poverty in Perspective: An Overview of Child Well-Being in Rich Countries (Innocenti Report Card 7)*. Florence: Unicef Innocenti Research Centre, 2007.

United Nations General Assembly. 'United Nations Declaration on Human Rights Education and Training'. New York: Office of the High Commissioner for Human Rights (OHCHR), 2011.

Verhellen, Eugeen. 'Children's Rights and Education'. In *Citizenship and Democracy in Schools: Diversity, Identity, Equality*, edited by Audrey Osler, 33–43. Stoke-on-Trent: Trentham, 2000.

10

Exercising Global Citizenship in the Family: The Case of Language Brokering

Ann Phoenix

Chapter outline

- Introduction
- Childhood language brokering
- The Study
- Enabling global citizenship within and across international borders
- Lifelong commitment to acts of global citizenship
- Processes of developing global citizenship
  - Language brokering as systemic belonging
  - Building confidence and skills
  - Recognition of unfavourable positioning in power relations
- Conclusion
- Note

Keywords: language brokering; acts of citizenship; transnational families; belonging; positioning; power relations

Introduction

The notion of global citizenship brings together ideas about identities, relationality and active engagement in communities, increased ease of travel and recognition of international ecological, political and economic interlinkages and new modes of communication. It, therefore, is concerned with global connectedness, social justice and cosmopolitan perspectives (Carter 2013). Israel (2013), from The Global Citizens Initiative, defines a global citizen as 'someone who identifies with being part of an emerging world community and whose actions contribute to building this community's values and practices'. Global citizens thus require knowledge, understanding and skills that enable them to function both within and beyond cultural communities and borders (Banks 2017), 'making connections across lines of difference and distinction ... while keeping and deepening a sense of one's own identity and integrity' (McIntosh 2005, 23).

While work on citizenship education has burgeoned (e.g. Osler and Starkey 2005), that research generally focuses on what children should be taught, rather than on what they do as global citizens in particular contexts. Yet, as Isin and Nielsen (2013) suggest, people become citizens through 'acts of citizenship'. In other words, citizenship is about practices, rather than simply a conferred status. In their everyday practices, young children (aged 5–13 years) have been shown to understand 'acts of citizenship', making rules about social behaviour and about how to contribute to the social good and exercised freedom to achieve their own rights (Larkins 2014). The fact that children can routinely exercise global citizenship is often evident as children engage in the work of language brokering, interpreting and translating for their parents and others. While children are often popularly considered to be obliged to do this work by their parents and due to their parental circumstances, research on childhood language brokering shows that they express agency about their work and are active negotiators, helping their families to settle and engage in employment in countries where they do not yet speak the local language. In doing so, their work affords their families access to resources and information as well as understanding of the society in which they live. Children help to 'make it possible for their family to live, eat, shop and otherwise sustain themselves as workers, citizens and consumers in their host country' (Orellana 2009, 124). They are undoubtedly part of what Israel (2013) calls an emerging world community whose actions contribute to building community values and practices and provide the knowledge and skills required for their families to function within and beyond cultural communities and borders (Banks 2017). Language brokering can thus be seen as a neglected example of children's everyday practices of global citizenship (Bauer 2010) and part of their general translanguaging practices (Orellana 2015).

This chapter focuses on childhood language brokering. It first briefly discusses current understanding of childhood language brokering then describes the study of adults looking back on their experiences of childhood language brokering that informs the chapter. The main part of the chapter illuminates why language brokering constitutes acts of citizenship of benefit to society and transnational communities. In particular, it explores how children use their knowledge and skills to maintain networks of relationship and connection (McIntosh 2005).

Childhood language brokering

Child language brokering is not a new phenomenon, but as migration has increasingly become part of public imaginaries in many countries, attention to children's contributions to their families' negotiations of everyday life in their new countries has also burgeoned. Available research publications give important insights into how childhood language brokering is enacted in different contexts, parent–child relations, how children feel about it and the skills they acquire and deploy in doing language brokering. Findings are somewhat contradictory with reports of children being unreasonably stressed from having to interpret in contexts that are difficult, or painful as in hospitals or banks. Others find that children mostly enjoy language brokering and are proud to do this work for their families (AKam and Lazarevic 2014; Hall and Guery 2010). Children have been reported in some studies to be 'adultified' through language brokering, with related stresses on parent–child relations and parents being unhealthily dependent on their children (Dorner 2017). Other studies report that parents and children develop close bonds where children are language brokers (Morales and Hanson 2005; Weisskirch 2010). Language brokers are also identified as active advocates of their parents' rights in complex situations (Morales and Hanson 2005, 494).

Very little is known, however, about what language brokering means to children, and the implications for their adulthood (cf. Orellana 2009). No research to date has explored how adults narrate their experiences as child language brokers, and how their perspectives on their language brokering experience change as they grow from children into adults. Additionally, the link between language brokering and citizenship contributions remains unexplored. For example, a major gap in the literature relates to children's engagement as citizens in their activities as language brokers. Orellana (2009) pioneered understanding that children's language brokering is skilled work that may sometimes be pleasurable and sometimes stressful, but that gives children skills their peers take longer to acquire, including how to listen and paraphrase meanings, or the nuts and bolts about employment, housing, shopping and medical care among other things (Dorner et al. 2007). What is evident from this burgeoning literature is that children have strong viewpoints about language brokering and that how they experience language brokering is contingent on context, their age perceived competence and how their brokering is received among other things (Cline et al. 2011, 2014). From her longitudinal study of child language brokers at home, school and in public settings, Orellana argues that the children's work helps to ensure that their parents can be good citizens, able to pay their taxes, obey the laws and maintain their employment and family lives.

Children frequently seek to protect their parents and other family members from humiliation. This aspect of childhood language brokering also receives relatively little attention. Yet, since McQuillan and Tse (1995) coined the term language brokering, it has been recognized that children also broker the culture when they convert meanings from one language into meanings in another language (Hall and Sham 2007). If little attention has been paid to children's contributions to their parents' citizenship practices, even less has been paid to children's citizenship practices in interpreting and translating for their parents. In a rare exception, Bauer (2010) suggests that in 'helping out' their families through language brokering, children are, as Orellana (2009) suggests, making productive contributions to society that may be seen as contributing to agentic citizenship 'as individuals who are creating particular roles, and effecting desired outcomes as active citizens, and not merely being passive in these situations' (143). In this process, they also learn about a variety of citizenship practices and how to challenge issues they disagree with and to be actively engaged in society.

This chapter focuses on the ways in which childhood language brokers exercise global citizenship through their work of interpreting and translating for their parents and others by examining the narratives of adults who have been language brokers as children. While retrospective studies cannot claim that participants are remembering exactly what happened when and in detail, such accounts demonstrate the contemporary significance of events in participants' current lives (Josselson 2009; Orellana and Phoenix 2017). The section below briefly describes the study that informs this chapter before discussing examples of adults looking back on their language brokering and considering its significance for their current lives.

The study

This study is part of a programme of research 'Transforming experiences: Re-conceptualising identities and "non-normative" childhoods' funded by the UK Economic and Social Science Research Council.[1] It focused on the ways in which adults from different family backgrounds negotiate their identities as they re-evaluate their earlier experiences. The family backgrounds central to the study are common for many families, but are often considered non-normative and non-ideal. Three sets of family experiences were examined, where children were (i) serial migrants who came from the Caribbean to rejoin their parents in the UK; (ii) households whose family members were considered visibly ethnically different and (iii) childhood language brokers, who interpreted and/or translated for their parents in childhood. All the participants were recruited through a variety of means that included posting notices in community groups, libraries, adverts in community newspapers and snowballing.

This chapter focuses on evidence from the third project. Forty adult language brokers (twenty-seven women and thirteen men) were interviewed individually in five countries and three group discussions with some of those interviewed individually were held in the UK and the United States. The aim was to focus on language brokering broadly rather than language brokers from any particular language group. The participants in the study enacted language brokering between English and fifteen other languages: Arabic, Bengali, Cantonese, Croatian, Greek, Gujarati, Italian, Mandarin, Punjabi, Self-constructed Sign language, Somali, Spanish, Swedish, Turkish and Urdu. A further participant interpreted and translated from Arabic to Swedish. Participants reported that they began interpreting at ages between five and thirteen years of age. Many continue to do language brokering work for their parents and other family members at the time of interview. Their mean age at the time they were interviewed was thirty-three years old. All the interviews were fully transcribed.

The participants were asked to look back on their childhoods and tell the stories of their language brokering in any way they chose. The aim was to understand the ways in which they re-conceptualized their experiences over time and the impact of those experiences on their identities. The interviews were first analysed thematically. Since narrative analysis is time-intensive, only some were analysed narratively. Interviews from each theme were selected for narrative analysis ensuring that participants in different countries were included. Particular attention was paid to the answer to the first question since the initial invitation to tell their stories frequently elicited mention of the themes elaborated in the rest of the interview and constituted the rationale for conducting narrative analysis on the first part of the interview (Phoenix et al. 2016). The participants below have been selected because they exemplify multiple ways in which language brokers enact global citizenship.

Enabling global citizenship within and across international borders

One of the reasons that the adults interviewed brokered language in childhood was because they were members of transnational families. In helping their families, they sometimes acted as language brokers for members of the family who lived in their families' countries of origin, particularly if they had family members who wanted to migrate to join them. The following extract is taken from the opening of an interview, conducted via Skype, with Fong, a woman in her mid-twenties, who is of Chinese origin and lives in California.

> And I remember at that time it was … when my mother was trying to petition her family, her two sisters and her brother over from China. … And you know, the (.) the entire immigration process is (.) is (.) takes a long, long time, I think I remember maybe it took ten years, the entire thing, … so I remember im- you know, translating immigration paperwork, calling immigration several times, um and (.) and being put on hold (laughs) several times for long periods of time. But I think having them arrive you know, you're seeing the fruits of your labour, I think it's (.) it's kind of rewarding in that sense um but you know, didn't see it for a long time … that was a big project um I think some of the smaller projects were just you know, writing cheques and things like that. Um and as a matter of fact, I think when my brother and I both went to [university] um she (.) my parents were you know, at home (.) without you know, anyone to language broker for them and that (.) that year was actually very difficult because um they didn't (.) they don't know how to use email quite … I think that's the reason why I (.) … I chose to move back down. Um just so that someone was there uh to do writing cheques, I also translate for (.) for the relatives now that they're here … I do more for the relatives now than I do for my parents.

Narrative is generally agreed to be 'defined … by sequences with a specific order' (Andrews et al. 2013, 13). Riessman (2008) describes this connecting of events into a sequence as accomplished because it is 'consequential for later action and for the meanings that the speaker wants listeners to take away from the story' (3). In narrative analysis, then, researchers need to pay attention to how participants sequence their accounts and the meanings that particular sequences allow and produce. It is, therefore, important that, at the start of her interview, Fong situates her account chronologically, explaining that she cannot remember doing very much language brokering until middle school. She then explains that she did a lot of language brokering until she went to university and that, after her brother also moved away to university, she transferred to a local university in order to help her parents by language brokering. At the start of the interview, she is clear that language brokering is both something she feels is one of her family responsibilities and an important part of her identity so that ensuring proximity to her parents is an important part of her language brokering story. She is, as McIntosh (2005) suggests, important to global citizenship, showing empathy in preserving a network of relationship and connection across family differences and in deepening her sense of identity in doing so. What she identifies as 'small project' work of everyday interpreting and translation enabled her parents to function in the US society and so facilitated their global citizenship.

One of the first stories Fong tells in the interview is of spending time, over maybe ten years, following up her mothers' petitioning to get her siblings to the United States from China. Fong could not do this work without considering relations between different countries and what it means to be part of a transnational family and reasons that people migrate. She also had to get to grips with immigration regulations and to mediate between them and immigration officials. It is irrelevant whether this took ten years or a different length of time, Fong's actions in relation to her aunts' and uncle's migration claim helped her to recognize herself as globally interconnected, contributing to social justice (Carter 2013), identifying with being part of an emerging world community and contributing to building this community's values and practices (Israel 2013). Fong's statement that 'I think having them arrive you know, you're seeing the fruits of your labour. I think it's (…) it's kind of rewarding in that sense um but you know, didn't see it for a long time … that was a big project', shows how she views what she did as large-scale, longitudinal, goal-oriented hard work that was successful and paid off. She has enabled her relatives' citizenship claims and human rights in rejoining the family, and engaged in long-term 'acts of citizenship' (Isin and Nielsen 2013), working to change social arrangements in agentic ways. Fong is undoubtedly functioning within and beyond cultural communities and borders (Banks 2017). In many ways, therefore, she was exercising global citizenship through her language brokering.

Lifelong commitment to acts of global citizenship

Fong's example shows how of language brokering work can enable global citizenship for people across the world and for the language brokers' parents. Childhood language brokering can also open language brokers' eyes to social injustice that leads them to form lifelong commitments to working to address social injustice. Many reported experiences of seeing the difficulties their parents and others faced because they were not fluent in the local language. They told stories of how they and their parents were denigrated as a result of the language they spoke and often subjected to racism. These experiences were extremely painful and often anxiety provoking. As children, they were sometimes working as language brokers in situations of consequence for their families. Those experiences animated their hearts and minds (Orellana 2015) and constituted turning points in their lives (Dorner 2017).

In the extract below, Matt, who was the first Australian child born to migrant parents from Italy, reflects on how his experiences of language brokering led to his social commitment to work with adults when he became adult.

> Matt: [A]nd then many years later, when I did a lot of immigrant work I- I worked for the unions for some years working with immigrant, mainly mi- immigrant women workers, Timorese refugees and Italian women workers in factories and stuff. ... and I worked for uh a kind of social welfare (pause) public support agency for immigrants and mainly volunteer work and uh I (pause) I didn't know why actually I was driven in to do- doing that, but then I (pause) I realised later why I was doing it. I was sort of um trying to (pause) psychologically trying to do something for my parents in a proxy way and uh but I remember I- being engaged in that process and thinking how very different it was an advocate there, it was a experientially, a completely different thing. And I often found like there was this double agent in my head you know, there was this kind of different person (pause) talking on behalf of other people um partly to re-present another experience that had occurred to me. Because I could see that it was really a (pause) a consequence of the social position of people ... (Matt, in his fifties)

Matt's explanation of why he spent much of his career in advocacy work with migrants almost suggests that he had no agency in the process but was impelled by unconscious forces. His account suggests that he realized in adulthood that he was symbolically trying to compensate his parents for what they had suffered through not speaking English in Australia. In the rest of his interview he describes many anxious occasions where he had to language broker in contexts that were consequential for his parents' health and financial affairs.

While Matt's account is striking, it fits with those of many others in the study who wanted to contribute to migrant communities in some way. Leung, for example, a student in his twenties in California, helps with medical screening programmes for people like his parents and grandparents.

> Leung: Well, because I think I grew up doing this and it (.) I've been doing it for a long time, I don't attach like too much significance to it but (swallows) um I

thought about because um I work with a community service group that does screenings for the underserved API, the Asian Pacific under-population in Los Angeles, and most of them are also first generation. My parents' age or older like my grandparents' age and they don't speak English and so we have to use like our knowledge of whatever languages we know to communicate with them./ ... /

As with Matt, Leung (in his twenties) suggests that he has not thought about what attracted him to working with people who come from the Asian continent and do not speak English. However, he links not attaching much significance to his childhood language brokering and his voluntary work as a teenager and young adult. The fact that his volunteering involves interpreting and translation suggests that his own experience has fuelled his commitment to making a civic contribution and exercising global responsibility as he works with international migrants who bring global relations into the US context.

Many participants performed informal language brokering for family friends, family members and as they got older, for children they noticed were language brokering. In the UK, Ambika explains how voluntary work can itself have an impact on family expectations and so pull language brokering further into citizenship work.

I felt it was my duty to support my mum and my dad ... and for example, my extended family live quite close ... so they'd often invite me round or if I had popped round there, this is more in my teenage years and during my time at the university when I'd come back and visit them, they'd ask me to translate information. For example, ... because they were aware that I used to volunteer at the Citizen's Advice Bureau, so therefore they thought I was a qualified and specialist advisor on every legal issue, but (.) even though I wasn't. So um like um completing DWP (UK Department of Work and Pensions) pension forms and how to claim in- c- carer's benefits for my uncle, my aunt often asked me about the procedures and protocols and what financial documents would be required. So I'd look through the kind of forms and things and explain to her what it meant and what [pause] what [pause] you know, who would be eligible and whether they should qualify, etc., so that [pause] that's another example. Um others included um I'd often suggest to my parents, especially now that they're retired and my aunts and uncles in their similar age group, that there's a lot of networking opportunities in the community and there's a lot of groups for Asian community people to join, if they wanted to kinda find out [pause] you know, develop links within the Gujarati community. ... signposting them to activities local authority led or voluntary sector led. ... So [pause] which I'm happy to help out so that's just an example.

It was not only that Ambika wanted to be involved with translating financial documents but that her volunteering served to identify her as someone skilled and willing to help in these areas. More than this however, Ambika saw her role as ensuring that her parents and other older Gujarati people stayed active and networked. She, therefore, facilitated opportunities for them to engage in activities and socialize.

Other participants went into professions, or worked in areas of their professions, where they could directly help migrants, children who were translanguaging or adults who required language brokering as well as campaign for changes in (local) language policies. This was the case, for example for Feyzi, a UK sports teacher in his forties, who came from Turkey as a child and chooses to work in multilingual schools. When asked to tell his story about language brokering, he responded:

> Feyzi: Well it [language brokering] doesn't [end] because um while your parents are (.) are alive, they continue (.) to need that support ... I never realised that I was really doing this until I got to secondary school um when uhhhh you'd have open evenings. And um it was clear that uh my (.) my stepfather couldn't get to open evenings. He was very committed to supporting us, and he was great as a stepfather, but he worked at nights so he couldn't get to open evenings, so it was my mother. And her view was 'well there's no point in me going because I don't understand what goes on' and when we did manage to get her to attend, uh her view afterwards was 'well they didn't really talk to me, you know, they'd talk to you' th- you know, and uh I remember her very clearly saying that 'well one teacher, he never even looked at me, you know, so what is the point of me going along?' So you (.) you start to you know, some of the thoughts going through my mind was about um the (.) the (.) the lack of respect, if you like, for (.) for my (.) for my parents and (.) and (.) and their attempt to support me in my learning. And I suppose that had some uh effect for me, in terms of my behaviour in that school, um in my secondary school ... And so as I got older and started sort of you, you know, beginning to make some sense of what was going on around me, that business about the lack of respect for my parents used to play on my mind a lot. ... But the ... experience ... of my family convinced me that um in (.) in terms of, you know, this lack of respect, the fact that they didn't understand English, didn't mean ... that they weren't interested in me and me doing well. You know, it was a huge commitment to making sure that all three boys did well in school, you know, um (swallows) meant that it has actually impacted big time in my thinking about when I came into teaching and start to find my way in teaching. Uh I was at (.) you know, I was determined that the kids that I was engaging with and (.) and their families, weren't going to have the same sort of experiences. ... And I remember very distinctly like in my first week in that school [in his first job] with a number of teachers saying to me 'well, you know,

you'll be alright with one or two of these kids but you know, the (.) the Asian families, they just don't get engaged with their kids and they're … not interested in sport.' And that was like um a challenge for me, you know, 'cos they were wrong, but it was (.) it was about how then I could do something about that and by the time I finished in that first year, um I had a dozen families come to every football, every netball game, every cricket game, every athletics events. Um, we ran parents and kids activities and … so on, and parents were turning up in … hundreds. … And it transpired we had a … mother from Trinidad who was … an international cricket player, you know, and we didn't know. So I started using her by having her coming along and coaching some of the kids. You know, and all of that just built up, so it was about you know, I could do something about this 'cos I had some sort of experience about what it felt like not being engaging with the kids because uh the system didn't allow it. … [I]t gave me a lot of incentive and drive to try and influence the system from within, if you like, and work in the system. Um yeah, so … that's … all I would say really in terms of that effect.

A key theme for Feyzi was the disrespect faced by his mother because she did not speak English. His indignation about what he came to see as the unjust and unwarranted equation of lack of interest and encouragement with not speaking English has permeated his life and career. While he allows for the possibility that the discrimination that rankles with him is unwitting, he indicates that such assumptions continue to be routinely held even in ethnically mixed schools where he has worked. He identifies himself as counterposing other teachers' assumptions that migrant parents are not interested in their children's education. His stories of engaging parents through sport serve both to show other teachers that such parents are interested in their children's schooling and that he values the contributions of parents from across the globe, with Asia and the Caribbean being specifically mentioned. In Israel's (2013) terms, he identified as a member of an emerging world community in the UK and was contributing to building this community's values and practices. He was, in addition, challenging the status quo in relation to views of translanguaging and making local shifts in how multilingual populations were seen. In doing so, he was enabling a wide range of parents take part, and be included in. their children's education and so to be part of society more generally. His acts of citizenship, therefore, helped parents from a range of ethnic backgrounds to engage in acts of citizenship.

The question of why it is that childhood language brokering engenders adult commitments to civic responsibilities that are part of exercising global citizenship are explored below.

Processes of developing global citizenship

From the language brokers' accounts, three factors seem central in the accounts above. First, many participants described language brokering as having given them a sense of belonging to, and responsibility for, their families and broader collectivities. Second, they had gained skills that made them feel efficacious and able to use their agency to improve the circumstances of people with whom they felt common cause, particularly children and young people. Third, language brokering gave many a keen sense of social justice because they came to recognize that they, or their parents were subjected to discrimination and racism because of their parents' lack of fluency in the local language.

Language brokering as systemic belonging

The extract below, from Amorita, a Californian language broker in her fifties from a Mexican family, shows how adults who had been language brokers could see themselves as part of a family system where children had their part to play.

> It was not a chore ... as I got older I felt it was a contribution ... I was helping my family help me ... I was helping my grandmother take care of me. I took great pride in that, and I always felt honoured that I was the one that got to do that ... it's such a natural order ... just like you come together to eat ... family help each other. And throughout the world, that means children help too. That's part of a family, is that everybody extends their hand and [pause] and that it's a good lovely thing to do and to experience. To [pause] to be needed in that way and to be helpful in that way.

From Amorita's retrospective view, language brokering is part of the reciprocal caring duties within families and one that she feels that helped her grandmother, who was responsible for her upbringing and spoke only Spanish, to take care of her. She describes her family unit, herself and her grandmother, in systemic terms, where helping each other, and belonging together, are both natural and lovely.

Building confidence and skills

Amorita's reported pride in language brokering was commonly reported by other participants, particularly when it seemed to go well (Orellana 2009). Sonita, in her twenties, with parents from Bangladesh, typifies the positive gains language brokers reported (Bauer 2010).

> Mm well I feel as though I've become much more confident ... I've learnt a lot about ... different people, like if you're interpreting for someone you do learn different things. That maybe if I hadn't interpreted I wouldn't have known. ... In general I think I ... interpreting has helped me a lot to understand different things, the way our parents think, the way our aunties, the older generation think. It does broaden your knowledge a bit, cos you know about other things. Whereas if you were associating with your age group you wouldn't know these things and you wouldn't think that far, or you wouldn't think that wide. ... I don't know how to say this, you wouldn't see it through whereas when you're like maybe interpreting for your parents, they go more in depth, certain things that, maybe we wouldn't realise until we were much older. So as a person it did make me more mature I think. Yeah.

Sonita identified social skills of understanding the older generation and their thinking as well as precociously learning 'other things'. The skills reported by participants and commonly described by language brokers related to understanding finance, housing and health care (Bauer 2016; Dorner, Orellana, and Li-Grining 2007). These skills are part of developing knowledge about citizenship practices. It is well established that language brokering, and translanguaging more generally, can build important academic skills, creativity and critical thinking and confidence for dealing with everyday practices (Bauer 2010, 2013; García and Wei 2015; Orellana 2009, 2015).

Recognition of unfavourable positioning in power relations

Language brokers often gained a sense of their own agency, efficacy and worth as well as skills that allowed them to understand that they could act on the world and ways in which it is possible to do so. This understanding is central to developing citizenship practices. Recognition that they and their families were positioned less powerfully than most others in society, subjected to discrimination or taken advantage of because of the intersections of their language, ethicized and racialized positioning, frequently catalysed acts to improve the circumstances of their families and others who faced similar issues. This recognition was even part of the reported experiences of those childhood language brokers whose narratives were overall very positive. For example, directly after telling stories about the acclaim he received for language brokering abroad, Omar told a story of how his confidence in his language brokering was used to exploit his parents.

Omar: Sometimes it was uh a pain, 'okay right, here we go translating again'. [Five seconds pause] I remember once also, there was a translation between a builder who wanted their paperwork signing off because we had some work done on the house on a grant and he wanted that form of completion. And he was adamant that it should be filled in and my father was saying that … he didn't want to sign it, so I was actually on [pause] I was probably stuck in the middle of these two. So finally convinced my father to sign the form, I didn't realise until later what that form was, that it was assumed [pause] the builder was saying that everything's built to a standard and he was happy with it and that's it, there's no issues. My father understood that but I didn't realise so [pause] so my father signed it and I remember a month later, the roof was leaking and the builder goes 'tough, you've already signed the uh got that signed.' So I didn't quite grasp the concept of what's going on there and I was trying to tell my dad 'look, he just wants it signed' I thought [pause] you know. You're stuck in the middle [laughs].

Omar's positive experiences in language brokering had given him sufficient confidence that, from the safe distance of more than two decades, he was relatively sanguine about remembering how the family linguistic positioning rendered them vulnerable to exploitation.

Other language brokers also told stories showing their early learning that they and their families occupied devalued positions. One concomitant effect of this was that they learned early to recognize injustice and to see it not just for their family, but across a range of groups. From their adult views, this early recognition was so strong that it permeated their consciousness. Leung, aged twenty-one years, explains:

Leung: And growing up in upstate New York, there wasn't a large Asian population and uh my teacher instead of, I guess, encouraging me to try harder to pick up the language at the same rate as my peers, she actually, I guess, kinda had pity on me in a bit [pause] and she didn't require the same amount of I think [pause] I guess standard from me, so I didn't have to work as hard or didn't have to get it as quickly as other students did. And it would be okay with her and for me, I knew that I that I was receiving some special attention in that way and I thought that was really great because I was like 'oh, you can get away with this'. But um when I was around five, they moved to California and that's when it completely changed because in Northern California, in the Bay area, there's a very large Asian American population. And I was thrown into the school district where [pause] I had a lot of peers that looked like me and they could speak English perfectly fine, so at that stage I could see that there was a problem there. And at the time, I was just thinking 'oh, like I won't be able to make friends' you know, but now thinking back on it, it's like you know, there's that difference there. So I entered some speech programmes um my English improved a lot and both for my parents I guess their language capacity mostly stayed around like pretty basic English.

Leung's disjunctive experiences led him to new understandings of his intersectional positioning in very early childhood. The memories he cites are iconic, saturated with emotion and retrospective evaluation. The accretion of such examples for all the sample members led to recognition that their families were unfavourably positioned in power relations and were often discriminated against. In response, childhood language brokers sometimes reported that they experienced acute embarrassment that took them some time to overcome.

The unequal power relations that the childhood language brokers described were exacerbated by the precariousness of many of their families' economic positioning so that many developed strong feelings of responsibility for their families and described language brokering as an overwhelming responsibility with the attendant anxiety that they would interpret or translate incorrectly with negative consequences (Bauer 2010, 2017).

Conclusions

This chapter has considered the ways in which adults retrospectively evaluate their experiences of having been language brokers in childhood. Many of their narratives illuminate ways in which childhood language brokering constitutes acts of citizenship that are of benefit to society and transnational communities. Childhood language brokering is recognized to enable parents to live everyday lives, managing issues as mundane as shopping and as consequential as health and mortgage affairs in ways that allow them to be good citizens in the country to which they have migrated. Language brokering was thus of benefit at the time to language brokers and their families and helped the brokers to engage in acts of citizenship as well as helping their parents and others to exercise their citizenship claims, manage their mobility and settle into their new country (Bauer 2010, 2017; Orellana 2009, 2015). When they grew up, the citizenship choices language brokers made often proved beneficial to society. More implicitly, language brokering enabled local language speakers who interact with childhood language brokers to do their jobs efficiently and, where relevant, to profit from those interactions. Language brokers make contributions to society through their unpaid work in institutions such as schools, tax and healthcare (Orellana 2009). As the mediating partners in such interactions, childhood language brokers learn skills and often gain confidence (even from situations that make them anxious) that are central to being able, as agents, to engage in acts of citizenship. Those acts are global in that they bring together people from different language communities who otherwise would have difficulty communicating with each other and sometimes they enable relatives from other countries to deal with immigration applications (cf. McIntosh 2005).

In adulthood, some participants constructed their experiences of language brokering in childhood as giving them the impetus to attempt to ameliorate the circumstances of migrants and/or people who required language brokering services both in voluntary capacities and sometimes in employment. From their accounts, there were three sets of reasons for the link between childhood language brokering and the responsibility and desire the participants felt to help others who are in comparable positions to those in which they had been. First, childhood language brokering gave them skills and confidence that they could act on the world and on other people's behalf. Second, it gave them keen senses of belonging both to their families and to wider collectivities. Third, it enabled them to recognize that they and their families, as well as others in their positions, were positioned unfavourably in power relations. The empathy and responsibility that childhood language brokers reported feeling for their parents, other family members and people disadvantaged through migration, linguistic difference or racism is not only the province of language brokering. Children living in poverty frequently also attempt to protect their parents from knowledge of how difficult they find this experience (Pugh 2009). Both are, therefore psychosocial, about the inextricable linking of structures and emotions. However, childhood language brokering as active citizenship enables the brokers creatively to make up practices to deal with the situations in which they find themselves. Their solidaristic *acts* of citizenship both allow them some autonomy and reflexivity that prepares them for adulthood and further contributions to global citizenship.

It follows from this that, although teachers are sometimes reluctant for children to broker language, that children themselves are sometimes committed to acting as language brokers.

Current research evidence highlights the importance of teachers checking whether children are happy to act as language brokers and for whom, as well as not taking them out of class for impromptu language brokering (Crafter et al. 2017). Equally important, teachers need to be helped to recognize the valuable linguistic resources that child language brokers bring to school. García and Wei (2015) suggest that this involves allowing children to use their full language repertoire (i.e. translanguaging) and 'to learn with and from their students, and to help their students deepen and broaden their capacities for using these linguistic tools' (Orellana, Martinez, and Martinez 2014, 312). As Rizvi and Lingard (2009) suggest, the citizenship functions of formal education need to take cognizance of the local, national and global work that citizens do. That work includes childhood language brokering.

Note

1   ESRC Award number: RES-051-27-0181. With thanks to the participants to the research for so generously sharing their time and stories. The research could not have been completed without the work done by Elaine Bauer and Stephanie Davis-Gill made important contributions to data collection. Thanks also to Meri Parkkinen at the Helsinki Collegium for Advanced Studies, Helsinki University for speeding the tedious task of formatting and checking the manuscript.

References

AKam, Jennifer and Vanja Lazarevic. 'Communicating for One's Family: An Interdisciplinary Review of Language and Cultural Brokering in Immigrant Families'. *Annals of the International Communication Association* 38, no. 1 (2014): 3–37.

Andrews, Molly, Corinne Squire, and Maria Tamboukou, eds. *Doing Narrative Research*. Los Angeles, CA: Sage, 2013.

Banks, James A. 'Diversity and Citizenship Education in Multicultural Nations'. In *Multicultural Education in Glocal Perspectives*, edited by Yun-Kyung Cha, Jagdish Gundara, Seung-Hwan Ham, and Moosung Lee, 73–88. Singapore: Springer, 2017.

Bauer, Elaine. 'Language Brokering: Practicing Active Citizenship'. *MediAzioni*, no. 10 (2010): 125–146.

Bauer, Elaine. 'Reconstructing Moral Identities in Memories of Childhood Language Brokering Experiences'. *International Migration* 51, no. 5 (2013): 205–218.

Bauer, Elaine. 'Practising Kinship Care: Children as Language Brokers in Migrant Families'. *Childhood* 23, no. 1 (2016): 22–36.

Bauer, Elaine. 'Language Brokering: Mediated Manipulations, and the Agency of the Interpreter/Translator'. In *Non-professional Interpreting and Translation: State of the Art and Future of an Emerging Field of Research*, edited by Rachele Antonini, Letizia Cirillo, Linda Rossato, and Ira Torresi, 359–380. Amsterdam, NLD; Philadelphia, NY: John Benjamins Publishing Company, 2017.

Carter, April. *The Political Theory of Global Citizenship*. New York, NY: Routledge, 2013.

Cline, Tony, Sarah Crafter, Lindsay O'Dell, and Guida De Abreu. 'Young People's Representations of Language Brokering'. *Journal of Multilingual and Multicultural Development* 32, no. 3 (2011): 207–220.

Cline, Tony, Sarah Crafter, and Evangelia Prokopiou. 'Child Language Brokering in Schools: A Discussion of Selected Findings from a Survey of Teachers and Ex-Students'. *Educational and Child Psychology* 31, no. 2 (2014): 34–45.

Crafter, Sarah, Tony Cline, and Evangelia Prokopiou. 'Young Adult Language Brokers' and Teachers' Views of the Advantages and Disadvantages of Brokering in School'. In *Language Brokering in Immigrant Families: Theories and Contexts*, edited by Robert S. Weisskirch, 224–244. New York, NY: Routledge, 2017.

Dorner, Lisa M. 'Turning Points and Tensions'. In *Language Brokering in Immigrant Families: Theories and Contexts*, edited by Robert S. Weisskirch, 270–293. New York, NY: Routledge, 2017.

Dorner, Lisa M., Marjorie Faulstich Orellana, and Christine P. Li-Grining. '"I Helped My Mom," and It Helped Me: Translating the Skills of Language Brokers into Improved Standardized Test Scores'. *American Journal of Education* 113, no. 3 (2007): 451–478.

García, Ofelia and Li Wei. 'Translanguaging, Bilingualism, and Bilingual Education'. In *The Handbook of Bilingual and Multilingual Education*, edited by Wayne E. Wright, Sovicheth Boun, and Ofelia García, 223–240. Hoboken, NJ: Wiley-Blackwell, 2015.

Hall, Nigel and Frédérique Guéry. 'Child Language Brokering: Some Considerations'. Manchester Metropolitan University, 2010. http://mediazioni.sitlec.unibo.it/images/stories/PDF_folder/document-pdf/monografia2010CLB/02%20hall_and_gury%20pp24_46.pdf.

Hall, Nigel and Sylvia Sham. 'Language Brokering as Young People's Work: Evidence from Chinese Adolescents in England'. *Language and Education* 21, no.1 (2007): 16–30.

Isin, Engin F. and Greg M. Nielsen. *Acts of Citizenship*. London: Zed Books, 2013.

Israel, Ron. 'What Does It Mean to Be a Global Citizen?' *Open Democracy*, February 2013. Accessed 6 April 2018. https://www.opendemocracy.net/ourkingdom/ron-israel/what-does-it-mean-to-be-global-citizen.

Josselson, Ruthellen. 'The Present of the Past: Dialogues with Memory over Time'. *Journal of Personality* 77, no. 3 (2009): 647–668.

Larkins, Cath. 'Enacting Children's Citizenship: Developing Understandings of How Children Enact Themselves as Citizens through Actions and Acts of Citizenship'. *Childhood* 21, no. 1 (2014): 7–21.

McIntosh, Peggy. 'Gender Perspectives on Educating for Global Citizenship'. In *Educating Citizens for Global Awareness*, edited by Nel Noddings, 22–39. New York, NY: Teachers College Press, 2005.

McQuillan, Jeff and Lucy Tse. 'Child Language Brokering in Linguistic Minority Communities: Effects on Cultural Interaction, Cognition, and Literacy'. *Language and Education* 9, no. 3 (1995): 195–215.

Morales, Alejandro and William E. Hanson. 'Language Brokering: An Integrative Review of the Literature'. *Hispanic Journal of Behavioral Sciences* 27, no. 4 (2005): 471–503.

Orellana, Marjorie Faulstich. *Translating Childhoods: Immigrant Youth, Language, and Culture*. New Brunswick, NJ: Rutgers University Press, 2009.

Orellana, Marjorie Faulstich. *Immigrant Children in Transcultural Spaces: Language, Learning, and Love*. New York, NY: Routledge, 2015.

Orellana, Marjorie Faulstich and Ofelia García. 'Language Brokering and Translanguaging in School'. *Language Arts* 91, no. 5 (2014): 386.

Orellana, Marjorie Faulstich, Danny C. Martínez, and Ramón A. Martínez. 'Language Brokering and Translanguaging: Lessons on Leveraging Students' Linguistic Competencies'. *Language Arts* 91, no. 5 (2014): 311–312.

Orellana, Marjorie Faulstich, and Ann Phoenix. 'Re-Interpreting: Narratives of Childhood Language Brokering over Time'. *Childhood* 24, no. 2 (2017): 183–196.

Osler, Audrey and Hugh Starkey. *Changing Citizenship*. Maidenhead, UK: Open University Press, McGraw-Hill Education, 2005.

Phoenix, Ann, Julia Brannen, Heather Elliott, Janet Smithson, Paulette Morris, Cordet Smart, Anne Barlow, and Elaine Bauer. 'Group Analysis in Practice: Narrative Approaches'. Vol. 17, 2016. Retrieved from http://nbn-resolving.de/urn:nbn:de:0114-fqs160294.

Pugh, Allison. *Longing and Belonging: Parents, Children and Consumer Culture*. Berkeley, CA: University of California Press, 2009.

Riessman, Catherine Kohler. *Narrative Methods for the Human Sciences*. Thousand Oaks, CA: Sage, 2008.

Rizvi, Fazal and Bob Lingard. *Globalizing Education Policy*. New York, NY: Routledge, 2009.

Weisskirch, Robert S. 'Child Language Brokers in Immigrant Families: An Overview of Family Dynamics'. *MediAzioni* 10 (2010): 68–87.

Part Four

Transnational Perspectives on Peace-building and Human Rights Education

11

The Possibilities of Postcolonial Humanism, Human Rights and Education in an Era of Globalization

Stephen Chatelier

Chapter outline

- Introduction
- UNESCO and the call for a new humanism
- Humanism and its contemporary predicament
- Postcolonial theory and the critique of humanism
- The possibilities for a reformulated postcolonial humanism
- From the postcolonial critique of humanism to that of human rights
- Humanism and the negotiation of globalization and education
- Edward Said and his democratic, cosmopolitan humanism
- Conclusion: UNESCO and the ethical imperative of humanist education
- Notes

Keywords: humanism; human rights; globalization; postcolonial theory; UNESCO

Introduction

The world in which we now live is one facing challenges and opportunities of a global nature such as climate change, large-scale involuntary migration, cyber security, diasporic workers, international collaboration, to name just a few. These phenomena have a significant impact on how people from various parts of the world respond to each other. That cultural norms, beliefs and ideologies are of inevitable and profound importance to how these matters are dealt with should come as no surprise. The World Economic Forum's 2016 'Global Risks of High Concern' report lists 'large-scale involuntary migration' as being seen by survey respondents as the most likely of risks to occur and one of the most serious in terms of impact (WEF 2016). Sociologists of globalization have been describing the shifting conditions of this world for more than two decades. It seems to me that we are required to acknowledge that our togetherness, mediated in various ways by the conditions of globalization, is a basic empirical fact of life that will continue into the future. For example, it is hard to argue against the likelihood of technology continuing to facilitate the economic, cultural and political intertwining of humanity. In this sense, the kind of 'togetherness' rendered by our global condition is not only about inter-subjective dialogue, nor about physical proximity (though both of these might also be true), but about our enmeshment. This enmeshment tends to become clearer when things go awry, as in the case of the 2008 global financial crisis.

While global challenges, as the rhetoric of Donald Trump suggests, might result in rising nationalist sentiment, it is nevertheless the case that the communities in which we are living are increasingly constituted by diversity (Kalantzis and Cope 2016). These conditions – in which we are increasingly seeing different ethnic, cultural and national groups interacting within a context which sees processes of globalization negotiated through frameworks of national interests and filiations – demand of us to make moral responses to both the challenges and opportunities that arise. This requires re-thinking and reformulating traditional approaches to moral and ethical decision-making. When transnational spaces constituted by difference are becoming the norm, we require some way of taking a moral stance on the challenges that arise. Such a task is not so easy in a world of intercultural connection. As this chapter will show, key moral resources utilized in the years after the Second World War – humanism and human rights – have been challenged on account of their 'false' and, at times, violent, universalist presumptions. Yet, an outright rejection of both the category of the universal, and notions such as humanism or human rights, risks creating a moral vacuum. Thus, the task for scholars, policy-makers and educators is to consider ways of thinking, being and doing that avoid cultural relativism on the one hand and cultural imperialism on the other.

UNESCO and the call for a new humanism

One organization within the field of education that has been concerned in recent years with how to find an alternative to either imperialistic or relativistic policy has been UNESCO. In 2010, its director-general, Irina Bokova, gave a talk in which she began to articulate the challenges and possibilities for a new humanism for the twenty-first century.[1] Subsequent to this has been a number of UNESCO publications on the matter including, more recently, a booklet titled, *Envisioning a New Humanism for the 21st Century: New Avenues for Reflection and Action*. It is clear that UNESCO, a significant player within the global policy space, sees the question of humanism as absolutely critical to its own activities, including that of education. That is, there is a strong desire and commitment on the part of Bokova and UNESCO to keep the ideals of humanism, and the functions of humanistic practice, at the heart of their work. What they recognize is that the humanism which inspired the founding of UNESCO seventy years ago 'must be adapted to the new demands of our time' (Bokova 2010, 1).

The key conditions to which humanism must adapt, Bokova suggests, include the processes of globalization, the ubiquity and significance of ICTs and digital technology, and the growing awareness of climate change and its consequences (2010, 1–2). We might wish to add to this the enormous increase in human mobility, both in terms of refugees seeking asylum in safer places, but also through business and leisure. One significant aspect of this is the way in which business diasporic communities function with dual – or multiple – national loyalties, the imbrication of different cultural traditions, and the exchange of knowledge and ideas across cultural and national boundaries (Rizvi et al. 2016). Children who grow up within such transnational communities and spaces find themselves confronted with very different realities to the children growing up in the middle of the twentieth century, for example.

The humanism that influenced the 1950s classroom in Melbourne, Australia, for example, was far less likely to be called upon to produce a response to the matter of cultural difference. Moreover, when it did, the almost unquestioned presumption was that its role was to support the civilizing mission to make the non-European more European, that is, more civilized and modern. The ensuing years have seen widespread decolonization in the political sense, with a lagging decolonization epistemologically and economically. However, as this chapter will suggest in regard to postcolonial thinking, not only is complete decolonization impossible, it is also not necessarily desirable. It remains that, where the asymmetrical structure of contemporary global relations functions to maintain the dominance of the Global North, critique of neocolonialism and its effects is indeed necessary. However, as Chakrabarty (2000) so eloquently put it, Europe is a gift to us all; one that should be accepted in a spirit of anticolonial gratitude (255). In this sense, the challenge for UNESCO and, indeed, for all of us implicated in formal education in particular, is to determine that within the continuing influence of European humanism which is a gift, and that which is violent and exclusive. For Bokova and UNESCO, the contemporary challenge is to reformulate a humanism that speaks to the challenges and opportunities of the world before us, in the hope that we might learn to live together.

Humanism and its contemporary predicament

While UNESCO's hope may sound overly idealistic, as already mentioned, Bokova acknowledges that any humanism that functions as a resource for peace in the world requires a reformulation. Despite its long and continuing influence within Western histories generally, and education more specifically, humanism has been a site of debate in more recent decades. This debate has meant that many of those who have wished to defend humanism have needed, at a minimum, to take seriously the potential problem of an a-historical, essentialized, humanism. Moreover, they have been given the burden to show why and how humanism might escape philosophical, ethical and political critiques. The distinguished philosopher Martha Nussbaum is one voice who has consistently defended humanism in her writings. In her *Cultivating Humanity* (1997), Nussbaum seeks to defend a humanism that prioritizes: critique; the acknowledgement of a common humanity that shares vulnerabilities, capabilities and problems; as well as the kind of imagination that allows us to enter into the stories and perspectives of those with whom we differ. This humanism, cultivated in the (American) university is conceived as necessary for students who will be able to engage the world without languishing in cultural conservatism on the one hand or moral relativism on the other.

In a later book, *Not for Profit* (2010), Nussbaum again takes up the problem of humanism within education but, this time, in response to the increasing marketization and commoditization of education. While the matter of humanism as a concept is not of primary concern for Nussbaum in this book, it nevertheless pervades the text as an underlying assumption for her overall argument. Focused more specifically on the role of the humanities for the nurturing of democratic citizenship, humanism for Nussbaum, especially as it is attached to education, represents an ethical and radical (political) approach to life. It is ethical because of its insistence that matters of human life remain central, and it is political because of the way in which it is integrally (if not necessarily) linked to democracy. Thus, prioritizing humanism as a powerful resource in articulating human rights agendas, responding to the needs of the Global South, and in the development of a critical democratic disposition in both individuals and societies continues to motivate certain scholars and practitioners today. The aims and motivations of humanists such as Martha Nussbaum are hard to criticize, and while her position is, of course, contestable, it is also defensible.

Yet, despite these kinds of robust justifications for a humanist position, there are many others who have, especially since the 1960s and 1970s, presented philosophical, ethical and political challenges to humanism. These critiques have come from within the discourses, among others, of structuralism, poststructuralism, feminist theory, critical race theory, animal studies, eco-philosophy, cultural studies and critical posthumanisms.[2] For example, the critiques offered by structuralism and poststructuralism share concerns regarding how humanism has been construed philosophically. That is, there are significant onto-epistemological questions that structuralists and poststructuralists bring to the notion of humanism. Given the primacy which structuralism attached to underlying structures or systems, the unity and essence of 'man' represented a very different view of reality, one in which humanity appeared to be somehow abstracted from the structures governing the rest of life. The poststructuralist perspectives tend to be more radical again insofar as they seek to undermine fixed ontologies more broadly, not least that of the human(ist) subject. For poststructuralists who built on the work of scholars such as Michel Foucault, the subject is formed discursively and, thus, humanism's essentialist and universalist assumptions, they might say, become untenable.

To provide an example of criticism arising from those who have been excluded by it, we might consider the case of feminism. Many feminists, including prominent voices such as that of Irigaray (1985), attach their concern regarding the presumed universalism of humanism to the way in which it keeps silent on the difference represented, and performed, by women. Moreover, given that initial feminist criticism was aimed at an Enlightenment version of humanism, which rather distinctively placed its hope in the 'triumph of man', it is not difficult to see why feminists began to question humanism as an epistemological and political foundation for their own emancipation. Indeed, humanism, one might argue, represents that which women are seeking emancipation from.

While these and other criticisms of humanism remain powerful today, given the focus this collection has on globalization, this chapter is particularly concerned with the challenge that postcolonial theories pose to humanism and, relatedly, human rights in education. This is because it was the colonial enterprise, some may argue, that gave rise to globalization and both moments in history have direct implications for humans living together, despite their many differences. For this reason, one could argue that it is the postcolonial challenge to humanism that is most relevant to the contemporary context of transnational connectivities, mobility and global interdependence.

Postcolonial theory and the critique of humanism

The postcolonial challenge to humanism is particularly significant in its relation to the problem of how we as humans live together. While postcolonial theorists tend to share much in common with the critics of humanism already mentioned, one point of difference between postcolonial concerns and those of other critics is the historical fact of colonialism and its effects on lived human life. This is significant because while globalization can tend to be dispatched as an ahistorical concept, it is perhaps better understood as a set of processes tied to the history of colonialism and its ongoing history in the form of various types of cultural, epistemological and economic imperialism (Rizvi 2007, 259–260). Today, lived life increasingly involves, for many in the world, not only connection with, but certain forms of dependence on, people from other cultural backgrounds. Some early theorists of globalization, in particular, have feared the homogenization of 'culture' through the spread of dominant Euro-American values, ideas and knowledge. What has become clear, though, is that cultural exchange – which assumes that the interlocutors are kept intact in some way at least – is often taking place in a way that resists, to some extent, Euro-American cultural imperialism. This is not to say that the exchange is equal but that, as the term 'exchange' necessitates, the relationship is not a one-way takeover. On the one hand, then, the fear of globalization as a reified force with agential intent might be assuaged to some extent. On the other hand, the fact that the world is structured in dominance (Radhakrishnan 2003) with global inequalities increasing rather than decreasing, opens up a space for postcolonial criticism. As such, any engagement with the philosophical problems of humanism by postcolonial theorists should proceed with the concerns of the lived life of the world's most marginalized people foregrounded.

Various scholars have claimed that humanism has functioned as a tool of colonial oppression (Alvares 2006; Jean-Marie 2008). As part of the programme of cultural imperialism that took place with colonization, humanism functioned as the moral impetus of colonialism's civilizing mission. In a variety of ways, not least the aims of colonial education, the civilizing mission sought to correct and improve the 'native', that they might modernize and develop a moral and rational relation to the world. Thus, whatever moral vision of the good society that humanism might have reflected and enacted in a local culture was to be radically undermined by its inextricable ties with colonial endeavours. In other words, what became clear with colonialism was the way in which humanism was able to be used to oppress the other, and to function as a boundary marker for judging the success of the civilizing agenda. Moreover, humanism-inspired colonial education legitimized colonial relations and their asymmetrical power structure. So it is that the postcolonial challenge to humanism becomes so problematic for a humanism that prioritizes the ideal of living together as core to its agenda.

Moreover, part of what the spatial movement of humanism through colonialism instigated was the problem of universalism. Indeed, much postcolonial theorizing turns on the debate between universalism and particularism. For example, the critique of human essentialism is necessarily related to this debate. Were particular cultural differences not a reality, then it would be much easier to assume an essentialist philosophical anthropology. Postcolonial concerns regarding epistemic violence and cultural violence – let alone territorial and physical violence – also revolve around an understanding of the particular as a challenge to universalist assumptions. Epistemic and cultural violence is violent because the imposition of European concepts and modes of knowledge, and of sensibilities and morality, takes place at the expense of indigenous or local ways of knowing, being and doing.

The possibilities for a reformulated postcolonial humanism

What the more sophisticated examples of postcolonial theorizing (as opposed to the strictly anti-colonial work) do is to work through the tensions of affirming a certain need for universals while also foregrounding and prioritizing the particular. For example, Chakrabarty reflects on the difficult tension when he writes that 'we need universals to produce critical readings of social injustices. Yet the universal … [produces] forms of thought that ultimately evacuate the place of the local' (2000, 254–255). In a related but different vein, Radhakrishnan (2003) engages in an extended critical reflection on the place of universalism in the context of a globalized postcolonial world. His argument is for working towards a certain kind of perspectival universalism which seeks justice in the name of all humanity, while ensuring that this is both negotiated across cultural difference and cognizant of political and structural dominance. As such, universality, he argues, 'should not be conceived of as the final and definitive resolution of perspectivism', but should be constructed and practised as 'ongoing processes of multilateral accountability to Alterity' (2003, 85). Radhakrishnan wants to ensure that the universal itself, along with universal notions such as justice, freedom or human rights, are not stripped of their historical provenance which often reveals that such concepts have been formed out of struggle or oppression. Indeed, in *History, the Human, and the World Between* (2008) – Radhakrishnan writes that 'the ontology of a universal humanism has to be perceived both as a promise and a possibility in itself and as that possibility that is being denied by the absurd rationale of the colonial world' (86). Thus, it is an ethico-political imperative that the particularities of lived experiences, often reflecting and embodying asymmetrical relations of power, remain in tension with the aims and contradictions of the universal.

It can now be seen, perhaps, that this relationship between the universal and the particular in postcolonial theory reveals, as briefly mentioned above, that while it shares with other critical perspectives on humanism a shifting away from the hubris of Eurocentric universalism, the nub of its critique revolves around the specific matter of colonialism and its effects on 'the subaltern' subject. Thus, as postcolonial theorists such as the Subaltern Studies group, for example, began to utilize and adapt the Gramscian notion of the subaltern in a political move to engage in a different historiography, the lived experiences of those previously excluded from, and without a voice in, history emerged as concrete challenges to abstract universalisms, including that of European Enlightenment humanism.

From the postcolonial
critique of humanism to that of human rights

The provenance of the notion of human rights is not without debate. Just as humanism may be traced to ancient Greece, so too could human rights. However, in terms of its relation to the dominant human rights discourse today, it is perhaps more accurate to trace its origins to the aftermath of the Second World War or, to go back a little further, the ideas and ideals of the Enlightenment. In any case, it would appear that when we speak of human rights, we refer to an idea that has emerged not only from Western history but also from Western reason. It would be easy, then, as some scholars have done, to offer a postcolonial critique of human rights because of its presumed Eurocentrism (Barreto 2013;

Bonnet 2015; Matua 2002). However, while the dominant understanding of human rights, especially after the Universal Declaration of Human Rights in 1948, ought to be challenged for its distinctively Western character, this is not the same thing as challenging human rights per se.

Yet, related to the critique of a Eurocentric version of human rights is, for many critics, the greater problem of its universalism. The description by Zembylas et al. (2017), citing Hopgood, of 'Human Rights (with capitalized letters) at the international level (as a sacred metanarrative discourse)', aptly portrays the imperialist risk of such a universalism. This criticism, as opposed to the charge of ethnocentrism, is not historical or contextual, but conceptual. In this sense, the key problem is that a transcendent notion of Rights, stripped of context, is one that is imposed indiscriminately. This has led some critics to reject the entire notion of Human Rights, with many others instead attempting to relativize Human Rights into human rights. While postcolonial theorists have fallen into both camps, the argument I am presenting here is that postcolonial concerns should lead one to seek a human rights discourse that emerges from the negotiation between the universal and the particular.

Indeed, if postcolonial theory seeks to prioritize the lived experience of the subaltern, as I suggested earlier, then it is difficult for the outcome of postcolonial theory to be the rejection of humanism and human rights. As the case of Malala Yousafzai, the Pakistani girl who at the age of fifteen was shot in the head by the Taliban because of her commitment to getting an education, reminds us, human rights are most important for the marginalized.[3] Thus, while it remains important to criticize human rights for being complicit with power in a world unevenly structured, it is *because* of this uneven world that we ought not to dismiss humanism and human rights too readily. The postcolonial challenge is, then, to see humanism and human rights as universal notions that need to be negotiated, and transposed, out of the particular experiences of those whose rights have too often been ignored. Or, as Spivak puts it, human rights' 'so-called European provenance is for me in the same category as the "enabling violation" of the production of the colonial subject. One cannot write off the righting of wrongs. The enablement must be used even as the violation is renegotiated' (2004, 524). This should not be read as a full embrace of human rights by Spivak, but an ambivalent relation to the idea, acknowledging its productive power both positively and negatively. Spivak's theoretical intervention through the coining of the phrase 'enabling violation' is, in my view, a recognition that the lived experiences of those whose rights as humans are being violated demands something other than an outright rejection of the notion of human rights.

Humanism and the negotiation of globalization and education

This notion of an enabling violation, similar to other important concepts in Spivak's work, such as 'strategic essentialism' and 'affirmative sabotage', is able to function in a way so that the critique of human rights does not lead to further violation of humans' rights. The rejection of humanism and human rights for its universalist hubris risks becoming a rejection of the normative and thus producing a kind of relativist logic in regards to ethics. As Spivak's theorizing of human rights as an enabling violation shows, however, such outright rejection of the category of the universal is not the only option. Indeed, postcolonial scholars such as Radhakrishnan and Chakrabarty have made the claim that the category of the universal maintains an important ethico-political function. But, they argue, the historical fact of colonialism and imperialism has shown us that the universal must be provincialized, and that this is not the same thing as dismissed or destroyed. And so, it is on the basis of this kind of postcolonial thinking that we might begin to imagine the humanist challenge of living together. Indeed, it just might be that a humanism reformulated out of the postcolonial critique is able to provide the moral justification for education's continued interest in human rights. And, it is on the basis of this kind of thinking that we may be able to imagine a humanist inspired education in the difficult context of contemporary globalization.

In their book *Globalizing Education Policy*, Rizvi and Lingard (2010) make a strong case for understanding policy as necessarily 'value-laden'. They argue that while the values inherent in policy have traditionally 'articulated national interests', in more recent times, 'global considerations now enter the articulation of values as never before' (16). Moreover, as they argue in chapter four of their book, education itself 'is a deliberate, purposive activity directed at the achievement of a range of ends' (71). Education thus has 'normative implications: it suggests that something worthwhile is being intentionally transmitted, and that something valuable is being attempted' (71). Whereas philosophical propositions and arguments from a particular cultural tradition have tended to be presented as the value basis for educational thinking, policy and practice, globalizing processes have functioned to ensure that the norms of education are negotiated across cultural difference.

However, the acknowledgement of education's normative and values-based implications is no guarantee that it will not capitulate to the logic of *the market*. As Rizvi and Lingard further demonstrate, the globalization of education policy has seen various values from different national and state imperatives become subsumed under a broad neoliberal social imaginary. In this sense, they argue, 'there is an unmistakable global trend towards a convergence in thinking about educational values' (72). This convergence, they suggest, is 'towards a neoliberal values orientation' (72) in which, as Wendy Brown (2015) puts it, *homo politicus* is transformed into *homo oeconomicus*. The point that Rizvi and Lingard wish to make is that the result of this globalizing of education policy is that 'policymaking is a fundamentally political process' of negotiation (72). As such, policies do not represent a simple, direct-line outcome of a philosophical moral principle. Rather than policies representing a particular value, then, they 'order, organise and enact' a range of values into a particular configuration (73). What this analysis suggests, therefore, is that the ways in which globalizing processes bring *differences* into contact with each other requires the universal and the particular to work on each other in mutually transformative ways. Such a notion is reminiscent of Ania Loomba's (2005) observation that 'both the coloniser and the colonised are affected by the processes of colonisation and decolonisation' (22). Moreover, Loomba notes the way in which postcolonial theory tends to bring in to focus the fact that this mutual-effect of colonization takes place according to an uneven power relationship – a point made previously in this analysis. While Rizvi and Lingard note the market-based logic that influences the process of contemporary policy formation, by demonstrating the necessary place of values within policy formation and enactment, they highlight the political and transnational stakes in policy negotiation.

This dominant articulation of globalization with the logics and norms of neoliberalism is one for which it is difficult to imagine an alternative. However, the fact that it is an articulation means that the relationship between globalization and neoliberalism is not a necessary one. Despite recent events such as the Brexit vote and various moves by Donald Trump such as his withdrawal of the United States from the Trans-Pacific Partnership, we are highly unlikely to leave the conditions of globalization behind and retreat to a world comprised of disconnected nation-states. Moreover, I share Rizvi and Lingard's view that a market-based logic pervades much globalization policy. Yet, if globalization is to persist as a condition of our existence but is not in any necessary sense wedded to neoliberalism, the possibility for articulating globalization to another set of logics remains. If there is a desire to attempt this, for the sake of social justice, the question becomes to what might globalization be articulated and how? Here, I am making the argument that a provisional, contingent and cosmopolitan humanism similar to that espoused by Edward Said can act as a moral resource within the context of globalization.

Edward Said and his democratic, cosmopolitan humanism

Said most explicitly addressed the problems with and possibilities for humanism in *Humanism and Democratic* Criticism (2004). Here, he makes clear that he is not interested in defending a Eurocentric humanism that exists to extol its own virtues to the exclusion of others. His humanism is not elitist, but democratic. Whereas elitism connotes imposition from on high – a kind of transcendentalism – democracy assumes a level of negotiation and co-construction that takes place between the past, present and future simultaneously. Said's version of humanism sees 'no contradiction at all between the practice of humanism and the practice of participatory citizenship' (22). Rather than being about withdrawal and exclusion, humanism's 'purpose is to make more things available to critical scrutiny as the product of human labour, human energies for emancipation and enlightenment, and, just as importantly, human misreadings and misinterpretations of the collective past and present' (22). That is to say, there is nothing that is beyond the scope of critique and nothing that, in any necessary sense, is any less open to critique due to its cultural provenance.

Said's critique of the version of humanism that is both Eurocentric and universalist leads him to espouse a democratic, cosmopolitan humanism. For him, Western universalist humanism is predicated on the idea of fixity and is, therefore, not equipped for an inclusive and open engagement with the world. That is, the kind of humanism privileges the West at the exclusion of others is also the kind of humanism that privileges that which has been fixed over that which is, or might be, emerging. And it is his commitment to a contingent and provisional humanism that ensures that he does not react to the universalist presumptions of Western humanism by advocating for an alternative form of humanism based on a similarly fixed logic. For example, Said (2004) notes that new fields of study in the later decades of the twentieth century such as 'postcolonialism, ethnic studies, [and] cultural studies' (14) risked being identitarian. While conservative humanists disapproved of these studies for distorting or sullying humansim, the issue for Said was not their newness or difference, but the potential of their identitarianism. So it is against the presumed opposition between canonical humanism and new intellectual movements, that Said (2004) contends, 'you will find that no great humanistic achievement was ever without an important component, relationship, or acceptance of the new' (23). Thus, between the dual enclosures of 'new' identity-politics on the one hand and 'old' ethnocentrism on the other – two sides of the same coin – Said (2004) argues for a humanism that sees cultural difference as the 'new norm', and the critical negotiation of this difference as key to its practice.

What Said (2004) proposes is a humanism that eschews its Eurocentric past in favour of a more open and integrated model. This requires the humanist to avoid affirming one tradition over the other and to instead 'open them all, or as many as possible, to each other, to question each of them for what it has done with the others' (49). This kind of work prioritizes the humanistic prospects for 'coexistence (as opposed to partition)' (49). Initially, Said does not elaborate at any great length on what this kind of humanistic work would look like, but instead elaborates on what it is that it needs to be distinguished from. That is, negative models of partition as evinced by 'nationalism, religious enthusiasm, and identitarian thought' (50). Nationalism, argues Said, produces the kind of views regarding national sovereignty that give rise to the idea of the clash of civilizations and the superiority of 'us' over them. It seeks to dismiss pluralism in favour of a manufactured, ahistorical essentialization of national identity. Said's humanism might be thought of as cosmopolitan if understood simply as an alternative to both nationalism, at a local level – which, as has been shown above, is closely related to identity thinking – and a kind of culturalism at a broader level, one version of which might be Eurocentrism. Both constitute a kind of identitarianism. Indeed, Said suggests that Eurocentrism is very often 'the nub' of the negative models of partition described above. According to Said (2004), the problem with Eurocentrism is 'the parochiality of its universalism, its unexamined assumptions about Western civilisation, its Orientalism, and its attempts to impose a uniformly directed theory of progress', which all end up 'reducing, rather than expanding, the possibility of catholic inclusiveness, of genuinely cosmopolitan or internationalist perspective, of intellectual curiosity' (53). The effects of Eurocentrism are, he deems, 'about as inappropriate to humanistic practice in the United States as it is possible to be' (52). However, if humanistic practice is to be marked by catholic inclusiveness and a cosmopolitan perspective, is it anything more than a trite affirmation of some kind of utopian 'love-in'?

Said (2004) anticipates this criticism and makes clear that he does not see cosmopolitan humanism as one that simply amounts to 'a lazy or laissez-faire feel-good multiculturalism', which, he states, 'means absolutely nothing to me as it is usually discussed' (50). Said (2004) is interested, rather, in a

> rigorous intellectual and rational approach that ... draws on a rather exact notion of what it means to read philologically in a worldly and integrative, as distinct from separating or partitioning, mode and, at the same time, to offer resistance to the great reductive and vulgarising us-versus-them thought patterns of our time. (50)

To guard against 'feel-good multiculturalism', this worldly, cosmopolitan, democratic humanism that Said describes has critique at its heart. If humanists are to stand for something, that is, to be politically engaged rather than cordoned off in their scholastic cloisters, then their practice must involve a worldly, not merely textual, critique. In the early 2000s, Said (2004) saw the time to be right for humanists to do this kind of work. He writes that 'the new generation of humanist scholars is more attuned than any before it to the non-European, genderised, decolonised, and decentered energies and currents of our time' (47). To be aware of such things, Said (2004) continues,

> means situating critique at the very heart of humanism, critique as a form of democratic freedom and as a continuous practice of questioning and accumulating knowledge that is open to, rather than in denial of, the constituent historical realities of the post-Cold War world, its early colonial formations, and the frighteningly global reach of the last remaining superpower of today. (47)

In other words, humanism is the practice of democratic critique that openly engages the raft of (geo)political, cultural and socioeconomic issues that are manifest in the world.

Just as the processes, tensions and configurations discussed in relation to policy by Rizvi and Lingard emerge through their negotiation according to political and economic interests, so too does a postcolonial, cosmopolitan humanism emerge as a negotiated construct. It assumes values, but these values cannot be considered to always be fixed. Education in a globalized context is required to be cognizant of the dominant logics ordering and shaping its agenda. Moreover, any normative pronouncements regarding its aims and aspirations are ones that must take into consideration not only the negotiated nature of the very pronouncements but the *negotiated* nature of their implementation. That is to say, statements of values are debated and negotiated at the philosophical level but also experience a *negotiation* through the way in which they are interpreted and implemented in different local contexts. Thus, as specifically humanist values travel from policy to education sites, the values themselves may be reshaped as they are articulated to each particular context. Indeed, the *telos* of this kind of postcolonial, negotiated humanism is the process of negotiation itself. Thus the end of humanism is not fixed but dynamic. Given the empirical fact of global interconnectivity and interdependence in socially material ways, the question remains as to how we will handle the inevitable challenges (and opportunities) that emerge. While education may not provide the answers, it has a role to play.

Conclusion: UNESCO and the ethical imperative of humanist education

Given that education suggests 'something worthwhile is being intentionally transmitted, and that something valuable is being attempted' (Rizvi and Lingard 2010, 71), and given the significant place that education occupies throughout the world, I would contend that it is uniquely placed to counter xenophobia, imperialistic dispositions and superficial relativism. Indeed, this is precisely what I deem UNESCO to be attempting to do. Under Bokova's (2014) leadership, UNESCO has been looking for ways to work towards a 'new, universal vision, open to the entire human community and embracing each and every continent' for which there is an 'aspiration to peace, democracy, justice and human rights; it is an aspiration to tolerance, knowledge and the diversity of cultures' (8). It is a lofty ideal, but as a postcolonial sensibility should remind us, a necessary one.

In the era of the modern nation-state and internationalism, the disciplines of philosophy (ethics) and political science (ideology, policy) were viewed as having the capacity to direct the world towards a peaceful and just future. However, Bokova (2014) argues it could now be reasonably suggested that 'no political or ethical doctrine has had the capacity to fully prepare today's decision-makers and individuals for the complexities, intricacies and changeability of the present world' (1). Instead, it is the view of UNESCO that it is a renewed humanism that is required to garner a sense of solidarity in a world that is interconnected and interdependent. The fact of the world's interconnectedness represents a challenge in the sense that 'our societies are more diverse than ever' and yet 'intolerance is on the rise' (Bokova 2013, 2). In such an environment, determining a foundation from which a new sense of common humanity can be realized is also more problematic. Nevertheless, Bokova (2014) suggests that 'cooperation has always formed the starting point of humanism, understood as a philosophy of education both for individuals and humanity as such' (2). The fact is that the world is connected across difference. The universal value that is required is the recognition of a common humanity as a moral foundation as we negotiate these connections. In other words, while it is one thing to invoke humanism or a common humanity, it is another thing to begin to describe some principles regarding what it means to be a humanist. Moreover, no longer can it be assumed that these principles can be decided by a male Greek philosopher or a group of French elites and simply imposed on the rest of the world. As Bokova (2014) makes clear, 'no matter how universally recognized the objectives of peace and prosperity may be, they must be constantly reviewed, renewed and adapted to the requirements of the present and the future' (2). Like Said, her call is not for a previous Eurocentric or classical humanism.

Rather, the provisional and contingent rendering of universal objectives such as peace and prosperity – 'this principle of constant "attuning"' – as Bokova (2014) puts it, 'is central to the New Humanism. Peace and shared welfare are two sides of the same coin. And humanism is that coin' (2). I would argue that Bokova's new humanism is about the manifestation of the ideals of traditional humanisms, enabled by the fact of globalization, as genuinely universal and cosmopolitan. That is, the various European humanisms (and those from other cultural traditions) that existed as an ethico-political imperative for both the betterment of the individual and of society are now able to realize their universalizability, not through colonial imposition, but global negotiation. However, it is at this point that the postcolonial challenge to humanism acts as an important interruption and reminder. The negotiation of humanism is one that takes place in a world structured asymmetrically and, therefore, a genuinely universal rendering of humanism is highly unlikely. Nevertheless, the imperative of critique from Said, or Bokova's insistence on constantly reviewing and adapting universal notions, go some way to de- transcendentalizing and, therefore, reducing the violence of a newly constructed humanism.

Yet, it remains unclear as to exactly what UNESCO might be able to reasonably expect of this new humanism. Elfert (2016) argues that UNESCO, with its humanist ideals and agenda, has actually had very little impact over the past seventy years. With her specific focus being on the concept of 'lifelong learning', Elfert (2016) notes that, despite UNESCO's clear humanistic understanding of the term, 'lifelong learning' has become a notion that is routinely seen as being operationalized in neoliberal terms (248–249). This is merely to say that humanistic intent will not necessarily manifest in humanistic ways. But more than this, UNESCO exemplifies the opportunities and limitations of being an international organization in a globalized world constituted by nation-states that remain powerful. That is, while it has a global platform from which to influence policy, the fact remains that policy is still negotiated and implemented at the level of the nation-state and according to its interests.

Thus, UNESCO's task is not so much to formulate ready-to-go policy, but to act as an intellectual and moral agent with a global agenda. Indeed, Bokova (2014) claims that UNESCO 'as an intellectual organisation ... must take the lead in humanist thinking in the international community' (8). It is this same kind of task that this chapter has tried to achieve in some small way. In this chapter, I have not engaged in an in-depth analysis of the possibilities for, and dilemmas within, a humanist pedagogy. Instead, I have made an attempt to provide an intellectual intervention in, and provocation for, how a negotiated humanism and, subsequently, notion of human rights, might continue to inform the kind of education that struggles for a world in which we learn to live together well.

Notes

1   See: http://unesdoc.unesco.org/images/0018/001897/189775e.pdf
2   There is not the space here to discuss all of these challenges. For a brief interaction with aspects of the posthumanists' challenge to humanism, see, Stephen Chatelier. 2018 (forthcoming). Beyond the humanism/posthumanism debate: The educational implications of Said's critical, humane praxis. *Educational Theory*, vol. 67, no. 6.
3   See https://www.theguardian.com/world/2017/aug/17/schoolgirl-campaigner-malala-yousafzai- wins-oxford-university-place

References

Alvares, Claudia. *Humanism after Colonialism*. Oxford: Peter Lang, 2006.

Barreto, José-Manuel. 'Decolonial Strategies and Dialogue in the Human Rights Field'. In *Human Rights from a Third World Perspective: Critique, History and International Law*, edited by José-Manuel Barreto, 1–42. Cambridge: Scholars Publishing, 2013.

Bokova, Irina. 'A New Humanism for the 21st Century'. UNESCO, 2010. http://unesdoc.unesco.org/images/0018/001897/189775e.pdf.

Bokova, Irina. 'New Humanism in the 21st Century – The Role of Education in Empowering Society'. Address on the occasion of the visit to the University of Malaya. 21 May 2013. UNESCO. http://unesdoc.unesco.org/images/0022/002209/220974E.pdf.

Bokova, Irina. 'Envisioning a New Humanism for the 21st Century'. UNESCO, 2014. http://unesdoc.unesco.org/images/0022/002278/227855E.pdf.

Bonnet, Sebastian. 'Overcoming Eurocentrism in Human Rights: Postcolonial Critiques – Islamic Answers?' *Muslim World Journal of Human Rights* 12, no. 1 (2015): 1–24.

Brown, Wendy. *Undoing the Demos: Neoliberalism's Stealth Revolution*. Brooklyn, New York: Zone Books, 2015.

Chakrabarty, Dipesh. *Provincializing Europe: Postcolonial Thought and Historical Difference*, 2nd edition. Princeton, NJ: Princeton University Press, 2000.

Chatelier, Stephen. 'Beyond the Humanism/Posthumanism Debate: The Educational Implications of Said's Critical, Humane Praxis'. *Educational Theory* 67, no. 6 (2018-forthcoming).

Elfert, Maren. 'The Utopia of Lifelong Learning: An Intellectual History of UNESCO's Humanistic Approach to Education, 1945-2015'. PhD diss., University of British Columbia, 2016. https://open.library.ubc.ca/cIRcle/collections/24/items/1.0228054.

Irigaray, Luce. *This Sex Which Is Not One*, translated by Catherine Porter. Ithaca, NY: Cornell University Press, 1985.

Jean-Marie, Vivaldi. *Fanon: Collective Ethics and Humanism*. New York: Peter Lang, 2008.

Kalantzis, Mary and Bill Cope. 'Learner Differences in Theory and Practice'. *Open Review of Educational Research* 3, no. 1 (2016): 85–132. Doi: 10.1080/23265507.2016.1164616.

Loomba, Ania. *Colonialism/Postcolonialism*. London: Routledge, 2005.

Mutua, Makau. *Human Rights: A Political and Cultural Critique*. Pennsylvania: University of Pennsylvania Press, 2002.

Nussbaum, Martha C. *Cultivating Humanity: A Classical Defense of Reform in Liberal Education*. Cambridge, MA: Harvard University Press, 1997.

Nussbaum, Martha C. *Not for Profit: Why Democracy Needs the Humanities*. Princeton, NJ: Princeton University Press, 2010.

Radhakrishnan, Rajagopalan. *Theory in an Uneven World*. Malden, MA: Blackwell, 2003.

Radhakrishnan, Rajagopalan. *History, the Human, and the World Between*. Durham: Duke University Press, 2008.

Rizvi, Fazal. 'Postcolonialism and Globalization in Education'. *Cultural Studies? Critical Methodologies* 7, no. 3 (2007): 256–263.

Rizvi, Fazal and Bob Lingard. *Globalizing Education Policy*. London: Routledge, 2010.

Rizvi, Fazal, Kam Louie, and Julia Evans. 'Australia's Diaspora Advantage: Realising the Potential for Building Transnational Networks with Asia'. In *Report to the Australian Council of Learned Academies*. Melbourne: ACOLA, 2016.

Said, Edward.W. *Humanism and Democratic Criticism*. New York: Columbia University Press, 2004.

Spivak, Gayatri Chakravorty. 'Righting wrongs'. *South Atlantic Quarterly* 103, no. 2–3 (2004): 523–581.

World Economic Forum. *The Global Risks Report 2016*, 11th edition. Geneva: World Economic Forum, 2016. http://www3.weforum.org/docs/GRR/WEF_GRR16.pdf.

Zembylas, Michalinos, Panayiota Charalambous, Constadina Charalambous, and Stalo Lesta. 'Toward a Critical Hermeneutical Approach of Human Rights Education: Universal Ideals, Contextual Realities and Teachers' Difficulties'. *Journal of Curriculum Studies* 49, no. 4 (2017): 497–517.

12

Peace Education in Pakistan: Challenges and Possibilities

Sarfaroz Niyozov and Munir Lalani

Chapter outline

- Introduction
- Historical background and the context
- Education as 'a promoter' of conflict and violence
- Education as a victim of conflict/violence
- Initiatives for promoting peace and harmony
- Curriculum and pedagogical approaches for peace education in Pakistan
- Contribution of Aga Khan University
- Implications: Seizing the potentials of peace education in Pakistan
- Conclusions
- Notes

Keywords: education and conflict; Pakistani society; peace education; curriculum and pedagogy; violence; initiatives for promoting peace

Introduction

Located in northwest of South Asia, the Islamic Republic of Pakistan occupies a great strategic geo-political importance. It is the land of varying landscapes, including five of the fourteen highest mountains in the world; five major deserts; and the Arabian Sea in its South, which provides transit link between European and Asian countries. Pakistan is also home to individuals from diverse ethno-linguistic backgrounds, including Punjabis, Pakhtuns, Sindhis, Balochs, Mahajirs and others. Its population is predominantly Muslims, but people adhering to other religions, including Christianity, Hinduism and Sikhism, as well as followers of some minor religions such as Kalash (specific to the people living in Pakistan's Kalash valley) and Zoroastrianism also inhabit the country (Halai and Durrani 2018). The birth place of Guru Nanak (founder of Sikhism) and many ancient sites of Hinduism and Buddhism are also located in Pakistan.

In world politics, Pakistan was titled as 'fort of Islam' by Colonel Gaddafi during the Second Islamic Summit Conference in 1974; it is the only Muslim country with the nuclear power, and enjoys close intimacy with China – a relationship that is popularly described as *higher than the Himalayas, deeper than the oceans and sweeter than honey*. Pakistan's army has played a major role in United Nations peace-keeping missions in the countries like Somalia, Kosovo, Ivory Coast, Congo, Western Sahara, Bosnia, Sierra Leone, East Timor Haiti and so on (Shoukat 2018). Pakistan has also played a vital role in leading the withdrawal of Soviet Union from Afghanistan (1979–1989) (Hilali 2017; Khan and Wei 2016; Malik 2016).

Unfortunately, all these riches, beauties, diversities and strategic positions have also been both sources and targets of conflicts. Historically and at present, Pakistan has experienced all sorts of conflicts and violence, ranging from domestic (e.g. gender abuse), to street-level (e.g. traffic, theft, robbery, cell-phone and purse snatching, pollution, loud noise), to economic (poverty and unemployment), to religious (Shi'a–Sunni, Muslim–Christian, Muslim–Hindu), to extremism-related (e.g. various and radical extremist groups), to geopolitical military (e.g. three wars and ongoing border skirmishes, Kashmir conflict, Afghan wars, wars of and against terror). In other words, Pakistan regrettably appears as a laboratory of conflicts. Against this background, the efforts on peace are insufficient, piecemeal and superficial. In fact, open, serious talk about many of the above-mentioned conflicts is not encouraged and can be seen as subversive to the country's self-projection as the land of peace and prosperity.

The rest of the chapter will present a brief historical background of the depth, nature, causes and effects of conflicts. This is followed by a section of education–conflict dialectical nexus. Next, we discuss some of the peace initiatives in formal and informal education, paying special attention to the work of the Aga Khan University's Institute for Educational Development (AKU-IED). We end with highlighting the need for using peacemaking and peace-building potentials in the country. Given the multiplicity of the forms of conflicts, their enduring nature, critical–formal engagement with conflicts and its inter-connected causes is vital for sustainable and contextually relevant peace education.

Historical background and the context

The contemporary challenges to peace education in Pakistan have their roots in the post-colonial historical and political events of becoming an independent country, managing its diversity, handling relations with its neighbours and positioning itself in the new world order, especially in the era of neoliberal globalization. Since time immemorial, the Indian subcontinent has been comprised of different territories and kingdoms, governed by various royal dynasties (McLeod 2002). The expansion of the British Empire and ensued colonialism resulted in creating an 'artificial unity' of these states under British Crown through its divide and rule policies. Consequently, the conflicts between the political parties and various communal groups, particularly between Hindus and Muslims, rapidly increased during the freedom movement. This finally led to the partition of British India into two sovereign states of India and Pakistan (Adnan 2006; Khan 2017; Majumdar 1968).

The newly born countries had to face violence and aggression from their very inception. Millions of Hindus and Muslims lost their right to live in their birthplaces and were compelled to cross the border and migrate on account of their religions. About 2 million people were murdered or underwent all forms of assault and harassment on their way to cross the borders (Sharma 2017; Yousafzai and Lamb 2013). Additionally, Pakistan has faced territorial disputes with Afghanistan and India. These were augmented by many internal conflicts between different communal groups on account of their religious or racial identity (Fair 2008). Peace-promoting speeches by the political and nationalist leaders such as Mohammad Ali Jinnah did not fully succeed to unite the people on one common ground, for many people believed that their nationalism was based on their provincial, ethnic, linguistic and/or cultural backgrounds. An outcome of such parochial world view was the major rupture in the history of Pakistan, that is, the fall of East Pakistan and the formation of Bangladesh as an independent country, following the 1971 Indo–Pak war (Biberman and Castellano 2018).

Pakistan is believed to be the world's first Muslim ideological state with about 97 per cent Muslim population constituting Sunni and Shia Muslims, each subdivided into additional sub-sects (Halai and Durrani 2018). The lack of inter- and intra-religious tolerance has led to the rise of sectarianism and militancy, especially by strong conservative forces who keep trying to forcefully impose their strict interpretation of Islam as the only correct one on the other Muslims and non-Muslims. These ultra-conservative forces were particularly strengthened under the Islamization policies of President Zia-ul-Haq, who, in the words of the Aga Khan, attempted 'to make Pakistan more Islamic than it was' and 'failed to answer a crucial question – what kind of Islam did he intend?' (Interview with His Highness the Aga Khan 2010) This sectarianism reached its peak during the Afghan migration in Pakistan and the rise of Taliban Various militant groups were especially armed and trained by the international agencies on Pakistani soil to support the United States and its allies during the 1979–1989 Soviet–Afghan War. Pakistan became a 'safe haven' for the religious zealots, who migrated here from their counties to get training and patronage (Ford 2017; Habib 2013; Halai and Durrani 2018).

Post-Soviet-Afghan war, different militant groups have continued penetrating Pakistan with different political agendas, disguised under religious coatings. After the terrorist attacks on the World Trade Center on 11 September 2001, Pakistan's government ended its ties with the Taliban regime in Afghanistan and supported the United States in its 'war against terrorism'. This stance of the Pakistan government outraged militant groups, who openly waged war against Pakistan's government. Pakistan's initial negotiation appeasement tactics with the militant groups did not work, and the Taliban kept occupying Pakistan territories such as the district of Swat, where they not only demolished ancient Buddhist statues, but also exploited the natural resources to get money from their illegal sales (Yousafzai and Lamb 2013). The militants started launching attacks on schools, mosques, shrines, cinemas and other public places in the major urban areas, causing deep damage to the image of Pakistan abroad and to law, infrastructure and socio-cultural fabric at home (ICG 2015).

Finally, in 2014, Pakistan army launched a military operation called *Zarb-e Azb* to disrupt he militants. The United States offered additional support by launching drone strikes on militant camps based in Pakistan. According to Ford (2017), during the Pakistan–American operations against the so-called extremists and militants, hundreds of civilians were also killed and thousands were displaced from their homes and on average, six civilians lost their lives for one militant in a drone strike. Admittedly, despite of all security measures and military operations, the violent attacks have not ended. In 2017 alone, Pakistan was the site of 370 extremist violent attacks, including twenty-four suicide attacks.

Ethnic tensions also contribute to violence and terrorism in Pakistan. Following the East vs. West Pakistan's ethnic war, in the 1980s Karachi became a victim of ethnic violence between Mahajirs and Pathans. Further conflicts have erupted in Balochistan, where Baloch nationalists continue separatist movements targeting Pakistani state, army and, at times, people who belong to other ethnicities.

In addition to ideological and military-motivated violence and conflicts, Pakistan is also rife with other hegemonic forms of violence: domestic violence against women; landowners', industrialists' and business holders' violence against farmers, workers and servicemen in their farms, factories, shops and corporations, and blasphemy-related violence against the liberal thinkers and non-Muslim sects. Other forms of violence and conflict, associated with gender, poverty, health, space limitation and pollution take place on a daily basis, without being considered as forms of violence and being reported (Ajmal, Umer Bin 2012; Habib 2013; Hyder Akram and Padda 2015, ICG 2014). Most cases rarely make it forward to the justice system, unless there is a huge noise raised locally and internationally, such as in the case of seven-year-old girl's rape in Kasur, Punjab.[1]

Education as 'a promoter' of conflict and violence

Educational systems can act to support, maintain or disrupt violence. The United Nations Declaration of Human Rights highlights the need to structure education so that it can promote tolerance among different social groups (United Nations 2015). Ironically, educational institutions around the world have been implicated for promoting prejudices and violence. The division of schools into private and public with streams and tracks within them, selective so-called merit only-based admission policies, exclusivist curricula that reflect the 'truths' of the dominant elite, authoritarian, disrespectful, biased teacher–student relationships, capital punishment, bullying, and stressful and decontextualized and meritocratic-only modes of assessment are just few examples of symbolic violence created by schools and education systems (Anyon 1980; Danish and Iqbal 2016; Grenfell 2014). The same can be observed in the Pakistani context, where the public, private and religious systems of education have a wide gulf in their philosophy, curriculum, mode of assessment and instructions. It has contributed to a fragmented Pakistani society with the people having divided interests and opposing goals (Rahman 2004). The school textbooks generally do not acknowledge the religious, ethnic and racial diversity existing in Pakistan. The books of Pakistan Studies generally provide a superficial outlook of a uniform Pakistani culture with minor regional differences. The Islamic Studies course does not discuss at any point the diversity and pluralism among the

Muslims in terms of their practices, traditions and beliefs. Therefore, there is less likelihood of appreciation of the differences existing in the society (Nayar and Salim 2005; Malik 2012).

In 2006–2007, the Federal Ministry of Education provided guidelines for the National Curriculum, which clearly state to not include any content that is prejudicial and controversial. However, this guideline was violated in the new textbooks published in 2013–2014 with many examples instigating biases against Christians, Hindus and Sikhs (Ahmed 2017; Paul 2014). For instance, history textbooks continue to glorify the acts of Muslim invaders, who had demolished temples or waged holy war against non-Muslims (Paul 2014). Paul (2014) argues that the hatred injected to the young minds in schools later contributes to the terrorist attacks and desecration of the religious places. The term jihad is hammered down on young minds, without explaining its context in Islamic history and its various meanings and true essence.

It is however not the government and local bureaucratic setup who are solely responsible for promoting violence and hate in the educational system. In certain cases, international agencies have also contributed to the spread of hate through curriculum. Malala Yousafzai, famous activist and educational campaigner, discusses in her book an example of how during the Soviet–Afghan war, the children in refugee camps were provided with the textbooks published by an American University with the hate-promoting contents. There were mathematical problems, which included devout Muslims fighting with and killing Russian 'infidels' (Yousafzai and Lamb 2013). This example clearly demonstrates how education has been used as a vehicle to inject hatred. Lall (2008) and Talbani (1996) have suggested that such hate and prejudices in the school curricula have increased with the rise of conservative religious parties in India and Pakistan.

Furthermore, the traditional, 'banking' pedagogy of teaching (Freire 2000/1970), which requires teachers to indoctrinate their students in prescribed textbooks' contents, further adds fuel to the fire. Assuming textbooks as the fountain of wisdom, sole authority or simply the most reliable texts for passing the low and high stake tests, as well as unequipped with critical analysis skills, both the teachers and the students generally do not question or challenge any information or idea expressed in them. A survey, conducted with eighty teachers from twenty different schools in Peshawar, has revealed that 100 per cent of the respondents viewed their curricula as not fostering reflective thinking skills among the students (Butt, Iqbal, Naseeruddin, Hussain and Muhammad 2011). These findings are similar to mainstream schools in other cities, even though the students and teachers in larger urban centres have access to alternative sources of knowledge, such as media and internet. While these alternative knowledge sources could enable teachers to bring in diverse views and develop critical thinking among students, the projection of violence in children's popular cartoon shows, political talk shows and action movies can also serve to counter peace values.

Education as a victim of conflict/violence

There are a number of ways by which education became a victim of violence and terror. The increase in militancy, particularly during the post-9/11 period, made education and educational institutions prime sites for conflict and violence. Militant groups tried to control education for their agendas.

Madrasahs were their first victims. Currently, about 2.5–3 million children are enrolled in around 14,000 madrasah schools (Iqbal and Raza 2015). Historically mosques have served not only as places of worship but also encompassed other functions such as centres of learning and cultural activities. However, over a period of time, the foreign and local militants tried to seize these centres of worship and learning so as to exploit religious sentiments of the faithful for their political agendas. Many of the unregistered madrasahs, in particular, became the centres of militant groups and their activities (Fair 2008). The siege of madrasah at the infamous Red Mosque (*lal masjid*) in Islamabad in 2007 by Pakistan's army revealed how militants strive to hijack religious and educational places to promote highly exclusive and destructive agendas.

Exploiting religious sentiments is an important source from which militants and populists hire people, who would freely work for their cause with loyalty and dedication. Sophisticated in rhetoric and use of the sacred texts, these populists and militants brainwash the illiterate and semi-illiterate masses proclaiming themselves as defenders of faith and mobilizing the faithful for violence against anyone they see as threat to their authority and political-economic interests (Khan and Wei 2016). A case in point was the 2017 murder of a young blogger Mashal Khan at Abdul Wali Khan University where religious militants planned accusations of blasphemy and apostasy on Mashal, which, he never committed.

Despite Islam's emphasis on '*huqooq-ul-ibad*' (faithfuls' rights), the notion of human rights is viewed by the Pakistani ultra conservatives as an externally planted idea aiming to destroying the integrity of Muslim communities (Abu-Nimer and Kadayifci 2011). There is a famous hadith of Prophet Muhammad, which says acquisition of knowledge is obligatory for both men and women. Yet, the militants and religious populists continue to target specifically girls' school, with an argument that the kind of education disseminated in these schools is not in accordance with the teachings of Islam, a message that is almost similar to that Boko Haram in northwest Africa (Ford 2017). Such kind of brainwashing can especially instigate the extremists to target the educational institutes and projects, which are established or funded by the Pakistani state with foreign aid. Studies by Talbani (1996) and Iqbal and Raza (2015) suggest that the unsupervised dissemination of distorted facts and prejudiced views in madrasahs sharply channelize sectarian conflicts. The contemporary subjects, modern literature, sports and co-curricular activities are a very limited (if any at all) part of madrasah education. Therefore, the students studying there do not have enough opportunities to broaden their mental horizons. On the other hand, majority of the madrasahs provide facilities of accommodation, free food and textbook and do not require students to pay fees. This attracts poor people to get their children enrolled in madrasahs.

Notably, regardless of the critique, there is little empirical ground to consider madrasahs as breeding grounds for terrorists. A survey report by Fair (2008) found that out of 141 militants from Pakistan (the survey's participants), only 12 per cent had attended madrasahs. With the exception of 6 per cent participants, all others had formal schooling from the mainstream schools. Ford's more recent analysis (2017) of forty BBC and CNN articles reveals that, many times, the terrorists have graduated from modern higher education institutions. This poses a number of serious questions such as why their higher education from national and international institutions has failed to transform their intolerant attitudes; importantly, is it the very modern education they received that has created their intolerant attitudes? Further studies are required to identify the elements that have motivated them for terrorist activities.

Post-9/11, when militants failed to get political, economic, military and moral support from the masses, they started terrorist attacks on schools, colleges and universities, with more frequent attacks on girls' schools. Between the years 2009–2012, there were 838 reported cases of terrorist attacks on schools in Pakistan, destroying not only the school buildings but also murdering students, teachers and other school staff (Ford 2017; GCPEA 2014). Federally Administered Tribal Areas (FATA) have been particularly vulnerable to suicide bombers (Basit 2010). During last three years, however Balochistan has become more heavily affected by the terrorist activities than FATA, with 44 per cent of all terrorist attacks in Pakistan (Pakistan Institute for Peace Studies 2018). Even though the attack on the Army Public School in Peshawar (December 2014), which murdered 149 people (including 132 students), finally compelled the government to devise strong actions against the terrorist acts (Ford 2017), attacks on educational institutions have continued. Examples are Baccha University in Charsadda (Khyber Pukhtunkhwa) in 2016, which killed twenty-one people (Bhattacharjee 2016; Halai and Durrani 2018).

In sum, education in Pakistan has been a major victim of violence, both symbolic and material: hardening the curricula, textbooks and student–teacher relationships though a particular form of Islamization, damaging physical structures, and killing of students, teachers and staff are some key strategies. These security concerns prompt the feelings of fear in the parents to send their children to schools and colleges. Unfortunately, in a country where there are still reportedly 22.6 million children out of school (UNICEF 2018), these terrorist attacks further create obstacles in the way of literacy.

Initiatives for promoting peace and harmony

During the 1960s, the Field Marshal Ayub Khan (who later became Pakistan's second president) took measures to upgrade madrasahs and established the *Islamic Research Institute*. The institute had a mission to give exposure of modern ideas to *ulemas*,[2] create bridge between traditional madrasahs and modern schooling, and reinterpret religion according to modern times. However, according to Sajjad, Christie and Taylor (2017), the conservative forces criticized the scholarly work of the institute and labelled it as western propaganda tool against Islam and organized many rallies and processions against it.

The post-9/11 period marked another period of reforms and initiatives for promoting peace and harmony. President Pervaiz Musharraf tried to minimize the negative influences of madrasahs by introducing new programmes and non-religious subjects. These included expanding the curricula of madrasah schools in order to bring them closer to the mainstream schooling and to add restrictions to madrasahs for enrolling foreign students. Iqbal and Raza (2015) argue that the National Education Policy, in its attempt at mainstreaming madrasahs, aimed to equate the madrasah *sanads* with the degrees of formal education.

The reforms required madrasahs to register with the government, submit a yearly report of educational activities and an audit report to the registrar. The reforms also restricted madrasahs from teaching and publishing any hateful materials, which might instigate religious intolerance, militancy and sectarian divide. However, most of these reforms were rejected by the representatives of the madrasahs. Sajjad, Christie and Tayler (2017) argue that these state's reform attempts backfired by provoking reactive radicalism. Another key activity, as Jamil (2009) notes, was the revision of the educational curricula to introduce diversity, remove hate and exclusivist messages, and rebalance religious content with topics on citizenship such as gender, ethnic, sectarian and other diversities that need to be acknowledged and respected. Realizing that future extremists and militants may also come from secular universities, the government's Higher Education Commission has proposed additional measures such as Character Building Societies, to de-radicalize Pakistani youth at universities and campuses (Jamil 2009).

It is important to note that some of these government initiatives are either supported or funded by outside actors such as USAID, World Bank and others. There is a global realization that the enormous youth bulge (60 per cent of 208 million Pakistanis are under twenty-five years[3]) needs to be provided with hope for decent education and employment, so as to avoid the youth's radicalization and ensuing social-political cataclysms. The external affiliations in this regards, however, have been a two-edged sword. On one hand, the provision of external funding, research and expertise has helped to strengthen policies and action plans. On the other hand, they have been limited and vulnerable due to accusations of carrying foreign, anti-Islamic agendas or being simply window-dressing tools for foreign aid and resulting in almost no change (Yusuf 2011).

In addition to the government, Pakistani civil society and some non-government organizations (NGOs) have made further efforts in peace education. Peace Education and Development Foundation (PEAD) was setup by Sameena Imtiaz in year 2013. This institution is working to create awareness on gender equality, peace-building, environmental wellbeing and conflict resolution. While arranging training sessions at madrasahs, members of PEAD have found that in Punjab, many madrasah heads have realized that Islam does not support terrorism (Abu Nimer and Kadayifci 2011). PEAD has also launched a programme with the name of Peace Network Pakistan (PNP) with the assistance of the NGO Save the Children-Sweden. PNP creates resources to challenge violence, fundamentalism and terrorism. Similarly, another organization Open Minds Pakistan, with the assistance of the Institute for War and Peace Reporting (IWPR), UK has facilitated the acquisition of vocational skills for madrasah students aged ten to nineteen years, so these young people may engage themselves in constructive work instead of destructive work and violence. The International Center for Diplomacy (IRCD) has attempted to improvise madrasahs by presenting the concepts of Human Rights and Peace, embodied within Islamic framework.

Regretfully, however, the workshops organized by IRCD for the madrasah teachers from Sindh, Balochistan and Khyber Pakhtunkhwa have not produced widespread curricular change in the respective madrasah (Abu-Nimer and Kadayifci 2011). However, in interviews conducted from a sample of participants, Abu-Nimer and Kadayifci (2011) found that many of the participants have integrated human rights and peace into their madrasah curricula, and 78.8 per cent of participants considered this as the most important outcome of the workshops. Through additional data from the interviews, Abu-Nimer and Kadayifci (2011) gained further insight into participants' understanding of the nature and extent of curricular and pedagogical change for peace education, including spreading the message in sermons that not every European is their enemy, refraining teachers from criticizing other sects, and establishing good relationship with non-Muslims.

Members of the Swat Youth Front (another NGO) organized workshops at schools on the concept of human rights and peace. Students were encouraged to express their views in a magazine Naveed-e-Sahar, which was specifically launched as a part of this project. However, despite of its success in intervention, the project was closed due to lack of funds (Ahmed 2017). Grammar School, Rawalpindi is the only private school in Pakistan offering peace education classes in accordance with the guidelines provided by UNESCO. Habib (2013) found that these classes have continued to run for over twenty years without depending on any funds from donor agency. However, over time, the use of innovative pedagogies by the teachers is reported to have been reduced. One of the reasons cited for this was the deficiency of funding for the professional development of the teachers in dissemination of peace education.

In sum, the initiatives of civil society for the promotion of peace in Pakistan are commendable. There is an increasing need for its enhancement and expansion. Collaboration with government and with other national and international education stakeholders to address issues of funding, sensitivity of the context, and innovation are important for its sustainability and outcomes in the long run.

Curriculum and pedagogical approaches for peace education in Pakistan

Improved quality of life is an essential ingredient for peace and development. This requires access of quality education that can build capacities and generate human capital. This also requires skill development of the learners to deal with contemporary and future challenges. For that besides teaching content, pedagogy is also important. The study of Afzal (2015), in Punjab, at the grade 9 and 10 level, found that rote learning and memorization, without conceptual understanding, are still dominant across public and private schools in Pakistan. The case of madrasah schools is even more wretched, where in most cases, the students are expected to memorize 400 or 500 years old commentaries, written by ulemas of that era, without using analytical skills (Iqbal and Raza 2015). This shows that the elements of higher order learning especially critical thinking is missing from the education. It is important to develop critical thinking among the students, so they do not blindly accept what they are being told to do, but question the practices that are unfair; create new solutions and become active members of their societies. They need to be actively engaged in the activities that help them realize the need of peace and its value. Similarly, the parents and teachers need to stop giving corporal punishment to children, as it gives them impression that they can also control others by being violent. There should not be inconsistency between what is taught and what is practised. It is not only the content, but also pedagogy, teaching style and strategies, that can transform the extremist mindset into liberal and tolerant ones.

Against this backdrop, there is almost no direct formal peace education in Pakistan. Schools and universities avoid issues of conflicts and violence. The public knows of school based conflicts through informal discussion, social networks, seminars and news channels. Journalistic articles in the newspapers give good attention to incidents of violence and conflict, without deep analysis of the cause and effects. Some universities, private schools and individual educators are involved in addressing issues of violence and conflict in the society. Below we discuss how peace and conflicts are engaged at the Aga Khan University's Institute for Educational Development (AKU-IED).

Contribution of Aga Khan university

The Aga Khan University is an international university situated in six countries (Afghanistan, Kenya, Tanzania, Uganda, Pakistan and the UK). A part of the Aga Khan Development Network (AKDN), the university is actively involved in the promotion of peace, tolerance and pluralism in Pakistan and the region. The network's head, His Highness, the Aga Khan has continuously emphasized the peaceful nature of Islam and the necessity of peace and dialogue for development and human survival. The network has taken a multi-institutional area development approach (MIAD) that emphasizes multi-generational, multi-sector engagement, inter-agency and holistic development approach where economic, educational, material-economic, ecological, cultural and psychological aspects of human struggle are simultaneously addressed.[4] Such an approach leads to a focus on common life issues and challenges, non-denominational, inclusive participation, wider benefits for all human beings.[5] Tajik (2017), in his study of AKDN work in Chitral, suggests that such approach to real life experiences of challenges and the development of local solutions lead to harmony and peace.

The Aga Khan University is very much part of this mission. Within the university, its Pakistan-based Institute for Educational Development (AKU-IED) is engaged in improving the quality of education though capacity development (of teachers and school leaders), school improvement, curriculum reform, research and knowledge production and policy recommendations (https://www.aku.edu/iedpk/Pages/Home.aspx). The Institute has played an instrumental role in contributing to peace education, through teacher education and resource development (Dean 2005; Dean, Joldoshalieva, and Sayani 2006). Dean, Joldoshalieva, and Sayani (2006) developed a teaching and learning resource for education for citizenship, human rights and conflict resolution. This comprehensive resource creatively engages teachers and students in understanding and nurturing concepts, skills, pedagogical strategies and values in democratic citizenship, human rights and conflict resolution.

AKU-IED faculty and graduate students have conducted research and published articles on the nature of peace and conflict in the country, including challenges, solutions and teachers' roles in the peace making and building processes (Dean 2005; Halai and Durrani 2018; Lalani 2017; Niyozov 1995; Shamsuddin 2016). In 1995, Niyozov highlighted the daunting challenges that stand in front of the application of conflict resolution and peace-making in Pakistani schools: these included weak teacher preparation and subsequent weak knowledge; lack of materials on the conflicting perspectives about issues and topic for discussion; exclusivist social studies and Islamiyah curricula; dominance of test/exam-based culture in schools; the unwillingness or the fear of listening to and acknowledging alternative and uncomfortable viewpoints (especially those that are not part of Pakistan's ideological and curricula framework); fear for being accused in blasphemy and apostasy by the religious establishment and zealots, and fear of being accused as unpatriotic by the government, military and religious apparatuses. These challenges have persisted, as Shamsuddin (2016) found through his study on teachers' understanding of peace and conflict, and their pedagogical solutions in northern Pakistan. Shamsuddin suggested that peaceful and rational interpretations of one's faith were a part of the sustainable peace-making in the region. Tajik (2017) identified the key features of the earlier-mentioned AKDN work that contribute to harmony and peace in Chitral, and suggested it as a model to replicate in the rest of the country.

Most recent research by Halai and Durrani (2018) again reiterated Niyozov's 1995 concerns, but also provided updated developments. Wider in scope and methodology, Halai and Durrani (2018) identified opportunities and insights on understanding and developing peace education model that are relevant and sustainable in Pakistan.

An experimental study by Lalani (2017) directly explored the efficacy of teaching concepts of peace education, in Pakistan, through the use of Anne Frank narratives to reduce children's attitudes of prejudice and discrimination in specific dimensions (i.e. ethnicity & race, religion and gender). Anne Frank was a young Jewish girl, living in Nazi-led Germany. As Kuitert (2010) notes, Frank's diary, has captured the minds people of different age groups across the world, making it most widely read non-fiction book after Bible. Lalani's study involved experimental and comparison groups of students of grades 5 and 6, with nearly similar age group and gender division from two elite schools in Karachi, which follow England's national curriculum. The groups were formed after matching characteristics and comparing the results of the pre-test, which showed high level of prejudice in both groups with no significant difference [$U = 12101$; $Z = -0.33$; $p = 0.73$].

The intervention named as ROYAL (Reading of Young Anne's Literature), were centred on the narratives of Anne Frank (Selected extracts from *The Diary of a Young Girl* and *Hannah Goslar Remembers: A Childhood Friend of Anne Frank*). One of the aims of using Anne Frank narratives, instead of using local literature, was to help the students to expand their perspectives from a narrow local context by developing a sense of world-mindedness. Secondly, the local issues of conflict, based on prejudice and discrimination, are difficult to directly address with the school students, in Pakistan, as it could evoke controversy. It was believed that the use of the Anne Frank's narratives would help students not only to sympathize with Anne Frank and those who lost their lives during wartimes, but also to reflect on the current cases of discrimination and prejudice in their own local contexts and elsewhere.

The interventions, based on the Anne Frank literature, were provided only to an experiment group for fifteen sessions, of one hour each, over a period of two months. During the intervention, besides reading and discussing the text, the students were also engaged in activities to help them reflect on contemporary and local cases of prejudice and discrimination, to provide relevancy to present and future. In other words, scaffolding was used to build notions of diversity, equity, and peace so as to allow students use their awareness and skills in discussing issues in Pakistan contexts.

In contrast, the comparison group studied the same concepts through discussions and debates, but without the use of Anne Frank literature. The post-test was taken after the completion of the interventions on both the groups. Post-test results revealed that the students in the experiment group exhibited more unprejudiced and nondiscriminatory attitudes as compared to their counterparts with a significant difference [$U = 333.5$; $Z = -6.33$; $p = 0.01$] and large effect size ($r = -0.63$). Admittedly, this was a small-scale study with participants studying in the elite international schools of Karachi. Moreover, it was not a longitudinal study, therefore, the results do not speak to issues of long-term changes in attitude and behaviours.

In addition to providing research and curriculum materials, the Institute for Educational Development has also offered various teacher training programmes, in which the theme of peace education is addressed. Issues and questions related to peace and conflict resolution are addressed in courses on social studies education, critical pedagogy, citizenship education and learning to live in twenty-first century. Courses under these titles are offered at both graduate and certificate levels. During these long and short term courses, the institute's students are exposed to local and international research on peace, conflict, human rights (including girls'), diversity and pluralism. More importantly, the participants' own beliefs, values and practices are critically constructively engaged. Research by critical and transformative pedagogues, such as Dean (2005) and Waghid (2014), suggests that these engagements and practices can promote various levels of transformation. The institute works with various international partners such as Global Affairs-Canada, Department of Foreign Aid and Trade-Australia, USAID, German Federal Enterprise for International Cooperation (GIZ), European Community, as well as local partners such as the Aga Khan Education Services, local government's Reform Support Unit, and civil society, such as The Citizen Foundation.

Implications: Seizing the potentials of peace education in Pakistan

Pakistan, including its education, have undergone huge challenges and damages, as far as peace and peace education are concerned. These damages are created by various direct and obvious and indirect and subtle ways. There are no quick models or magic spells to tackle the causes of violence and terrorism. While education is critical, it is also critical to not simply educationalize issues of conflict and peace. Solution can not solely reside in changing the educational structure and curricula. Peace and conflict are larger structural and political-economic issues, involving the local and global stakeholders. Even within education, there is a need for all stakeholders concerned about peace-building, to cooperate and work together. Schools and other educational institutes need to be made safe and secure places. Increased access to education cannot be attainable, if educational institutions are vulnerable to the threats of violence and terrorism. While school and campus securitization is important, beefing heavily armed security personnel at the campuses may not be a sustainable or even morally right solution.[6]

The political parties or individuals supporting the cause of terrorism also needs to be held accountable by their citizens and the international community. However, some actors within the international community also need to be held accountable, as well. While Pakistan has been applauded for taking actions against terrorists by the international community, the question arises as to who provides arms and ammunition to the terrorists? From where do they get resources, enabling them to fight against state and its army? The terrorists and terrorism could not have flourished to the extent they do, without the sponsorship from international agencies, institutions and individuals. The international community, the government of Pakistan and educational institutions have to work collaboratively to end the menace of terrorism. How is peace possible, if on one hand, the international community conducts conferences on promoting peace and refugee education, and on other hand, weapons of mass destructions are being manufactured and sold out to terrorists? The following questions raised by twelve-year-old Anne Frank (2003) in the context of the Second World War are still worth reflecting:

> Why is England manufacturing bigger and better airplanes and bombs and at the same time churning out new houses for reconstruction? Why are the millions spent on war each day, while not a penny is available for the medical science, artists, or the poor? Why do people have to starve when mountains of food are rotting away in the other parts of the world? (278)

Notably, Malala (Yousufzai and Lamb 2013) has also been asking similar questions to the world powerful authorities, asking them to stop producing and selling arms and increase the building of schools, production of books and educational materials and work for peace.

The role, priorities and policy initiatives of the Pakistani government with regard to peace education need to change for significant changes to occur. It is vital to recognize that education sits within a multi-faceted policy context in Pakistan and the issues of violence and conflict cross these sectors. There are serious gaps between the rhetoric of cross-sectoral policy documents and the realities of implementation of peace education in the country. If well-qualified people are not getting jobs, if poor people are deprived of health care because of not having sufficient money, if people are unable to get married and have sustainable families due to poverty, if people are dying because of heat or cold, lack of clean water and other basic necessities, then they have no choices but to break rules and laws, be angry and mentally upset, engage in unlawful and harmful activities that are destructive to them and others around them (Krueger 2017).

Peace education in Pakistan appears futile, there is a need to acknowledge, respect and engage the differences between the people belonging to different castes, ethnicities and religions in the formal curriculum. Although the National Curriculum mentions the need for awareness of multi-cultures, this element is largely missing from the textbooks, creating superficial depiction of a homogenous society. Despite the education policy's recognition of the need for a peace education programme, it has not been integrated in school curricula and biases. Hatred, prejudice and discrimination continue to appear in school textbooks. Similarly, celebrating International Peace Day or organizing occasional programmes like theatre performance, art and poetry that touch on the theme of peace is not sufficient to eliminate conflict and bring peace in the country. A much more substantive programme of peace education is needed, with particular emphasis on reducing prejudice and discrimination, global citizenship, pluralistic outlook, conflict resolution and environmental wellness. While religious precepts of harmony, forgiveness, supplication, alms-giving, and deeper adherence to Islam are valuable, these need to be accompanied by materialist political economic analysis of the structural and cultural roots of violence and development solution. Peace education programme requires not only formulating objectives and printing of the textbooks, but also critical pedagogical approaches and assessment strategies to evaluate the outcomes of the program.

Building on more local research about youth and their needs and perspectives can help to build peace-building programmes with stronger contextual relevance. A uniform programme of education cannot be applicable for all the people as people belonging to various classes and subcultures have their own sets of norms and values. For instance, an educational programme advertised as being affiliated or funded by any American or European country might attract youth from the urban areas. On contrary, such an advertisement could have counter effect in tribal areas, where many people might view foreign aid or involvement with suspicion. One of the reasons for the success of the Swat Youth Front's peace education programme was catering directly to the needs of local community affected by the terror strikes of Taliban and at the same time not publicizing that source of aid received for the project. On the contrary, as Ahmed (2017) notes, the training sessions for the teachers on peace education in Karachi, organized by the Charter for Compassion, Pakistan, are said to have created less impact in education for having not taken into consideration the ethnic and sectarian issues of Karachi. Sajjad, Christie and Taylor's 2017 survey of 386 participants from seven regions of Pakistan informs that the youths supported more religious ideas in contrast to western secular ideas. However, when choosing between liberal and conservative religious ideas, the youth accepted the liberal Islamic ideas, norms and practices. This type of local contextual research is vital to better inform the need, applicability and possibilities of Peace Education Programmes in Pakistan.

Although the Pakistani government has made provisions for bridging the gulf between madrasahs and the mainstream schools, the actual integration still seems far away as there is a great difference in terms of their philosophical ideals, which determine the goals, objectives, content and pedagogy of teaching and learning. There is also a major difference in terms of formal curriculum, system of enrolment and assessment, infrastructure and facilities and overall organization and management. Still, all these differences could be minimized if ulemas are willing to cooperate. Iqbal and Raza (2015) assert that when the government of Pakistan promulgated the *Pakistani Madrassas Education Ordinance 2001*, to standardize the curricula of all madrasahs functioning in Pakistan, the ulemas did not cooperate with the government. Therefore, their inflexible attitude failed the enforcement of this ordinance within the country, which could have at least brought the level of madrasahs on a par with each other. Similarly, Iqbal and Raza (2015) found that many of the other reforms, introduced by the government of Pakistan, have not been accepted by the ulemas. The ulemas viewed these standardization and mainstreaming attempts as American conspiracy to secularize their education system, undermine their sole authority on these institutions, and diminish their 'unique Islamic identity'.

Similarly, the government needs to address the issue of hate-speech by the ulemas in their hate provoking sermons. The role of informal education could play a role here, to help to both inform and possible change mindsets. They need to bring those aspects of religion that unite people and respect differences and highlight the importance of peace in their sermons. Instead of labelling certain group as infidel (*kafir*), they need to harness the message of love and fraternity for all humanity. As it appears from the past experiences, ulemas would probably not participate in the sessions organized by non-clergy educators, assuming it as conspiracy of international community (Yousuf 2011). However, the state could hire the services of enlightened ulemas to speak to other ulemas on value of peace and tolerance. Ahmed (2017) found that Jamia Naeemia madrasah in Lahore, Punjab, has arranged workshops related to peace education among mosque leaders and ulemas. The lectures involved a range of topics, including the devastating impact of sectarian conflicts, Islam's emphasis on peace and the lectures' role for guidance in matters pertaining to polio vaccination campaign. Although the effect of these sessions on the participants have not been assessed, Ahmed (2017) noted that these lectures received positive response from the participants. Such programmes in all conflict-affected regions needs to be organized on regular basis.

Peace-building programmes require not only the efforts of politicians, but also inclusion of intellectuals including philosophers, sociologists, psychologists, educationists, historians and educationists for their success. Similarly, they require the participation of both male and female citizens. In most of the cases, women are generally not involved in decisive processes of establishing peace. Habib (2013) has cited examples of women's peace initiatives in many countries of the world, including Liberia, Bosnia, South Africa and Cyprus. It is worthwhile to mention that Malala Yousafzai, the youngest recipient of Nobel Prize for Peace, is a Pakistani citizen. Therefore, the role of women in such initiatives is especially critical for consideration. Peace-building programmes need to be designed and executed under the leadership of men and women intellectuals on merit basis.

Conclusions

Peace is vital for Pakistan and other developing countries' survival, progress, and prosperity. Peace education can play important role by developing skills, knowledge and dispositions among the students, teachers, parents and communities. Regardless of the multiple challenges, peace education appears to be gaining recognition and momentum in Pakistan among the government, civil society, and private institutions. Increasingly, government, civil society, private institutions and international agencies are commingling in their promotion of peace, pluralism, and tolerance through formal and non-formal education and other social services. AKU IED Pakistan appears to be a pioneering institution in peace and tolerance education. Situated within AKDN's value framework, the Institute has developed courses and programmes, resources and research around this tasks.

However, peace-making and peace-building are much larger and broader tasks: they require political-economic restructuring and cultural transformation of the current neoliberal-driven Pakistani society into a more equitable and inclusive one, where peoples' quality of employment, health, law and order, human rights and education is improved and hope is made more affordable.

Notes

1   https://tribune.com.pk/story/1615933/1-kasur-murder-case-prime-suspect-arrested-zainabs-neighbour/.
2   *Ulema* stands for Islamic religious scholars.
3   2017 Census of Pakistan. Wikipedia https://en.wikipedia.org/wiki/2017_Census_of_Pakistan
4   See Mary Drinkwater (Chapter 2, this book) for some strong connections between *robust global democracy* principles and the MIAD approach.
5   Drinkwater (Chapter 2, this book).
6   Children, especially from private schools, are escorted to and from their schools with heavily armed guards. Affording such security escorts is not possible to the majority of the children. More so, it provides wrong message about how peace is built and sustained in society.

References

Abu-Nimer, Mohammed and Ayse Kadayifci. 'Human Rights and Building Peace: The Case of Pakistani Madrasas'. *The International Journal of Human Rights* 15, no. 7 (2011): 1136–1159.

Adnan, Abdullah. 'Pakistan: Creation and Genesis'. *The Muslim World* 96, no. 2 (2006): 201–217.

Afzal, Madiha. 'Education and Attitudes in Pakistan - Understanding Perceptions of Terrorism (Special Report)'. 2015. Accessed 10 January 2018. https://www.usip.org/sites/default/files/SR367-Education-and-Attitudes-in-Pakistan.pdf.

Ahmed, Zahid Shahab. 'Peace Education in Pakistan'. 3 March 2017. Accessed 10 January 2018. https://www.usip.org/publications/2017/03/peace-education-pakistan.

Anyon, Jean. 'Social Class and the Hidden Curriculum of Work'. *Journal of Education* 162, no. 1 (1980), 67–91.

Basit, Abdul. *Attacks on Educational Institutes*. Islamabad, Pakistan: USIP, 2010.

Biberman, Yelena and Rachel Castellano. 'Genocidal Violence, Nation-Building, and the Bloody Birth of Bangladesh'. *Asian Security* 14, no. 2 (2018): 106–118.

Bhattacharjee, Dhrubajyoti. 'The Terrorist Attack on Students at Charsadda, Pakistan'. Indian Council of World Affairs, 10 February 2016. Accessed 15 January 2018. http://www.icwa.in/pdfs/VP/2014/ TerroristAttackStudentsCharsaddaPakistanVP10022016.pdf.

Danish, Malik Haqnawaz and Asma Iqbal. 'Corporal Punishment and Its Effects in Pakistan'. *International Research Journal of Arts and Humanities* 44, no. 44 (2016): 11.

Dean, Bernadette L. 'Citizenship education in Pakistani Schools: Problems and Possibilities'. *International Journal of Citizenship and Teacher Education* 1, no. 2 (2005): 35.

Dean, B., R. Joldoshalieva, and F. Sayani. *Creating a Better World*. Karachi, Pakistan: Aga Khan University, Institute for Educational Development, 2006.

Fair, C. Christine. 'The Educated Militants of Pakistan: Implications for Pakistan's Domestic Security'. *Contemporary South Asia* 16, no. 1 (2008): 93–106.

Ford, Kieran. 'The Insecurities of Weaponised Education: A Critical Discourse Analysis of the Securitised Education Discourse in North-West Pakistan'. *Conflict, Security & Development* 17, no. 2 (2017): 117–139.

Frank, Anne. *The Diary of a Young Girl: The Definitive Edition*. New York: Penguin Books, 2003.

Freire, Paulo. *Pedagogy of the Oppressed* (30th Anniversary ed.). New York: Continuum, 2000. Original work published 1970.

Global Coalition to Protect Education from Attack (GCPEA). 'Education under Attack 2014 Country Profiles: Pakistan'. 2014. Accessed 19 January 2018. http:// protectingeducation.org/sites/default/files/documents/eua_2014_country_profiles_ pakistan.pdf.

Grenfell, Michael James, ed. *Pierre Bourdieu: Key Concepts*. London: Routledge, 2014.

Habib, Zehra. *Women's Perspectives of Peace: Unheard Voices from Pakistan*. Fairfax, USA: George Mason University, 2013.

Halai, Anjum and Naureen Durrani. 'Teachers as Agents of Peace? Exploring Teacher Agency in Social Cohesion in Pakistan'. *Compare: A Journal of Comparative and International Education* 48, no. 4 (2018): 535–552.

Hilali, A. Z. *US-Pakistan Relationship: Soviet Invasion of Afghanistan*. Taylor & Francis, 2017.

His Highness, the Aga Khan. 'The Power of Wisdom'. Interview by Jean-Jacques Lafaye. *Politique Internationale*, 18 August 2010. Accessed 16 January 2018. https://simerg. com/about/voices-%E2%80%9Cthe-power-of-wisdom%E2%80%9D-%E2%80%93- his-highness-the-aga-khan%E2%80%99s-interview-with-politique-internationale/

Hyder, Shabir, Naeem Akram, and Ihtsham Ul Haq Padda. 'Impact of Terrorism on Economic Development in Pakistan'. *Pakistan Business Review* 839 (2015): 704–722.

ICG (International Crisis Group). *Revisiting Counter-terrorism Strategies in Pakistan: Opportunities and Pitfalls*. Asia Report, 2015. Accessed January 17, 2018. http://old.crisisgroup.org/en/regions/asia/south-asia/pakistan/271-revisiting-counter-terrorism-strategies-in-pakistan-opportunities-and-pitfalls.html.

ICG. *Policing Urban Violence in Pakistan*, Asia Report N°255, 23 Jan 2014. Accessed 17 January 2018. http://old.crisisgroup.org/en/regions/asia/south-asia/pakistan/255-policing-urban-violence-in-pakistan.html.

Iqbal and Raza. 'Madrassa Reforms in Pakistan: A Historical Analysis'. ISSRA Papers, 2015. Accessed 17 January 2018. http://www.ndu.edu.pk/issra/issra_pub/articles/issra.

Jamil, B. R. 'Curriculum Reforms in Pakistan – A Glass Half Full or Half Empty?' In *School Curriculum Policies and Practices in South Asian Countries* conference, NCERT Delhi, India, 10–12 August 2009. Accessed 16 January 2018. http://www.itacec.org/document/nep09/NCERT%20Pakistan%20paper%20BRJ.pdf.

Khan, Muhammad Khalil and Lu Wei. 'When Friends Turned into Enemies: The Role of the National State vs. Tehrik-i-Taliban Pakistan (TTP) in the War against Terrorism in Pakistan'. *Korean Journal of Defense Analysis* 28, no. 4 (2016): 597–626.

Khan, Yasmin. *The Great Partition: The Making of India and Pakistan*. Yale University Press, 2017.

Krueger, Alan B. *What Makes a Terrorist*. Princeton, NJ: Princeton University Press, 2017.

Kuitert, Lisa. 'The Publication of Anne Frank's Diary'. *Quaerendo* 40, no. 1 (2010): 50–65.

Lall, Marie. 'Educate to Hate: The Use of Education in the Creation of Antagonistic National Identities in India and Pakistan'. *Compare* 38, no. 1 (2008): 103–119.

Lalani, Munir. *Reducing attitudes of prejudice and discrimination through literature in 'personal, social health education (PSHE) classes: A Quasi experiment on the upper key stage 2 students of the British Schools in Karachi*. Unpublished Master's thesis. Aga Khan University: Karachi, Pakistan, 2017.

Majumdar, Ramesh Chandra, ed. *The Age of Imperial Unity*. Vol. 2. Mumbai: Bharatiya Vidya Bhavan, 1968.

McLeod, John. *The History of India*, Santa Barbara, CA: Greenwood Publishing Group, 2002.

Malik, Akhtar Hassan. *A Comparative study of elite-English-medium schools, public schools, and Islamic madrasahs in contemporary Pakistan: The use of Pierre Bourdieu's theory to understand "inequalities in educational and occupational opportunities*. Unpublished PhD thesis. University of Toronto: Toronto, Canada, 2012.

Malik, Hafeez. *Soviet-Pakistan Relations and Post-Soviet Dynamics, 1947–92*. Dordrecht, NLD: Springer, 2016.

Muhammad Naeem Butt IER, K. U. S. T., Muhammad Iqbal SUIT, K. U. S. T., Muhammad Naseer-Ud-Din IER, Ishtiaq Hussain, and Niaz Muhammad. 'Infuse Concept of Peace in Curriculum Development'. *Contemporary Issues in Education Research* 4, no. 2 (2011): 27.

Nayyar, Abdul Hameed and Ahmed Salim. *The Subtle Subversion: The State of Curricula and Textbooks in Pakistan Urdu, English, Social Studies and Civics*. Islamabad, Pakistan: Sustainable Development Policy Institute, 2005.

Niyozov, Sarfaroz. *Controversy as a Strategy for Social Studies in Pakistan*. Unpublished Master's thesis. Aga Khan University: Karachi. Pakistan, 1995.

Pakistan Institute for Peace Studies. *Pakistan Security Report 2017*. Islamabad: Pak Institute for Peace Studies. Accessed 17 January 2018. https://www.pakpips.com/web/wp-content/uploads/2018/01/sr2017-overview.pdf.

Paul, Anjum James. *Biased Pakistani Textbooks*. Islamabad, Pakistan: Pakistan Minorities Teachers' Association, 2014.

Rahman, Tariq. *Denizens of Alien Worlds: A Study of Education and Polarization in Pakistan*. Karachi: Oxford University Press, 2004.

Sajjad, Fatima, Daniel J. Christie, and Laura K. Taylor. 'De-radicalizing Pakistani Society: The Receptivity of Youth to a Liberal Religious Worldview'. *Journal of Peace Education* 14, no. 2 (2017): 195–214.

Shamsuddin, Noor. *Social Studies' Teachers' Perceptions and Enactment of Peace Education: An Exploratory Case Study from Chitral*. Unpublished Master's thesis. Karachi, Pakistan Aga Khan University, 2016.

Sharma, Manoj. 'Cinematic Representations of Partition of India'. *People: International Journal of Social Sciences* 3, no. 3 (2017).

Shoukat, Sajjad. 'Pakistan's Peacekeeping Role'. In *Pakistan Observer*. 24 October 2016. Accessed on 17 January 2018. https://pakobserver.net/pakistans-peacekeeping-role/.

Tajik, M. A. 'Building Communities by Building Schools in the Rural, Mountainous Regions of Pakistan'. In *Educational Policies in Pakistan, Afghanistan, and Tajikistan: Contested Terrains in the Twenty-First Century*, edited by D. Ashraf, M. Tajik, and S. Niyozov, 121–144. Lanham: Lexington Books, 2017.

Talbani, Aziz. 'Pedagogy, Power, and Discourse: Transformation of Islamic education'. *Comparative Education Review* 40, no. 1 (1996): 66–82.

Umer Bin, Ajmal. A. 'Domestic Violence'. 25 April 2012. Accessed 17 March 2018, https://www.dawn.com/news/713192/domestic-violence-2.

UNICEF. Pakistan Education Statistics 2017. Islamabad: Premier Printers Islamabad, 2018. Accessed 16 June 2018. http://library.aepam.edu.pk/Books/Pakistan%20Education%20Statistics%202016-17.pdf

United Nations. *United Nations Declaration of Human Rights*. 2015. Accessed 20 March 2018. http://www.un.org/en/udhrbook/pdf/udhr_booklet_en_web.pdf.

Waghid, Yusef. 'Islam, Democracy and Education for Non-violence'. *Ethics and Education* 9, no. 1 (2014): 69–78.

Yousafzai, Malala and Lamb, Christina. *I am Malala*. London, UK: Salarzai Limited, 2013.

Yusuf, Huma. 'Conspiracy Fever: The US, Pakistan and Its Media'. *Survival* 53, no. 4 (2011): 95–118.

13

Education for Democratic Peace-building Amid Gendered Violence: Youth Experience and Schooling in Mexico, Bangladesh and Canada

Kathy Bickmore

Chapter outline

- Introduction
- Education and social conflict
- Contexts and research methods
- Findings
  - Mexico
  - Bangladesh
  - Canada
- Discussion and conclusion

Keywords: social conflict; violent environments; publicly funded schools; peace-building; citizenship education

---

Introduction

Social conflicts – disagreements, misunderstandings, competing interests – are natural aspects of human life anywhere. However, conflicts (problems) are not equivalent to violence (inflicting harm), even though conflicts may carry the risk of escalation into violence. Democratic mechanisms for handling conflicts – such as participatory decision-making, equitable gender identity norms and redress of injustice – are directly and indirectly impeded by violence, yet essential to building sustainable peace. The (un)democratic nature of any social context, in turn, shapes people's opportunities for both conflict-related learning and citizenship agency.

What are the main elements shaping the escalation and persistence of difficult, large-scale social conflicts? Norwegian peace studies scholar Johan Galtung (1990, 1969) identifies mutually reinforcing *direct* (physical) and *indirect* (systemic) forms of violence. Indirect violence includes *social-structural* patterns of inequitable access to resources and political power – such as poverty and discrimination – and *cultural* beliefs, attitudes, norms and narratives legitimating direct violence, oppression and/or enmity. Other conflict theories also emphasize social-structural factors impeding people's opportunities to meet their human needs, as roots of the escalation and intractability of large-scale, persistent violent conflicts (Burton 1979, Burton and Dukes 1990). US cultural studies scholar Rob Nixon (2011) updates this theory, pointing to the globalized complexity, fluidity and incremental characteristics of indirect harms such as ecological damage, often invisible to the privileged, which he calls 'slow violence'. Similarly, US political scientist Marc Howard Ross (1993, 2007), based on anthropological evidence from many cultures, distinguishes two dimensions causing (de-)escalation of inter-group *conflicts*: (1) social-structural: communities' unequal access to resources and power for fulfilling tangible interests and (2) (psycho-)cultural: communities' identity-rooted, emotion-laden narrative interpretations of themselves and Others, including trust, fear and enmity. Together, these theories articulate the major factors animating *conflicts*, whether or not these escalate into armed *violence*.

Meaningful *peace* is more than the absence of direct violence. Galtung (1976) distinguishes 'negative peace' (absence of direct violence, for instance, stopping abuse or war) – very valuable, but insufficient to prevent recurrence because causes are unresolved – from sustainable 'positive peace' (presence of justice, through ongoing processes transforming social-structures and cultures into peaceful human–world relations). Thus, inclusive and equitable democracy and human security are essential to meaningful, sustainable peace. As Canadian scholar Ursula Franklin explained in a 1985 lecture (2006, 76–77), 'peace is indivisible:' when some people do not have (just, positive) peace, then nobody can really hold onto peace.

Nancy Fraser's theory of justice (the opposite of indirect systemic violence) includes, similar to the conflict theorists above (social-structural) *redistribution* and (cultural) *recognition* dimensions (2004, 2005). Her later work adds the principle of (democratic) *representation*, referring to inclusive voice in direct, communicative confrontation and transformation of conflict (ibid). I interpret this representation dimension as the nonviolent analogue to what Galtung calls direct violence: some direct episodes of *conflict may be handled nonviolently*, through various forms of dialogue, negotiation, restorative and transitional justice, and other collective problem solving (Bellino, Paulson, and Anderson Worden 2017). Fraser's principle of representation names the challenge of making conflict transformation dialogue inclusive and equitable in form and substance, and creates analytical space for direct encounter with Others (Davies 2014) and communicative praxis (Freire 1970).

John Paul Lederach (2003) affirms the importance of this third dimension, in combination with the other two:

> [Peacebuilding through conflict transformation is] rooted in the communicative abilities to exchange ideas, find common definitions to issues, and seek ways forward toward solutions ... both creating and addressing social and public spheres where human institutions, structures, and patterns of relationships are constructed. (27)

The work of Lopes Cardozo and colleagues (2015) applies comparable comprehensive theory to diverse cases of youth-engaged peace-building action and education from around the world. Following Fraser, they articulate the three dimensions of (social-structural resource) redistribution, (cultural identity) recognition and (democratic) representation introduced above. They add a fourth dimension, *reconciliation* – which, below, I incorporate into a broadened understanding of the direct encounter/representation dimension. Putting these theories together enables us to discern the potentially nonviolent and transformable conflicts underlying each dimension of violence – direct, social-structural and cultural.

Focusing attention on the *conflict* problems underlying the violent symptoms enables us to discern and create *potential spaces for human action* to resist and alleviate 'limiting conditions' (Freire 1970) – that is, for conflict transformation towards building sustainable positive peace (Lederach 2006). In turn, discerning potential spaces for (democratic) peace-building action *highlights the potential for education, to build young people's agency* – their capacities, opportunities, motivations and sense of competence – for citizenship action aimed at deep-structure democratic peace-building. Thus, *to educate for positive peace* is to prepare for and engage in constructive conflict communication, resolution and transformation – to try to stop violence by addressing systemic and direct causes, but not to avoid conflict.

Dimensions of Conflict & Peace-Building (Education)

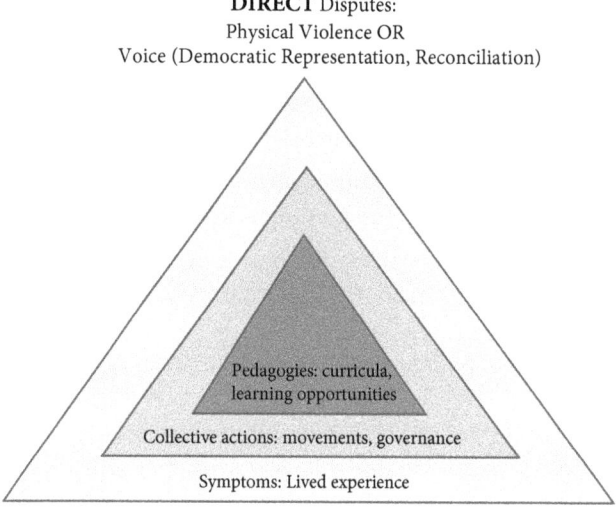

Figure 13.1 Dimensions of Conflict and Peace-Building (Education).

Figure 13.1 illustrates dimensions of conflicts and peace-building. The outer triangle presents three dimensions of feet-first lived experience of social conflicts (whether violent/unjust or peaceful/just). The inner triangle articulates the analogous learning opportunities both experienced and needed for peace-building citizenship. The middle triangle shows the democratic peace-building challenge: the intersection of personal experience with collective action (towards violence or peace). Each dimension feeds or mitigates the other dimensions.

All these dimensions of peace-building – in, for and potentially resulting from educational change – require transitional justice processes, grounded in education to face the social divisions and injustices embedded in 'difficult pasts' (Bellino, Paulson, and Anderson Worden 2017; Davies 2017; Paulson 2015). For each dimension of peace-building, Lopes Cardozo and her colleagues (ibid) articulate cognitive and procedural knowledge and attitudes, and the approaches of educational programming that may contribute to youths' development of those tools for agency. Educational activities to enable (social-structural resource) redistribution include work-related programming; (cultural identity) recognition education includes inter-communal arts and sport; education for (democratic) representation and reconciliation includes citizen activism and voice initiatives, including inter-group encounter and historical memory activities.

Gender-sensitive perspectives are crucial to analyses of conflict, peace-building and education for peace-building (Alden 2010; Cook 2007; Davies 2004; Hudson 2009; Lopes Cardozo, Higgins, and Le Mat 2016; Reardon and Snauwaert 2015; Sandole and Staroste 2015). Gender roles, experiences and hierarchies (including gender-based violence, maternal resources and health care, questions of sexuality and autonomy) intersect in differentiated ways with other social identities. The significance of gender beliefs/norms and social hierarchies is too often ignored or oversimplified in peace-building citizenship/ agency and education theory and practice. Yet hegemonic forms of masculinity and femininity are deeply entrenched in practices and ideologies of violence and expectations of deference or silence (Caprioli 2000; Connell 1995; Dunne and Leach 2007; Hahn 1996; Manaan 2011; Mlamleli et al. 2000; Tannen 1998).

While many of the theorists cited above present relatively optimistic possibilities for democratic peace-building education within informal (e.g. media networking) and non-formal (e.g. voluntary workshop and employment training) sectors, my own work focuses on uncovering the (thin but broad) spaces for social transformation within publicly funded formal schooling.

Education and social conflict

Formal education inevitably is shaped by – and helps to reinforce or reshape – the patterns of social conflict, violence, enmity and social-structural (in)justice in any context. As Novelli and Lopes Cardozo (2008) argue (citing Bush, Saltarelli and Davies):

> The evidence suggests that education cannot solve conflict on its own – embedded as it is within a complex global political economy, the effects of which can often override any 'positive' peacebuilding measures in the sector. Nor can education systems be seen as mere 'victims' of those processes. Education actors, systems and processes can play an active role in both increasing and mitigating [destructive] conflict. (481)

Clearly, education alone cannot resolve entrenched structural and cultural injustice conflicts, such as maldistribution of resources, Othering and concentration of power. However, some feasible changes in public education can help to mitigate and avoid reinforcing such harmful conflict. Schools may give diverse learner populations opportunities to recognize and challenge dominance, violence, exploitation and the paralysis of disengagement – adding constructive options to people's repertoires for collectively participating in democratic peace-building citizenship – that is, in managing the inevitable conflicts of life.

Patterns of gender and intersecting inequities influence the perceived authoritativeness of diverse citizens' voices in confronting and discussing conflicts (Bickmore 2011a; Delpit 1995; Simon 1992). Declarative statements and assertive voice are viewed as masculine in various cultures, and hesitant and qualified statements as feminine (Gordon 2006; Weikel 1995). Such gendered cultural expectations create differential pressures on diverse citizens' (and students') speech, and on their (in)attentiveness to others' speech, in contexts of conflict. Thus, gender is embedded in the ways conflict may be addressed to bridge differences, or to encourage hostility – in ostensibly peaceful racialized contexts such as North America (e.g. Schultz, Buck, and Niesz 2000) and in divided societies (e.g. Bekerman, Zembylas, and McGlynn 2009).

Young people's capacities and opportunities to participate in addressing the causes and remedies of (direct and systemic) social conflict are learned 'feet-first' (McCauley 2002), in particular in lived relationships to others and to social and political institutions. Implicit lived experience with social hierarchies and roles, conflict management, discipline and governance may complement or contradict the messages of explicit curriculum lessons, and vice versa. Inevitably, such feet-first learning experiences would reflect cultural and social-structural hierarchies of gender, including differentiated experiences of direct violence.

However, as Ross (2010) argues, many broadly disseminated explicit peace education emphasizes 'hearts and minds' learning goals – inculcation of individually oriented psycho-cultural attitudes and skills for conflict avoidance or resolution – and glosses over the cultural and (socially structured) tangible interest-based dimensions of conflict that are experienced feet-first by the haves and especially the have-nots. Official citizenship and peace (education) discourses may emphasize behaving as good individuals (often differentiated by gender, socio-economic status and other social identities), rather than engaging public institutions or collective action to solve conflicts or improve social justice (Davies 2011, 2008; Young 2007; Young 2011).

Citizen security initiatives, like national security, legitimize the state's authority to (ostensibly) protect citizens through surveillance and force (Peetz 2011). Securitization frames threats as primarily internal, representing certain social identity groups (such as unemployed youth) as bad people (Pearce 2010). In contexts of violence and marginalization, citizenship education and related development initiatives may function as securitization measures, rather than encouraging democratic engagement (Novelli 2011). Many anti-violence initiatives in schools, similarly – even in relatively peaceful contexts – tend to distrust particular populations of youth, focusing on surveillance, control and punishment instead of education, resolution or transformation of underlying problems (e.g. Skiba et al. 2002). Many anti-bullying and conflict management initiatives in Canadian schools have emphasized such *peacekeeping* control to inhibit violent symptoms, far more than addressing – or helping students and staff learn to themselves address – the *causes* of violence, via post-incident *peacemaking* problem-solving dialogue or proactive comprehensive *peace-building* transformation (Bickmore 2011b).

Globalized discourses embedded in educational materials may discipline students into a Western neoliberal, individualist view of the citizen as responsible, economically useful and law-abiding (implicitly male and autonomous) individual, alienated from the historical context of injustices and from possibilities for collective action (Apple 2010; Cox et al. 2014; Espínola et al. 2005; Kennelly and Llewellyn 2011; Quaynor 2012). Such securitization, applied to education, would block possibilities for learning and exercising democratic peace-building citizenship. Thus, the analytical framework applied below (represented by the middle-level triangle in Figure 13.1) points to participants' repertoires of social-scale dynamics and organizational spaces for citizen action, precisely because those rarely explicit democratic ingredients would represent precious resources for peace-building transformation.

Could the Spanish and Latin American concept of *convivencia* offer an alternative? Roughly translated as (inter-)communal cooperative coexistence, *convivencia* refers to mutually respectful, cooperative, peaceful relationships among diverse people living together in communities (Díaz-Aguado 2002). The broader concept of *convivencia democrática* (democratic *convivencia*) emphasizes human rights and power sharing, well beyond mere tolerance or negative peace (Carbajal Padilla 2013).

> School is the first location of citizen *convivencia* … where students are presented with the confrontations of society, with its threats of exclusion, marginalization, and aggression on one hand, and with the opportunities to learn ways to handle them, on the other. (Hevia 2009, 11)

However, the discourse of *convivencia* has been appropriated in recent years by governments, reimagined in a compliant form that would reinforce oppressive hierarchies. For instance, in the central Mexican state of Guanajuato where some of the research below took place, a new *Convivencia* School Regulation in June

2014 – one of a wave of similar laws enacted across Latin America – emphasizes regulation and punishment far more than equity or inclusion.

Public schools are key sites where democratic *convivencia* – or, in contrast, top-down citizen *securitization* – are modeled and practised. This education may build upon – or contradict – students' experiential knowledge, rooted in their gender and other identities and in particular community contexts. So, how may education facilitate learning for peace-building social transformation – including gender justice? Lederach (1995) articulates how resources for peace-building transformation of conflict are rooted in each community's cultural narratives and languages, implicit feelings as well as thoughts: these may be named and probed in informal and formal learning settings. Comparative international qualitative study, too, can elicit and recognize this wide variety of experiences, insights, questions and critical perspectives on the risks and opportunities in local-global classrooms.

The challenge, in making such research useful, is to identify with participant's possibilities (and impediments) for transformation – not mere addition of skill-building or content expectations – on a concrete level that could be felt in the lived curriculum. This requires investigating the implemented curriculum practices embedded in teachers' daily work, in dialogue with the feet-first understandings and sense of agency for handling conflicts that emerge from the lives of diverse marginalized students living in violent surroundings. Thus, the conceptual framework (represented by the outer triangle in Figure 13.1) is applied below to compare participants' notions of social conflict dimensions, including their repertoires of potential responses, with the implemented curriculum – teachers' and students' examples of what and how teachers taught.

Contexts and research methods

The perspectives in this chapter are based on research in contexts that are neither war zones nor divided societies, distinct from the contexts most often studied. Until recently, transnationally influential peace education theory and research have emerged primarily from zones of relative tranquility, and of relative social-economic privilege – whereas the poor and marginalized, and those surviving in armed conflict situations, are often most vulnerable to violence (Bar-Tal, Rosen, and Nets-Zehngut 2010; Salomon 2011). Mexico, for instance, is not typically recognized as a violent conflict zone, yet is ranked low (140 out of 163 countries) on the Global Peace Index (IEP 2015, 2016), as something over 80,000 people have been killed and more displaced by drug gang (and associated police/ military activity) in the last couple of decades – more than in Afghanistan during the same period. Bangladesh is ranked in the middle (83) of the Global Peace Index (IEP 2016), due to fairly high rates of social exclusion and direct violence, including escalated violence between supporters of rival political groups. Even in relatively peaceful countries such as Canada, marginalized, high-poverty communities endure considerable direct and indirect violence that may remain largely hidden from privileged neighbors (Doob and Cesaroni 2004; IEP 2016).

John Paul Lederach's (1995) notion of culturally 'elicitive' (vs. prescriptive) conflict transformation education informs the methodological and analytical framework of the research project drawn upon below. It was designed to facilitate participants' reciprocal, constructively critical articulation and reflection on education's relation to social conflict, as experienced by marginalized youth in particular contexts.

2014–16 fieldwork involved purposively selected public schools in Ontario, Canada (three schools in one city); Guanajuato, Mexico (two schools with grades 7–9 and two with grades 5–6 participants, in one city), and Bangladesh (a boys' and a girls' [grades 6–9] school in each of two cities – one wealthier and experiencing more political violence, the other poorer and experiencing less direct violence). A comparable later study in Colombia is not covered here. Focus group conversations engaged several sets of four to five students (age 10–15) per school (totaling eighty-one Mexican, thirty-six Bangladeshi and fifty-five Canadian), eliciting their experienced understandings and concerns about social conflict and violence, what they believed citizens could do about these problems, and what relevant education they had had in school. Sessions with teachers (twenty-one Mexican, sixteen Bangladeshi and fourteen Canadian, in groups of four to six) in each of the same schools, enabled comparison of students' understandings with the possibilities and obstacles in their classroom learning opportunities. This chapter selects Mexican, Bangladeshi and Canadian data, focusing on participants' narratives about gender-based conflicts.

Each student focus group discussed social conflict problems of particular concern, chosen from among a (fluctuating, locally relevant) set of image prompts (cartoons and photos) presented to them. The young people worked like reporters, naming and discussing the 'who-what-where-why-how and now what' of those conflicts – the stakeholders affected, what they thought had caused or exacerbated the problems and what they thought authorities and ordinary citizens could do about those problems. Students communicated their sense of agency for encountering, understanding and handling various types of social conflicts, and how their experienced school curricula had (and had not) addressed those concerns, and offered suggestions for teachers.

A series of four or five teacher focus group discussions in each school, a few months apart, began with their examples and explanations of what and how they were already teaching, and their understandings of various conflict issues, peace actions and constraints in their contexts. Teachers also helped to recruit student volunteers (the research team requested diverse participants representing each school's whole population). They vetted and suggested adjustments to the sets of image prompts to be used in workshops with their students to improve their local comprehensibility and relevance. In later teacher sessions, the research team presented (draft, anonymized summary) results from the student focus groups in their school to invite teachers' collective reflections on how their implemented curriculum content and pedagogies might respond to students' understandings and concerns. Later, teacher focus group sessions were animated by the research team's summary analyses of official curriculum guideline documents in the relevant jurisdictions, prompting further conversation about the (mis-)fit between democratic peace-building goals and the curricular spaces available within teachers' work.

The comparisons within and among participants, schools and urban communities especially affected by violence in multiple countries shed light on factors that may contribute to (and impede) young people's development of citizenship agency for democratic peace-building. Thus, this chapter links peace education with democratic citizenship education with young people's lived conflict experiences, in a range of conflict zones that are not (post-)war zones. The research questions: How did these young people understand and feel about various kinds of social conflict (including factors underlying direct and indirect violence) affecting their lives? What challenges, roles and repertoire of possibilities did they see for democratic peace-building citizenship activity to help re-make their worlds? How did they view their schooling as helping them (or not) to overcome those challenges? How did these perspectives compare with those embedded in their teachers' implemented curricula?

Below, I present selected findings from students' (and briefly from teachers') focus groups to highlight participants' perspectives on questions of *gender*-based violence and other gender equity conflicts. Gender conflicts highlight the interplay among the three dimensions of conflict, peace-building and education in each context – rooted in *culture* (misogynistic identity misrecognition, beliefs and attitudes), with evident *direct* (violent and also nonviolent voice-representation struggles) and *social-structural* (inequity and discrimination) dimensions.

Findings

The sets of images used to prompt conversation in student focus groups varied from site to site, but always included an image of gender-based domestic violence. The photo depicts a large clenched fist, apparently male and of indeterminate ethno-racial identity, and a blurry image of a person cowering. Most students identified the cowering image as a woman, some (also or instead) as a child.

Every group of students in every school in each country recognized the image as depicting gender-based violence (named in various ways, including domestic violence and woman abuse – framing men as the main perpetrators and women and children as victims), and said that this phenomenon was among their most prominent lived concerns. Many students elaborated by describing gender-based and/or homophobic harassment and assault outside the home. All participating student focus groups, in all the school sites, easily identified the direct participants in gender-based direct violence: men (almost always as perpetrators), women (almost always as victims) and children (as witnesses and victims). Some students in many contexts identified other actors – such as neighbors, police, courts or protest movements – who might (but usually did not effectively) intervene to address episodes or patterns of gender-based exploitation and violence.

Some students, in nearly all focus groups in all three countries, also recognized some indirect (cultural and social-structural) forms of gender injustice conflict, although unsurprisingly direct violence experiences were elaborated in more detail. Nor did they show confidence in any repertoire of potential actions for confronting or mitigating such problems. For instance, the young people frequently named sexism and male chauvinism, viewing these attitudes and beliefs as perpetuated by family and community models and norms. A few also mentioned misrepresentation or invisibility in media as another cultural perpetuator of gender injustice. Many students in each context also recognized gendered status and occupational hierarchies in their communities, in which women tended to hold jobs that were low-paid relative to male-dominated work categories, to have limited mobility and to carry primary responsibility for child rearing and care-taking.

Few students, and no teacher in any research site, mentioned collective or citizen action against gender-based violence or discrimination, with two exceptions: two Canadian teachers taught a short lesson about Pakistani hero Malala Yousafzai's advocacy for girls' education, and two Mexican teachers mentioned briefly in a history lesson women's acquisition of the right to vote after the Industrial Revolution. Gender equity conflicts, like other social conflicts, were often avoided as learning opportunities by participating teachers – addressed symptomatically (simplified and at a distance) with an emphasis on persuading students to desist from individual aggressive or intolerant behaviour.

Mexico

The vast majority of students showed clear familiarity and concern with domestic and other gender-based *direct* violence: most student focus groups in one intermediate school and one elementary school chose this as a priority concern for discussion; in the other two schools, this was somewhat eclipsed by other implicitly gendered concerns (gang violence, pollution, and economic exploitation of women, children and others). Some girls said their freedom of mobility was severely curtailed by the risk of violence and associated curfews. Boys and girls mentioned rape as an additional risk for female migrants traveling north to seek work. Many Mexican students also described peer fighting, bullying and street (gang) violence as a major problem in their communities, suggesting that most (not all) perpetrators were male.

Several male and female students in all the Mexican schools narrated, with emotion, stories of domestic violence by men against women and children – sometimes saying, or implying through inclusion of vivid details, that they were describing their own families. 'Sometimes my dad hits my mom'; 'My aunt lives next to a man who killed his wife with a gun'. The similar discourses voiced by Mexican students and teachers, and the contents of the official civics/ethics textbook teachers followed in the upper elementary grades, suggest that the pervasiveness, some roots and negative consequences of domestic gender-based violence were presented in a few lessons. An intermediate teacher had learned about students' experiences of abuse by having them write autobiographically, but she did not open class lessons on those issues.

Some teachers taught about husband–wife domestic relations primarily as disputes (rather than violent imposition), highlighting the value of interpersonal communication. One had students create skits portraying the perspectives of each party, using a story they read involving a marital conflict over money. Two intermediate teachers reported teaching self-care, empathy and mutual respect in sexuality relations. In one unusual intermediate class, students had organized issue panels, one choosing to talk about sexuality from perspectives of parents, children, psychologists and sociologists. While they nearly always referred to aggressors as 'he', teachers and students almost never named the gendered aspect of most direct violence problems.

Mexican participants characterized a *culture* of normalized, frequent gender-based and domestic violence repeated (learned) in a generational cycle (a few also mentioned media misrepresentation). Girls and boys said it was fueled by *machismo* (male chauvinism and sense of superiority), exacerbated by drug use and stress or arrogance. An elementary girl: 'Men ... want to feel like kings ... Sometimes men hit women for no reason.' Similarly, an intermediate school girl: men 'are, according to them, the best, and they believe they have the right to hit women'. Some boys and many girls mentioned *machismo*; boys were more likely than girls to mention alternate causes such as stress or alcohol, occasionally even blaming women for provoking violence. These narratives were similar across schools and between teachers and students, although students usually showed more concern about the prevalence and seriousness of gender violence problems than teachers. While most participants spent little or no class time on this issue, one elementary teacher described a 'debate' she had facilitated among her students about prejudice and gender-based violence, in which three of her male students had said that women sometimes deserved to be beaten: she had allowed them to voice these views, but had voiced her disagreement with them.

A few elementary and more intermediate students mentioned *structural* dimensions of gender injustice conflicts – women's disproportionate economic vulnerability and dependency –as itself a problem and as a reason they might be unable to escape domestic violence. A few intermediate students in multiple groups also mentioned prostitution and 'slavery' as gender exploitation problems linked to drug trafficking and gang activity, or pointed to intersections between gender discrimination and the structural disadvantages facing rural indigenous people. Some teachers said that several of their students had told the class that their mothers did not complete school because they planned to get married.

By far the most common *response* to domestic and gender-based violence suggested by Mexican teachers or students was persuasion towards (male) self-control, such as telling perpetrators that violence was wrong. Another response commonly suggested by youth was to denounce perpetrators to law enforcement (police and jail), although one elementary girl suggested there were no such laws: 'we need a law to protect women.' However, whenever this arose, peers voiced dismay and distrust – saying that police would not come, would accept bribes or would do nothing to protect the women or children nor to punish perpetrators. One or two girls in some groups advocated physical constraint or direct retaliation against perpetrators by neighbours or friends. Several students in one elementary school mentioned psychotherapy for abusers, or that the spouses could talk out their conflict instead of using violence. One elementary boy (like these peers, implying equivalent power, or that the woman was equally to blame) suggested that a grandmother could intervene: ' … could talk to them and calm them down and ask them why they fight and hit each other.' A very few Mexican girls mentioned building community awareness to resist gender-based violence, directly or through public protest: 'Until women realize that men can't do that, men will continue doing it.'

In one intermediate school and both elementary schools, teachers' main pedagogical goals expressed were to quell indiscipline, student peer aggression and sometimes student acceptance of direct violence in their homes. They framed these goals in terms of instilling values, not skills. One intermediate teacher did mention a history unit about social change following the Industrial Revolution, including the movement for women's right to vote. Teachers in the other intermediate school, in contrast, emphasized discussing issues more than discipline. There, some teachers and students reported a lesson on gender-based violence, legal equality and discrimination in a mandatory civics course, although students complained that it had been brief, not addressing the problem nor potential solutions in any depth. Thus, over all in Mexican sites, discussions of gender conflicts focused predominantly on patterns of direct aggression, especially domestic violence, presented as individual disputes between males and females that should be handled differently.

Bangladesh

All but one of the student focus groups (in the boys' school in the smaller, less affluent, less overtly violent city) identified *direct* gender-based violence and harassment as a very serious problem. Most female students, especially in the smaller city, narrated personal experiences of gender-based harassment and violence in their own families and neighbourhoods: '[Men] beat women for small mistakes' and 'spoilt boys harass girls'. They expressed outrage that females were often stigmatized after assaults, elaborating that economically powerful men were particularly abusive. Girls in the larger city also acknowledged the gender-based violence and sexual harassment in their communities; for instance, one said that her uncle frequently battered her aunt. Another lamented, 'we always see women get beaten'. Boys in both cities also said '[Gender-based violence] happens a lot in my neighbourhood' and 'When husbands do not like something about their wives, they beat them'. Boys in the larger city also said sexual harassment was pervasive. In general, all participants in the two cities were familiar with direct male violence against women and girls, at least as witnesses. Students showed considerably more concern about it than most of their teachers. Many participating girls located themselves in close proximity to this conflict, as victims and quite often as resisters; a few boys in the bigger city located themselves as allies in resisting gender-based violence.

A few teachers in both girls' schools, and in the larger city's boys' school, said they taught about sexual harassment, although the students did not mention having experienced this in class. Echoing the voices of the girls above, a teacher said he warned that 'there will be naughty and spoilt boys on the street, trying to harass you', and others said these offenses were widespread. As to what caused or exacerbated such problems, teachers and students virtually all named (other people's) bad attitudes and faulty morals.

As for *cultural* dimensions of gender-based conflicts, girls especially said that girls were often less valued than boys in their communities, with their activities limited by sexism. In the smaller city, girls named grandmothers and family in-laws as holding such views. Like the girls, students in the larger city's boys' school (but not in the smaller city) decried the 'common' patriarchal view that women were expected to 'serve and satisfy men' or even to be 'sex slaves', and agreed that abused women were stigmatized: 'If a woman, being abused, goes to the police station, people of the society look down upon her. They call her disobedient.' In contrast, a voice in one group in each of the boys' schools argued that corruption and inefficacy in Bangladeshi politics were worse because the country's prime minister was female.

Participants framed the religious culture of about 90 per cent of Bangladesh's population, Islam, as an antidote, more than as reinforcing sexist cultural practices. One boy explained, 'In Islam, women must wear hijab and veil, and men cannot legally touch or look at women even if they are not wearing veil and hijab. [Sexual harassment] happens mainly because of [women or men] violating this Islamic law.' Similarly, a voice in the smaller city girls' school: 'Men and women are equally respected in the *real* Islam.' The Hindu minority students remained silent, neither affirming nor contradicting this view.

Girls in the smaller city focus groups and boys in the larger city mentioned *social-structural* gender discrimination problems reinforced by cultural beliefs (nobody admitted to holding these views themselves) that in turn reinforced direct gender-based violence: girls frequently being denied access to beyond-basic education, and the demand for dowry bride prices by husbands' families. A few (female) students but no teachers mentioned girls' unequal access to education.

Teachers taught a mandated social studies chapter about the inappropriateness of dowry practices and disrespectful gender relations. A male teacher elaborated that 'because of dowry, women get physically beaten or killed'.

As in Mexico, by far the most common *response* to gender-based abuse suggested by any Bangladeshi participant was individual self-control, to be inculcated via moral education about proper exercise of religious values, occasionally also mentioning punishment. Students in the big-city boys' school and in both girls' schools agreed that sexual harassers and woman abusers should be arrested and strictly punished. However, multiple students expressed hopelessness about formal political remedies, arguing that some men got away with violating women's rights by paying bribes. Several students also addressed cultural and social-structural aspects of sexism and direct violence, suggesting collective mobilization to generate community awareness: 'Common people have to [become] aware, so that they never disrespect women and never oppress women.' Several girls in the smaller city, and one boy in the big city, argued optimistically that they themselves could take collective action to challenge patriarchal attitudes towards justice for women: 'We can make changes in our society by using the power of rallies to protest and raise people's awareness.'

Canada

Student participants in every Ontario, Canada, school chose *direct* gender-based and domestic violence as an issue of primary concern. Majorities in one school, and many in the other schools, also expressed vivid concern about implicitly gendered experiences of interpersonal aggression (direct and cyber-bullying), calling this frequent in their schools and communities. They told stories of women being murdered by men, of a woman having been raped and beaten on the street near one of the schools, and of a teacher recently dismissed from another of the schools due to alleged sexual abuse of female students. Students said physical aggression was predominantly perpetrated by males targeting weaker boys and girls. Several identified themselves as personally victimized, including a boy and a girl (in different focus groups in one school) shedding tears while describing persistent patterns of aggression against themselves.

In contrast to participants in Bangladesh and Mexico, young people in two of the Canadian schools raised concerns about bias-based homophobic/transphobic harassment, sometimes identifying their family members as targets. Students selected to discuss gender-based violence, yet often their conversations diverted into discussions of heterosexism aggression. Several noted intersections between gender-based aggression and ethno-cultural bias, such as harassment of *hijab*-wearing Muslim women and murdered indigenous women. However, at one school, several students also blamed (male) members of one particular immigrant group for much of the aggression they suffered in school. Some teachers there also exhibited distrust regarding the same immigrant community.

Participating Canadian youth quite often mentioned *cultural* dimensions of gender injustice conflicts, such as representations of females and males in news media and school climates that normalized aggression. They said they often heard 'stereotypical' expressions such as 'don't cry like a girl, don't hit like a girl'. A few mentioned mental illness and biology (hormones, physical strength) as factors exacerbating gendered violence. As in the other jurisdictions, these young people recognized and distanced themselves from ideologies of sexism. A girl sighed: 'Boys ... consider themselves stronger than girls, which is not true.' A boy in another school explained: '[Male students] are just trying to prove they are better than [female students] ... through violence.' They said that boys not conforming to dominant masculinity norms, too, would be bullied. Students identified media representations (movies, sports coverage) as exacerbating sexism and male aggression, but also argued that alternative media representations could counteract such attitudes. Although teachers spoke little about gender conflicts, two mentioned that domestic violence was learned generationally through experience in the home.

Students and occasionally teachers made rare, brief references to *social-structural* patterns of discrimination against women, such as employment and wage inequity. They were more engaged and specific in describing heterosexism. Most of these students had attended school presentations by NGO guest speakers opposing homophobia; fewer had encountered these issues in class with their teachers. One teacher mentioned social-structural dimensions, saying females could be constrained from fleeing violence because of financial dependence on men.

In Canada – in contrast to Mexico and Bangladesh – most students were aware of one or more places to which people victimized by gendered violence could turn for help, such as an anonymous (phone and internet chat) helpline and domestic violence shelters. One also mentioned self-defense classes. However – in contrast to Mexico and Bangladesh – neither teachers nor students in Ontario reported any classroom lesson about gender-based violence. Two teachers voiced personal worry about students in their school victimized by domestic violence, and another said that about two thirds of her students lived in economically marginalized female-headed households. Teachers typically referred to perpetrators of student aggression as 'he', and one said a boy in her class called a female peer a 'whore'. However, the only reported Canadian lesson about gender discrimination, in one grade in one school, was a global education lesson about Malala Yousafzai, as an individual hero working for girls' right to education in parts of the world 'less fortunate' than Canada. Beyond the rare mentions of Malala's work and post-incident help resources, neither students nor teachers named personal, social or institutional action to combat gender injustice conflicts. Students' main suggestion of what could be done in response to gendered aggression – as in Bangladesh and Mexico – was surveillance and punishment by authorities. One teacher suggested that they 'should' teach respectful gender relations, but colleagues replied that such 'personal' issues were too sensitive to voice in the classroom.

Participating students in Canada, like peers in Mexico and Bangladesh, showed and felt that their repertoires of responses to gendered (direct and indirect) social conflict were limited. They expressed their wishes to discuss conflict and violence issues more often and in more depth in classrooms, to learn about the roots and solutions of gendered and other conflict problems. Others requested relationship-building and creative arts pedagogies, such as role plays about how to handle disputes and aggression. Some argued for less individual blame by teachers and more voice in equitable conflict problem solving. Others, however, wanted adults to exercise more peacekeeping surveillance and punishment of aggression. Although they typically referred to aggression perpetrators as 'he' and showed (to varying degrees) awareness of sexism and discrimination, participants often were not explicit about the gender dimensions of conflict challenges.

Discussion and conclusion

In sum, gender-based direct violence, and to a lesser extent sexist beliefs and discrimination, were a prominent concern of students in all participating Mexican, Bangladeshi and Canadian schools. Female and male students in all three jurisdictions vividly portrayed frequent face-to-face experience with serious symptoms of *direct* gender-based conflict and violence, and with implicitly gendered (male) aggression. Students and teachers also showed some awareness of the *cultural and social-structural dimensions* of gendered exploitation. Yet, these problems were almost entirely silenced in the experienced curriculum reported in the Canadian schools, and mentioned only rarely in

Mexican or Bangladeshi classrooms. Thus, similarities were more prominent than differences among the three national urban contexts.

Only in the Canadian schools were some students aware of any social institution, such as a crisis line or shelter, where those victimized by gendered violence could go for help. Most students in all jurisdictions understood that gender-based violence, and discrimination against girls and women, were illegal in their countries; however, especially in Mexico and Bangladesh, most expressed scepticism or deep distrust that those legal structures would be upheld or enforced. In Canada, youth were aware of some recently achieved legal protections for same-sex couples, although none mentioned the collective action or political processes that would have led to that protection. A few students in Mexico and Bangladesh – primarily girls – expressed some rather optimistic ideas that people could collectively protest injustice and change community awareness and legal structures, but none showed awareness of any particular mediating institutions or social movements that might mobilize such action for change. Widespread distrust of governments and (ineffective and unjust) securitization policies exacerbated students' fear and frustration. So, participating youth had had few opportunities to witness or participate in communicative peacemaking or problem mitigation, much less in the larger-scale social transformations needed to address indirect dimensions of conflicts underlying gendered violence.

A few teachers in many participating schools did touch upon some of these gendered conflict dimensions – a little. A few curriculum mandates or textbooks – in civics, ethics or moral education, occasionally language or history – evidently had created some small spaces and incentives to recognize gendered social problems and/or to teach critical analysis or communicative conflict resolution. While Canadian pedagogies tended to name injustice conflicts and justice-peace-building actors elsewhere, avoiding attention to local injustices, Mexican and Bangladeshi teachers described a few lessons examining local problems and (more rarely) solution efforts. However, in all three jurisdictions, teachers seemed to be weighed down by a neoliberal individualism: they framed teaching-learning goals in terms of individual values, morality and character, rather than concept or skill development. There was little evidence of guided practice in analysing or discussing (even interpersonal-level) gender-related direct or indirect conflicts, much less in developing exposure to social-political actors, options or capacities for constructive conflict work towards co-creating collective solutions.

Perhaps these few lessons emphasizing face-to-face cultural and skill/attitude dimensions comparable to those emphasized in development aid-driven peace education (Ross 2010), plus the acknowledgement in Bangladesh and Mexico of some social-structural gender inequity dimensions, constitute small but significant building blocks towards youths' agency for direct participation in confronting (gendered) conflict – especially because these publicly funded schools were accessible to essentially everybody in these communities. Some curriculum guidelines and textbooks in all three jurisdictions did at times encourage teachers to address gender-based conflicts that they might ordinarily avoid, including some social-structural and cultural as well as direct conflict symptoms. Further, the schools themselves brought students together, potentially enabling them to share what they had learned from life experience with gendered conflict. Further research can uncover more ways in which young voices, as well as institutional supports, can contribute to their teachers' opportunities and courage to face the direct and indirect dimensions of gendered conflicts and violence.

References

Alden, Amie. 'A Continuum of Violence: A Gendered Analysis of Post Conflict Transformation'. *POLIS* 3 (2010): 1–37.

Apple, Michael W. *Global Crises, Social Justice, and Education*. New York: Routledge, 2010.

Bar-Tal, Daniel, Yigal Rosen, and Rafi Nets-Zehngut. 'Peace Education in Societies Involved in Intractable Conflict'. In *Handbook of Peace Education*, edited by Gavriel Salomon and Ed Cairns, 121–133. New York: Psychology Press/Taylor & Francis, 2010.

Bekerman, Zvi, Michalinos Zembylas, and Claire McGlynn. 'Working toward the De-essentialization of Identity Categories in Conflict and Postconflict Societies: Israel, Cyprus, and Northern Ireland'. *Comparative Education Review* 53, no. 2 (2009): 213–234. Doi: 10.1086/597482.

Bellino, Michelle J., Julia Paulson, and Elizabeth Anderson Worden. 'Working through Difficult Pasts: Toward Thick Democracy and Transitional Justice in Education'. *Comparative Education* 53, no. 3 (2017): 313–332. Doi: 10.1080/03050068.2017.1337956.

Bickmore, Kathy. 'Education for 'Peace' in Urban Canadian Schools: Gender, Culture, Conflict, and Opportunities to Learn'. In *Critical Issues in Peace and Education*, edited by Peter Pericles Trifonas and Bryan Wright, 88–103. London: Routledge, 2011a.

Bickmore, Kathy. 'Policies and Programming for Safer Schools: Are 'Anti-Bullying' Approaches Impeding Education for Peacebuilding?' *Educational Policy* 25, no. 4 (2011b): 648–687.

Burton, John. 'Institutional Values and Human Needs (Chapter 3)'. In *Deviance, Terrorism and War: The Process of Solving Unsolved Social and Political Problems*, edited by John Burton. New York: St. Martin's Press, 1979.

Burton, John and Franklin Dukes, eds. *Conflict: Readings in Management and Resolution*. New York: St. Martin's Press, 1990.

Caprioli, Mary. 'Gendered Conflict'. *Journal of Peace Research* 37, no. 1 (2000): 51–68.

Carbajal Padilla, Maria Patricia. 'Convivencia democrática en las escuelas. Apuntes para una reconceptualización'. *Revista Iberoamericana de Evaluación Educativa* 6, no. 2 (2013): 13–35.

Connell, Robert. *Masculinities*. Sydney, AU: Allen & Unwin, 1995.

Cook, Sharon Anne. '"Sisters Are Doin' It for Themselves": The Price of Ignoring Gender in Modern Peace Education'. *Peace Research: The Canadian Journal of Peace and Conflict Studies* 39, no. 1/2 (2007): 59–74.

Cox, Cristián, Martín Bascopé, Juan Carlos Castillo, Daniel Miranda, and Macarena Bonhomme. 'Educación ciudadana en América Latina: Prioridades de los currículos escolares'. In *IBE Working Papers on Curriculum Issues*. Geneva: UNESCO International Bureau of Education/Oficina Internacional de Educación, 2014.

Davies, Lynn. *Education and Conflict: Complexity and Chaos*. London: Routledge/Falmer, 2004.

Davies, Lynn. 'Interruptive Democracy in Education'. In *Comparative and Global Pedagogies: Equity, Access and Democracy in Education*, edited by Joseph Zajda, Lynn Davies, and Suzanne Majhanovich, 15–31. Netherlands: Springer, 2008.

Davies, Lynn. Can Education Interrupt Fragility? Toward the Resilient Citizen and the Adaptable State'. In *Educating Children in Conflict Zones: Research, Policy and Practice for Systemic Change – A Tribute to Jackie Kirk*, edited by Karen Mundy and Sarah Dryden-Peterson, 33–48. New York: Teachers College Press, 2011.

Davies, Lynn. 'Interrupting Extremism by Creating Educative Turbulence'. *Curriculum Inquiry* 44, no. 4 (2014): 450–468.

Davies, Lynn. 'Justice-Sensitive Education: The Implications of Transitional Justice Mechanisms for Teaching and Learning'. *Comparative Education* 53, no. 3 (2017): 333–350. Doi: 10.1080/03050068.2017.1317999.

Delpit, Lisa. *Other People's Children: Cultural Conflict in the Classroom*. New York: New Press, 1995.

Díaz-Aguado, María José. 'Por una cultura de la convivencia democrátca'. *Revista Interuniversitaria de Formación del Profesorado* 16, no. 2 (August 2002): 55–78.

Doob, Anthony and Carla Cesaroni. *Responding to Youth Crime in Canada*. Toronto: University of Toronto Press, 2004.

Dunne, Máiréad and Fiona E. Leach. 'Gender Conflict and Schooling: Identity Space and Violence'. In *Education, Conflict and Reconciliation: International Perspectives*, edited by Máiréad Dunne and Fiona Leach, 188–202. Oxford; New York: Peter Lang, 2007.

Espínola, V., A. Osler, H. Starkey, F. Reimers, E. Villegas Reimers, C. Cox, and L. Gómez-Morín. *Educación para la ciudadanía y la democracia para un mundo globalizado: Una perspectiva comparativa*. Washington, DC: Inter-American Development Bank, 2005..

Franklin, Ursula. *The Ursula Franklin Reader: Pacifism as a Map*. Toronto: Between the Lines, 2006.

Fraser, Nancy. 'Recognition, Redistribution and Representation in Capitalist Global Society [Nancy Fraser interviewed by H. Dahl, P. Stoltz, & R. Willig]'. *Acta Sociologica* 47, no. 4 (2004): 374–382. Doi: 10.1177/0001699304048671.

Fraser, Nancy. 'Reframing Justice in a Globalizing World'. *New Left Review*, 36 (November–December 2005): 1–19.

Freire, Paulo. *Pedagogy of the Oppressed*. New York: Seabury Press, 1970..

Galtung, Johan. 'Violence, Peace, and Peace Research'. *Journal of Peace Research* 6, no. 3 (1969): 167–192.

Galtung, Johan. 'Three Approaches to Peace: Peacekeeping, Peacemaking, Peacebuilding'. In *Peace, War and Defense: Essays in Peace Research (volume 2)*, edited by Johan Galtung, 297–298. Copenhagen: Christian Ejlers, 1976.

Galtung, Johan. 'Cultural Violence'. *Journal of Peace Research* 27, no. 3 (1990): 291–305.

Gordon, Tuula. 'Girls in Education: Citizenship, Agency and Emotions'. *Gender and Education* 18, no. 1 (2006): 1–15.

Hahn, Carole. 'Gender and Political Learning'. *Theory and Research in Social Education* 24, no. 1 (1996): 8–45.

Hevia, Ricardo. Introducción: Jornadas de cooperación Iberoamericana sobre educación para la paz, la convivencia democrática y los derechos humanos. San José, Costa Rica: Oficina Regional de Educatión de la UNESCO para América Latina y el Caribe, y Instituto Interamericano de Derechos Humanos, 2009.

Hudson, Heidi. 'Peacebuilding through a Gender Lens and the Challenges of Implementation in Rwanda and Côte d'Ivoire'. *Security Studies* 18, no. 2 (2009): 287–318. Doi: 10.1080/09636410902899982.

IEP, Institute for Economics and Peace. Mexico Peace Index 2015: Analyzing the Changing Dynamics of Peace in Mexico. Mexico City: Institute for Economics and Peace, 2015.

IEP, Institute for Economics and Peace. Global Peace Index 2016: Ten Years of Measuring Peace. Sydney, New York, Brussels and Mexico City: Institute for Economics and Peace, 2016.

Kennelly, Jacqueline and Kristina Llewellyn. 'Educating for Active Compliance: Discursive Constructions in Citizenship Education'. *Citizenship Studies* 15, no. 6–7 (2011): 897–914.

Lederach, John Paul. *Preparing for Peace: Conflict Transformation across Cultures*. Syracuse: Syracuse University Press, 1995.

Lederach, John Paul. *The Little Book of Conflict Transformation*. Intercourse, PA: Good Books, 2003.

Lederach, John Paul. 'Defining Conflict Transformation'. *Peacework* 33, no. 368 (2006): 26–27.

Lopes Cardozo, M. T. A., S. Higgins, E. Maber, C. O. Brandt, N. Kusmallah, and M. L. J Le Mat. *Literature Review: Youth Agency, Peacebuilding and Education*. Amsterdam: Research Consortium Education and Peacebuilding, University of Amsterdam, 2015.

Lopes Cardozo, Mieke T. A., Sean Higgins, and Marielle L. J. Le Mat. Youth Agency and Peacebuilding: An Analysis of the Role of Formal and Non-formal Education Synthesis Report on Findings from Myanmar, Pakistan, South Africa and Uganda. University of Amsterdam: Research Consortium Education and Peacebuilding, 2016.

Manaan, Emily. 'Gender, Violence, and Peacebuilding in Northern Uganda'. *Beyond Intractability*. March 2011. Accessed 18 March 2017. https://www.beyondintractability. org/library/gender-violence-and-peacebuilding-northern-uganda.

McCauley, Clark. 'Head First versus Feet First in Peace Education'. In *Peace Education: The Concept, Principles, and Practices around the World*, edited by G. Salomon and B. Nevo, 247–258. Mahwah, NJ: Lawrence Erlbaum Associates, 2002.

Mlamleli, O., P. Mabelane, V. Napo, N. Sibiya, and V. Free. 'Creating Programs for Safe Schools: Opportunities and Challenges in Relation to Gender-based Violence in South Africa'. *McGill Journal of Education* 35, no. 3 (2000): 261–277.

Nixon, Rob. 'Introduction'. In *Slow Violence and the Environmentalism of the Poor*, 1–44. Cambridge, MA: Harvard University Press, 2011.

Novelli, Mario. 'Are We All Soldiers Now? The Dangers of the Securitization of Education and Conflict'. In *Educating Children in Conflict Zones: Research, Policy, and Practice for Systemic Change – A Tribute to Jackie Kirk*, edited by Karen Mundy and Sarah Dryden-Peterson, 49–65. New York: Teachers College Press, 2011.

Novelli, Mario and Mieke Lopes Cardozo. 'Conflict, Education and the Global South: New Critical Directions'. *International Journal of Educational Development* 28 (2008): 473–488.

Paulson, Julia. '"Whether and How?" History Education about Recent and Ongoing Conflict: A Review of Research'. *Journal on Education in Emergencies* 1, no. 1 (2015): 14–47.

Pearce, Jenny. 'Perverse State Formation and Securitized Democracy in Latin America'. *Democratization* 17, no. 2 (2010): 286–306. Doi: 10.1080/13510341003588716.

Peetz, Peter. 'Youth Violence in Central America: Discourses and Policies'. *Youth and Society* 43, no. 4 (2011): 1459–1498.

Quaynor, Laura. 'Citizenship Education in Post-Conflict Contexts: A Review of the Literature'. *Education, Citizenship and Social Justice* 7, no. 1 (2012): 33–57. Doi: 10.1177/1746197911432593.

Reardon, Betty A. and Dale T. Snauwaert. 'Betty A. Reardon: Key Texts in Gender and Peace'. In *SpringerBriefs on Pioneers in Science and Practice*. Cham: Springer-Verlag, 2015.

Ross, Marc Howard. *The Management of Conflict: Interpretations and Interests in Comparative Perspective*. New Haven: Yale University Press, 1993.

Ross, Marc Howard. *Cultural Contestation in Ethnic Conflict*. Cambridge, UK: Cambridge University Press, 2007.

Ross, Marc Howard. 'Peace Education and Political Science'. In *Handbook of Peace Education*, edited by Gavriel Salomon and Ed Cairns, 121–133. New York: Psychology Press/Taylor & Francis, 2010.

Salomon, Gavriel. Four Major Challenges Facing Peace Education in Regions of Intractable Conflict'. *Peace and Conflict: Journal of Peace Psychology* 17, no. 1 (2011): 46–59. Doi: 10.1080/10781919.2010.495001.

Sandole, Dennis J. D. and Ingrid Staroste. 'Making the Case for Systematic, Gender-based Analysis in Sustainable Peace Building'. *Conflict Resolution Quarterly* 33, no. 2 (2015): 119–147. Doi: 10.1002/crq.21147.

Schultz, Katherine, Patricia Buck, and Tricia Niesz. 'Democratizing Conversations: Racialized Talk in a Post-desegregated Middle School'. *American Educational Research Journal* 37, no. 1 (2000): 33–65.

Simon, Roger. *Teaching against the Grain*. Toronto: OISE Press, 1992.

Skiba, Russell J., Robert S. Michael, Abra Carroll Nardo, and Reece L. Peterson. 'The Color of Discipline: Sources of Racial and Gender Disproportionality in School Punishment'. *The Urban Review* 34, no. 4 (2002): 317–342.

Tannen, Deborah. 'The Roots of Debate in Education and the Hope of Dialogue'. In *The Argument Culture: Stopping America's War of Words*, edited by D. Tannen, 256–290. Toronto: Random House, 1998.

Weikel, Brenda. '"Girlspeak" and "boyspeak": Gender Differences in Classroom Discussion'. In *Gender Tales: Tensions in the Schools*, edited by Judith Kleinfeld and S. Yerian, 7–11. New York: St. Martin's Press, 1995.

Young, Iris Marion. 'Structural Injustice and the Politics of Difference'. In *Multiculturalism and Political Theory*, edited by Anthony Laden and David Owen, 60–88. Cambridge, MA: Cambridge University Press, 2007.

Young, Iris Marion. *Responsibility for Justice*. New York: Oxford University Press, 2011.

Index

Lightning Source UK Ltd.
Milton Keynes UK
UKHW020634240820
368726UK00003B/78